COUP

COUPLES WHO KILL

Terrifying True Stories of
the World's Deadliest Duos

Selected, with an Introduction
by RICHARD GLYN JONES

This edition published in Great Britain in 1993 by
True Crime
an imprint of Virgin Publishing Ltd
332 Ladbroke Grove
London W10 5AH

This selection, Introduction and commentary © Xanadu
Publications Ltd 1987

First published as *Killer Couples* in 1987
by Xanadu Publications Ltd

The moral right of the author has been asserted

This book is sold subject to the condition that it shall not,
by way of trade or otherwise, be lent, resold, hired out or
otherwise circulated without the publisher's prior written
consent in any form of binding or cover other than that in
which it is published and without a similar condition
including this condition being imposed upon the subsequent
purchaser.

A catalogue record for this book is available from the
British Library

ISBN 0 86369 633 3

Typeset by TW Typesetting, Plymouth, Devon

Printed and bound in Great Britain by
Cox & Wyman Ltd, Reading, Berks

CONTENTS

List of illustrations — vii

Introduction — ix

Bruce Sanders
THE INCREDIBLE LOVERS — 1
(*Raymond Fernandez and Martha Beck*)

Max Pemberton
THE DOUBLE LIFE OF EDITH THOMPSON — 32
(*Edith Thompson and Freddie Bywaters*)

Miriam Allen deFord
SUPERMAN'S CRIME — 54
(*Nathan Leopold and Richard Loeb*)

Rupert Furneaux
THE AMATEUR GANGSTERS — 73
(*Karl Hulten and Elizabeth Jones*)

Lew Louderback
CLYDE, BONNIE, BUCK AND THE BOYS — 81
(*Clyde Barrow and Bonnie Parker*)

George A. Birmingham
IN THE INTERESTS OF SCIENCE — 126
(*William Burke and William Hare*)

Janet Flanner
THE MURDER IN LE MANS — 150
(*The Papin Sisters*)

Charles Franklin
ALMA RATTENBURY 157
(*Alma Rattenbury and Percy Stoner*)

H. B. Irving
THE WIDOW GRAS 177
(*Jenny Amenaide Brécourt and Nathalis Gaudry*)

Edgar Lustgarten
THE KRAY TWINS 196
(*Reggie and Ronnie Kray*)

Leonard Gribble
CORSETS AND CHLOROFORM 201
(*Ruth Snyder and Judd Gray*)

Tom Gurr and H. H. Cox
DEATH IN A CATHEDRAL CITY 211
(*Pauline Parker and Juliet Hulme*)

Jay Robert Nash
A LITTLE WORLD ALL OUR OWN 229
(*Charles Starkweather and Caril Ann Fugate*)

Malcolm Muggeridge
THE TERRIBLE FATE OF MRS STAUNTON 236
(*Lewis Staunton and Alice Rhodes;
Patrick and Elizabeth Staunton*)

Judge Gerald Sparrow
THE PASSION OF PERVERSION 249
(*Ian Brady and Myra Hindley*)

Postscript by Richard Glyn Jones 262

Sources and Acknowledgements 270

ILLUSTRATIONS

Raymond Fernandez and Martha Beck, the Lonely Hearts Killers (*Associated Press*)
Eddie Bywaters, lover of Edith Thompson – and murderer of her husband (*Popperfoto*)
Nathan Leopold and Richard Loeb (*Hulton Deutsch*)
Karl Hulten and Elizabeth Jones (*Topham Picture Source*)
Bonnie and Clyde pose tough for a friend's camera (*Hulton Deutsch*)
Burke and Hare, the original Bodysnatchers (*Hulton Deutsch*)
The execution of Burke (*The Mansell Collection*)
The murderous Papin sisters, Christine and Léa (*Topham Picture Source*)
Alma Rattenbury and Percy Stoner (*Popperfoto*)
Nathalis Gaudry, cold-heartedly used by Jenny Amenaide Brécourt (*Bibliothèque Nationale*)
Ronnie and Reggie Kray as young contenders (*Popperfoto*)
Tiger Woman Ruth Snyder and corset-salesman Judd Gray (*Topham Picture Source*)
New Zealand's strangest murderers: Pauline Parker and Juliet Hulme (*Hulton Deutsch*)
Charlie Starkweather and fourteen-year-old Caril Ann Fugate, whose murder trip inspired the movie *Badlands* (*Associated Press*)
Lewis Staunton and Alice Rhodes, who replaced Lewis's wife before she was dead (*Hulton Deutsch*)
Myra Hindley (*Hulton Deutsch*)
Ian Brady (*Popperfoto*)

Introduction

There have been many collections of murder cases, but this is the first to concentrate exclusively on murderous *couples*. Most killers operate on their own or involve other people only incidentally, and – despite what the media suggest – murder is still a fairly unusual occurrence, so in considering killer couples we are looking at something that is rare within an activity that is itself rare. Nevertheless, there have been a fair number of such couples, and I have selected what I believe to be the most interesting of them for this book – and an extraordinary collection they make.

Burke and Hare, the archetypal body-snatchers, were allied only for business purposes, but in all the other cases there is a strong emotional tie between the parties. They are genuinely 'couples'. Quite a few of them were simply adulterous lovers – two sides of the classic triangle – and in cases such as those of Edith Thompson and Freddie Bywaters, Mrs Rattenbury and Percy Stoner, Ruth Snyder and Judd Gray, the set-up and the motive are fairly clear-cut: a no-longer-wanted spouse simply had to be removed. The fascination of these stories lies in the circumstances of the murders, and their consequences.

In more casual associations like those of Bonnie and Clyde, Hulton and Jones and the Starkweather/Fugate relationship (superbly portrayed in the movie *Badlands*) we get a first hint of craziness, and this reaches much greater proportions in four truly bizarre cases; those of Leopold and Loeb, the Papin Sisters, Parker and Hume, and – most appalling of all – Brady and Hindley. Here we are faced not with some heat-of-the-moment outburst or one-off aberration, but with systematic murder that seems to be the product of *two* deeply distressed minds. In fact, one mind usually influences the other, and although this is a little-understood phenomenon, often it is clear that one of the partners would have been psychopathic anyway while the other might have lived a reasonably normal life if the association had not existed. Psychiatrists call this *Folie à Deux*, and one finds it in a milder form when, for instance, a husband adopts and believes in the delusions of his paranoid wife. Ian Brady has explained what happened when he moved in with Myra Hindley:

> A meshing into one took place. We didn't need to speak. Just a gesture – something had got to be done, something would happen.... It was so close, we knew exactly what was in each other's mind. We were one mind.

This would be quite touching, if the 'one mind' had not had the aim of devising sadistic ritual killings of children for its sexual gratification.

Further generalisation is impossible for, as suggested earlier, here we are looking at something that is, thankfully, extremely unusual. Perhaps this is what gives these cases their particular fascination.

R.G.J.

Bruce Sanders

THE INCREDIBLE LOVERS

Delphine Downing was a widow and forty-one, but as she paused with her hand outstretched to the handle of the door she was forgetful of such harsh realities. She felt girlish and coy and imagined herself in love with Ray, who was in the room on the other side of the door. True, she didn't care for Ray's sister Martha. She was nothing like Ray. She was gross and fleshy and her colouring wasn't Ray's dark Latin tinge, which Delphine found so attractive, especially when she remembered the pale charms of the husband who had not returned from a war the world was already allowing to slip into history.

There was Rainelle, twenty months old, asleep in her cot. But a daughter less than two years old did not belong to the exciting present, when love was unfolding like a tropic bloom in her mother's bemused brain. Rainelle slept on, blissfully unconscious that tropic blooms existed or could be lethal in their flame-bright attractiveness.

In that modest house on the outskirts of Byron Center, near Grand Rapids, in South-west Michigan, love walked on tiptoe that night – at least, as far as the door opening under Delphine's hand.

She stepped into the lighted room and the tropic bloom of middle-aged passion died at a glance.

The glance was thrown at the man seated in the armchair reading a newspaper. He was relaxing in his shirt-sleeves and his tie was loosened and he had kicked off his shoes. However, in a desire to be comfortable he had removed something else and had forgotten to lock the door, and that piece of negligence was going to cost four lives and send Raymond Fernandez's name humming along a million miles of telephone lines.

'Why, you're bald!'

At the words he dropped the paper and sprang to his feet.

Too late, he glanced at the toupee he had removed from its accustomed perch and placed on the table. His dark shoe-button eyes swung to the graven look of horror and dismay twisting the powdered and painted face of Delphine, standing just inside the room with one plum hand raised helplessly.

Desperately he strove to recover a situation permanently lost. He moved towards her, ignoring the shrinking of her body and the fresh loathing on her pink-and-white doll face.

'Look, honey, you don't have to act this way because I cover a bald patch. Heck, it's no crime, Delphie.'

She had liked Delphie and the way he made the senseless diminutive sound like something secretly shared. But not now. Not with the light of real awakening reaching through the scales he had draped over her faded-blue near-sighted eyes. He felt the first touch of fear. For the first time he saw how thin her lips were when compressed. She had been too generous with the lipstick, using it like camouflage to conceal the mean shape of her mouth. Maybe some scales were falling from his own eyes now there was no need to pretend.

'Honey,' he began again in the wheedling tone she liked, giving rounder shape to broad American vowels, 'I tell you –'

She shrank back.

'Don't touch me, you – you impostor! You lied to me. Why, you're old. Old!'

She poisoned the word and hurled it at him like a javelin, and her aim was true. He recoiled, wounded where the hurt was unseen but deep, in his pride.

'Well, Delphie, come to that –'

'You had better leave, both of you. I want you out of my house tonight.'

'Delphie, you can't mean it. Stop acting crazy, sweetheart.'

Anger poured through her in a molten stream, burning away caution and reason.

'Don't call me sweetheart, you common trickster!' Her voice lifted in a scream. There were tears in her eyes, blinding her to the changes taking place in his face. 'And don't say I don't mean it, I do. You both leave tonight. I'm –'

Then his groping hands reached her. They were not the hands of a lover, they brought no caress for her body. They were rough and they brought pain. They struggled, and she broke from him. He reached to his jacket, thrown across a chair. The door burst back against the door-stop, shuddered. Martha stood there, nearly twenty stone of feminine curves, all of them blunted and in the wrong places for beauty except in the eyes of one man, Raymond Fernandez, who was levelling the gun he had taken from his jacket pocket as Delphine screamed again.

Scream and shot blended. Delphine collapsed, blood pouring from her shattered head. There was silence for some moments, broken by the crying of an infant, lonely and afraid and wanting the comfort of a mother's presence.

The man shook his head, like a person trying to clear a befuddled brain.

'Martha,' he said, a choking sob in his voice, 'she saw me without the toupee, and said I was old. She didn't want me. She said we had to leave tonight. Martha, you don't think I'm old – not too old?'

At the pleading in his voice the smile that always brought him strange comfort shivered across her bank of fleshy chins and dug furrows into the mounds of tissue under her bright, jewel-like eyes, almost lost under the massive brows. Her weighty arms opened and he went into them gratefully. She pulled his troubled head down on to her mighty bosom and a hand like a broom stroked his head. Her pursed clammy lips touched the bald patch on the crown of his head.

'Never mind, darling boy, we'll fix things, like we always have.'

Her voice was plumby and deep and soothing to his jangled nerves and pierced pride. He clung to her, wanting the reassurance of her mountainous body, and an ecstatic light stole into the gem-bright eyes. They stood there, clinging to each other, the most incredible lovers in the twentieth century, people belonging to a nightmare, living characters no novelist or playwright could employ in a plot with any pretence of reality. And yet they were real enough, horribly so.

All that was required to switch them back to their own grim reality was Rainelle's crying.

The man pushed back.

'I can't stand her crying, Martha. It tears at me. We've got to do something.'

'Sure, Ray, we'll do what's necessary. Ain't that how it's always been, huh?'

She patted him, walked to the door. 'Just you dig a hole in the cellar, honey, and make it deep enough for both of them.'

Raymond Fernandez looked at the unlovely woman he loved with bizarre passion. He smiled. Martha was like that. She always seemed to know what to do when something had to be done. And there was always something to be done. Like now.

He went back to the chair, sat down and put on his shoes. Martha turned on feet surprisingly light for a person of her weight. She went out, and the door closed behind her. The man in the chair lit a cigarette, and sat smoking. The fingers he lifted to his face from time to time trembled.

He went to the door and opened it, stood listening. The crying had stopped. There was another sound, of a tap running. It remained running a long time, and he knew Martha was filling the bath.

Frowning, he went out of the room and down to the cellar. He smashed some of the thin surface of cement, cleared it aside, and began digging a hole. When it was big enough he went back to the room where he had left his gun and gathered the dead woman in his arms. He walked with her to the cellar and lowered her into the dark hole. He looked up and saw Martha with Rainelle in her arms. The little body was strangely inert, and water dripped from the sodden nightgown and pooled among the rubble on the cellar floor.

Rainelle was placed with her mother. The rubble was pushed back over them. Choking dust rose in the cellar and Martha coughed like a woman with weak lungs. She did not leave until the man was finished filling in the grave. Then she spoke.

'What do you feel like doing, Ray boy?' Her voice told him she was anxious to please him.

'How about taking in a movie?' he suggested.

She nodded. 'Fine. You get the car out, I'll put my coat on. We'll drive in to Grand Rapids. Should be something worth seeing when we hit the bright lights, Ray darling.'

'Yeah.'

He turned obediently and made his way to the garage. When she joined him the house was dark and silent. On the ride into the bright lights of a town where a hundred and forty thousand people lived, without a thought that soon they would fill ringside seats in a murder drama that would be headlined from one coast of the United States to the other, Martha let her head drop on Ray's shoulder.

They parked the car, entered a cinema, and found the flavour of the entertainment fare to their taste. They sat on and saw the picture through for a second time. Afterwards they drove back to the silent dark house. Ray garaged the car and followed Martha inside. He did not see dark figures moving across the road beyond the front gate, converging on the house. The rap on the door was unexpected. When the door was opened some policemen pushed their way into the house.

Martha's calling voice came to him. 'What is it, Ray? Who's there?'

He did not reply. He couldn't. The muscles of his throat were suddenly not functioning, and his lungs felt starved. He looked into the hard faces of the men marching into the house as though to take possession. He couldn't speak because he was puzzled and confused. These policemen coming into the house knew nothing of the bodies in the cellar.

One of the policemen spoke. His face was a blur as he said, 'You Raymond Fernandez? You ever know a Mrs Janet Fay?'

The face was becoming more blurred as a commotion near the kitchen dragged attention away from Ray. Martha, the light of battle polishing her eyes, was advancing with fists clenched and menace in her manner.

'Hey, what is all this?' she demanded, and for a long moment the surprised cops stood in their tracks just staring at the enormous woman.

Ray opened his mouth to speak, but the words wouldn't form. All air suddenly left his lungs. He started to slide down the wall, and might have made it all the way if a muscular arm in blue serge hadn't caught him.

'Leave him alone. Don't you goddam cops touch Ray or I'll –'

He didn't hear the terrible obscenities mouthed by the woman who loved him as the dawn loves sunlight, but the chances are he had just enough wits left to realize the gates of his crazy charnel-house of a Paradise had just slammed in his face.

The Michigan policemen searched the house and found the double grave in the cellar. They were not squeamish men, but the sight shocked them, possibly because the crime was so recent and the flesh of mother and child barely cold. Further, the discovery was unexpected. They had traced Raymond Fernandez and Martha Beck from information sent by the police of New York. The arrested pair were sent to Kent County Gaol, in New York State. By that time Ray was near to collapse, and Martha was suffering from reaction. They met County Prosecutor McMahon, a man prepared to be shocked by what he learned from questions he asked. But his preparations were not sufficient.

Within hours of the arrival at the gaol the story of one of the most fantastic murder courtships ever told broke in newspapers in every State of the American Union. Dark limelight spun dizzily over the incongruous figures of the thin Spaniard and his obese paramour. The names of Raymond Fernandez and Martha Beck were uttered with loathing. The story of their lives and loves was read with spine-chilling horror. Psychiatrists, doctors, neurologists, and even priests were consulted by reporters and newsmen after fresh angles to write up. For that story was not merely a nine-days wonder. It was a whole consecutive series of nine-days wonders.

The United States was still bemused by wonderment when the story finally terminated, on March 8th, 1951.

It began in Hawaii, where Raymond Fernandez was born eight days before Christmas in 1914. Several worlds away Christmas gifts for British Tommies about to spend the season of goodwill in Flanders trenches were arriving from the Princess Royal. Beyond the barbed wire limitations of No Man's Land grey-clad Germans were penning Christmas letters to their families. It threatened to be an anxious Christmas for scores of thousands of families in Europe. But for Señor and Señora Fernandez in Hawaii, a mother and father with a little son Raymond, it was promising to be the most wonderful Christmas of their lives. Already they were learning to look upon themselves as Mr and Mrs Fernandez. They had christened their youngest son Raymond, not Ramón. He would be an American citizen. The family had high hopes that Christmas in 1914.

When Ray was three the family had journeyed thousands of miles to Bridgeport, in Connecticut, where living among Yankees did something to Papa Fernandez. Possibly he found the journey had been a mistake and he himself a misfit. With his broken accent and aquiline brown features he certainly stood out in a Bridgeport crowd. The only jobs offered him were low-paid, and his family were often in want. Adversity did not reveal hidden strength in the bread-winner's character. It laid bare his many weaknesses. Fernandez took to cheap liquor as an escape from brooding and a retreat from everyday reality. When drunk he beat his small son Ray, who became a target for the man's frustration and inherent brutality. Ray was dragged up rather than brought up. He became light-fingered, and at fifteen was gaoled. Not only for stealing chickens, but because his drink-sodden father had refused to take custody of his son.

In Fairchild County Gaol the world turned upside down for Ray Fernandez, alone with bitter thoughts and a mind filled with one urgent desire, to escape from the Yankee Doodle tradition in which he neither shared nor had a place. His thoughts turned eastward across the Atlantic to the land of his ancestors, the land from which had sailed Columbus and the Conquistadores who had won a whole hemisphere by force of arms. Within the stone walls of a New England gaol he found a desire to return to Spain – return, although he had never been within nearly four thousand miles of the country. The sixty days in the county gaol passed in hard work by day and dreaming of Spain by night. When the youth was again free his mind was made up. He worked to save passage money, and he sailed to Spain and found his way to the home of family relatives in Orgiva. Ray the American became a Spaniard. Five years after the dream in gaol he was twenty, handsome, and physically robust. He had tried his hand and brain at a number of tasks, and discovered that he had no great talent. He was content.

He read of depression in the United States and thanked his

stars he had got out ahead of industrial trouble and a scarcity of jobs. But one day a letter came from his family. His father had a mind to patch things up with his youngest son. He also had a mind to bring the family and join him in a land where a dollar could be exchanged for a handful of pesetas, and where a peseta could go a long way if one was careful. The Fernandez family was reunited on the ancient soil. Ray allowed his wandering glances to remain on the smiling face of Encarnación Robles, and found encouragement in the curve of her lips. It was a good match for the son of a family that had drifted like flotsam half across the world. The Robles family was of good standing. Ray became a father in the fullness of Encarnación's time. But following the pattern of a previous generation, he quarrelled about his son, and in a fit of pique, or to demonstrate his independence, or just to cut loose from too much vine-clinging family, he sailed back to the United States, where news caught up with him that his son was dangerously ill. The later generation had a better understanding of fatherhood than the former. Ray turned about in his tracks and sailed home, to get caught up in the turbulence of civil war, which dispersed his family and left him serving in Franco's forces.

Victory in a bomb-shattered homeland peopled with the halt and the lame and the arrogant with guns on their grey-green hips meant for Raymond Fernandez walking from one brief job to the next. He was a gardener and a collector of city refuse. He polished cars and he carried bales of merchandise. He lived through bitter years of waste and saw another war growing like a cloud beyond France's eastern frontier. He decided he could do better for himself than gardening when hostilities broke out. He made his way to Gibraltar, and in the summer of 1939 was selling ice-cream to British sailors and soldiers and tourists.

Then Europe was again standing to arms waiting for the first real move in a death struggle to be made. Ray began to ask questions, and one day the ice-cream vendor found himself closeted with a dead-pan British Intelligence agent.

'We can use you provided you are capable of obeying orders and being discreet, Fernandez,' he was told.

'Just tell me what I have to do,' he said. 'I shan't be fool enough to risk my neck by letting my tongue wag.'

A few days later, when the ice-cream season was nearly over, he received his first instructions. He proved satisfactory to his new masters. He did nothing materially to shorten the war, but he was useful, and when the conflict was over he was given a testimonial that must have proved exceedingly gratifying. In part it read:

'Raymond Fernandez was entirely loyal to the Allied cause and carried out his duties, which were sometimes difficult and dangerous, extremely well.'

The ex-spy didn't return to selling ice-cream. Possibly years spent in the service of a maritime power had given him the notion of becoming a seaman. Anyway, he signed on as ordinary seaman aboard an oil tanker and sailed to Curaçao, where his land-lubber's sluggishness almost cost him his life. He was slow in moving, and a hatch cover slammed down across the top half of his body. He was rushed in a pulpy condition to hospital two days after Boxing Day in 1945. When he left, on March 15th, he looked a different person. His cracked skull and torn flesh had mended. But the repair work was visible. Most of his dark hair had gone. There were deeply grooved scars across his scalp. There were apparent changes. Others were not apparent. They were the more important. His personality had been impaired by the effects of that severe blow on the head. His assurance was replaced by a furtiveness, which he sought to conceal behind a simpering front of anxiousness to please. He secured a berth on an oil tanker leaving for Mobile, in Alabama. His light fingers that had taken him to gaol in his youth returned him there. He stole some articles stamped 'U.S.' from the tanker, and they were found concealed in his clothes when he tried to step ashore. He learned that the United States Government had little liking for unauthorized persons picking up its property and less for persons who had a previous gaol record. Raymond Fernandez, with his scars hardly mended, and his cranium full of aches and bewilderment, arrived in the Federal Penitentiary of Tallahassee, the capital city of Florida.

In case he had read the currently popular posters about going to sea, he was certainly seeing the world, and from some unusual angles.

His sentence was for a year and a day, which has a distinct

medieval flavour. When it had been served he didn't take the opportunity to tour the Everglades or try his luck in Miami, he sped north to Brooklyn, where one of his sisters was settled. He arrived a stranger to her. Daily he complained of crushing headaches, and his temper reminded her of their father. When he sat around the house Ray was morose and sullen, and when conversation was forced on him he became bitterly argumentative and inconsistent in his arguments.

He tried to get work, but his glowering expression and carved-up pate were against him. There was work for others, not for Raymond Fernandez. He was in danger of becoming as much a misfit as ever his father had been. His room in his sister's house became a smelly sanctuary where she was not allowed to tread. He built some crazy kind of Voodoo altar in the corner by the window, where light and shade gave the best effect, and he went from room to room muttering noises that could have been strange jungle incantations. They weren't calypso rhythms, and the words were unintelligible. His sister began to have suspicions about her brother's sanity.

When he claimed supernatural powers those suspicions were certainly not lessened. But he backed up the claim with a fantastic story about learning Voodoo spells and rites from a prisoner in Tallahassee with whom he had become friendly.

'What sort of spells, Ray?' his sister wanted to know.

'I can hypnotize folks from a distance.'

It sounded like bragging. She smiled, but asked, 'Anything else?'

'I can make women do what I want by thought concentration.'

That was sobering information. She changed the subject.

Shortly afterwards Ray had a big idea. He bought some notepaper and wrote to half a dozen lonely hearts clubs. He received some replies in due course, studied them carefully, paying great attention to the information they conveyed. He replied to one, written by a Mrs Jane Lucilla Wilson Thompson, who described herself as a dietician. They met, and from that moment Ray became an actor. In his part a good actor. He set himself to charm and to please his new lady friend. His success was surprising even to himself. He found he had acquired a new glibness. What he could not do naturally, he could perform by consciously acting and keeping to his self-induced role. He also practised inducement on his new friend, who had money in the bank and wanted to see the world and taste some of the more tantalizing flavours life had to offer those with the spirit and will to adventure. She paid for tickets to Spain, and travelled with Ray as his wife. They arrived at La Linea, where the genuine Mrs Fernandez was living with her son. What his real wife thought of Ray's reappearance complete with a stranger's looks and another stranger calling herself his wife has never been recorded. But she did and said nothing to arouse the lady dietician's fears that she was being played for a sucker, in the words of her own countrymen.

In fact, Encarnación had developed into a woman of considerable accommodation. She allowed herself to be introduced as Señora Robles, and was accepted as an old friend of Ray's. The husband from the past who was posing as someone else's husband now began squiring both women. They went to theatres and restaurants and bullfights, a laughing, carefree trio - on the surface. Then the veneer of camaraderie cracked and flaked. On the night of November 7th, 1947, there was a quarrel. At its most acrimonious and wounding, Ray left the hotel. He did not return, but in the morning the American woman who had been accepted as Mrs Fernandez was found dead. She had died from taking an overdose of digitalis.

Suicide or murder?

Before they could answer such a question the Spanish police decided they must confer with Mr Fernandez. There were some questions he should answer. One rather pressing question high on the list was where had the digitalis been procured?

But Raymond Fernandez was not available for questioning. While the police spent several fruitless days trying to discover where he had taken himself he had procured passage on a ship to the United States. He was growing used to leaving one side of the Atlantic in a hurry for the other.

He arrived back in New York with, apparently, a plan of operation. He went straight to the closed apartment of Mrs Thompson and let himself in with a key he had thoughtfully remembered to bring from Spain. He sat down at a writing desk and began to experiment with pen and ink. He was experimenting for several hours, but when he rose he held in his hands a document signed by a dead woman. By the terms of this document all her furniture and effects were left to her very dear friend Raymond Fernandez.

It was not a very original piece of forgery, but it sufficed to deceive Mrs Wilson. This old lady was Mrs Thompson's mother.

'I shall see that you are not disturbed,' the kindly attentive Mr Fernandez informed her. 'Things for you will continue just as before.'

Mrs Wilson, thankful to have a roof over her head, did not create difficulties of her own by asking embarrassing questions. She accepted Mr Fernandez for what he purported to be, allowed him to install himself permanently in her dead daughter's apartment, and for a while there was a semblance of the even tenor of life continuing unbroken.

The break came when an enormously fat woman accompanied by several large pieces of luggage and two children arrived one day at the apartment.

When Ray saw her he had trouble with his breathing. When the words came they were a whining demand.

'What in God's name are you doing here, Martha?'

'Can't you see?' said the woman scathingly. 'Moving in, buster.'

Martha Beck had arrived in Ray Fernandez's life for the duration.

The fat woman with the tough manner and the heart that longed secretly and passionately for romance was six years younger than Ray. She had been born with a freak's body encasing some of the heat that burning Sappho knew. She first saw the light of day on May 6th, 1920, in the State where Ray had served his second gaol term and where he had claimed to meet the Voodoo expert. She enjoyed, if that is a valid term in the context, a most unhappy childhood. A pituitary ovarian deficiency had resulted in the child suffering from considerable glandular disorders. She very quickly became overweight and fat, and the object of piercing ridicule by her classmates in school. Life was not made any easier when her father, Holland Stanley Seabrook, tired of the dual role of father and editor-owner of the *Milton Gazette*. He forsook the editorial chair and the father's seat at the head of the table at the same time. He was a man who seemingly preferred to cut strings himself rather than suffer loose threads to ensnare his itching feet. He packed a bag and took off. It was not a specially large bag, but it was a permanent removal of his person from the small township of Milton.

Somehow the remainder of the family kept themselves beneath a single roof, although there were moments of tribulation and stress. For instance, when Martha was thirteen. She learned the facts of life abruptly and crudely when assaulted by her brother Dudley. Such untoward events did not disrupt her normal studies sufficiently to wreck her prospects of 'graduating', as the Americans term passing senior form examinations, at the local high school.

With schooldays thankfully behind her she knew what she wanted to do next. It had been on her mind for some time, for she knew the disadvantages of her size in any normal sphere of activity. She applied to the Pensacola School of Nursing to become a trainee, and after an interview was accepted, and began her probationary period. She was ungainly and awkward, but she had a determined patience and she could be surprisingly gentle with her bulbous fingers. Her nurse's uniform could not lend grace to her graceless adiposity, but it gave her authority, and that was something new in the life of Martha Seabrook, growing out of her teens and without realizing it becoming a woman without ever having enjoyed youth. Somewhere in the passage of years those glandular deficiencies had tricked her out of maidenhood. She passed in development from the physical status of a child to that of a grown woman. It would have been frightening had she known. It was yet to be frightening because she did not know, and could not understand the desires and hungers that could be awakened in her quivering mass of flesh.

Her final examinations took two days, March 2nd and 3rd, 1942. She passed with high marks, and donned her green belt with pride. She was eager to begin real nursing, for the United States was in a war, and Pearl Harbor was a recent searing memory.

Now she had to take disillusionment, bitter and galling and

terribly mangling to her pride. No hospital wanted a comedy nurse weighing nearly three hundred pounds avoirdupois. Some of the refusals at the end of painfully short interviews were accompanied by ill-concealed grins. Some terminated with looks of pity. She hated both. She was a trained, highly efficient and capable nurse, and no medical superintendent would employ her. The only job offered came from an undertaker.

He didn't actually call her 'Fatso', but his leer was a rubber stamp of the hated nickname, and his attitude was unequivocally 'Take it or leave it.'

The fat nurse took it. She wanted her first job. Even more, she wanted the chance to prove that she was as good as the next woman in her chosen profession. The work offered by her first employer hardly satisfied that secret hunger, for the task entrusted to her was the most menial of all nursing chores. She was responsible for preparing corpses for the undertaker's attentions. The work was not the kind to call for great skill, and there was no demand for that tenderness which eases away pain. The corpses she washed and combed were past suffering. She found she could envy them that great negation of all feeling. She also found such a life of dreary, ghoulish monotony demanded a palliative to make continuance possible.

She began to read avidly all the true-romance magazines she could buy or borrow. The more lurid the cover the greater the promise of lavish emotional gymnastics. Martha Seabrook became a person living two lives. One with the dead who were finished with living. The other with the living who had never lived. Both were fantastic and abnormal and calculated to produce in time a dangerous neurosis in the mind of a young woman whose physical growth was not normal.

In time the bright covers of the true-romance magazines won out against the corpses in the undertaker's parlour. Eight months after taking the job Martha quit, with enough cash in her purse to buy a ticket to California's sunshine, oranges, and surplus male population. She packed her bags, said goodbye to the indifference of dead folk and the amused tolerance of the living, and went westward. Apparently there was a shortage of nurses in California. She did not have to make many applications before securing a post as floor nurse, as American ward nurses are called, in the Victory Memorial Hospital. Maybe the hospital's name was significant. Martha had won a victory for herself. She had at last been accepted in a world of normality. She began to work with true healing in her fat fingers.

But the true-romance magazines were not an opiate that lost its potency with the passage of time. Martha, having won victory, yearned to continue the winning sequence. She wanted love, with all its physical fulfilment, and she wanted a mate who would be hers in the sight of God and man, but especially in the sight of Martha Seabrook.

Searching for her own true romance in her off-duty hours, she drifted into a casual hole-and-corner affair with a bus driver, who allowed himself to become her husband in the sight of Martha Seabrook, but who omitted to take her to church or to publish the banns of matrimony. Martha found herself pregnant with no comforting band of gold on her third finger. This was a situation that had never developed in such a harsh realistic way in the true-romance magazines. Martha had to find her own solution and she did so by waylaying her lover and demanding marriage. The bus driver became scared. He stalled to gain time. With time to consider the alternatives he decided suicide was preferable to being Martha's husband. Having taken the resolve, he put it into swift execution. He got drunk and jumped off a pier. But the inscrutable Providence that has a special care for fools and drunks did not allow the salt Pacific water to siphon all the air out of his lungs before some well-meaning but meddling rescuer pulled him back to *terra firma* and the attentions of an ambulance crew. But not to Martha. Whether he was too shame-faced, or knew too intimately the cross-continental bus routes, is not known, but her shabby lover vanished as soon as the first opportunity arrived.

Martha was rid of him, and for a time of herself.

She was picked up in San Francisco, obviously in physical and mental distress. She didn't know her own name and could give no account of her actions or background. She was sent to hospital suffering from acute amnesia. Doctors and psychiatrists went to work on her outsize person. One recorded in her case history: 'She was not oriented to her own person, and remote memory was extinct except for hazy recollections.' She was kept in that hospital, closely watched, for four days, then she was released. She found work in another hospital, but the sense of victory was gone, and the weeks wore away with a swiftness that filled her mind with panic. She had to contemplate a future when she would be a mother.

She turned eastward, and journeyed to Pensacola, where she had trained to become a nurse. Now she wore a phony wedding ring and claimed to be the wife of a soldier fighting overseas. This fictitious hero she named Joe Carmen, and after a suitable lapse of time she sent herself a telegram announcing that Joe Carmen was another victim claimed by the little yellow men on some Pacific assault beach. She showed the telegram around to friends and acquaintances, the war widow winning a ready sympathy never previously given to a fat girl who looked like a model for a comic postcard artist.

The story found its way into the local papers, and lost nothing in the re-write process. It is possible that the long lonely hours spent at the wheel, watching a two-way tide of humanity ebb and flow, makes bus drivers sensitive beings with responsive sympathies. Or possibly bus drivers are allergic to thin women. However it may be, a second bus driver entered Martha's life. He came full of sympathy for the war widow with her young baby.

He was Alfred Willard Beck, and his proposal of marriage was the most exciting Christmas present Martha had ever received. The fat woman who claimed to be a war widow, and the sympathetic bus driver, who was about to become stepfather to another busman's child, were married twelve days before Christmas, 1944, and before the New Year had arrived the marriage was permanently fractured. The happy bride and groom who had been wedded in Escambria County Courthouse were strangers to the angry, disillusioned partners who decided to dissolve their partnership in the following May. As may be expected by the cynical, the request for a divorce came from the husband. Judge Ernest E. Mason heard the case in the Chancery Court, and duly granted the divorce.

Martha Beck was again without a man about the house. She had a child, and would in due course become the mother of another, but, any way she considered it, life had handed her a raw deal. There was a mature bitterness overlaying her years-old resentment when she secured work in a hospital. When her second child was due she remained in the hospital, and after the confinement she had three months to fill and only the same pair of fat hands to earn the necessary money to buy food and provide shelter.

At this stage many a woman, less crudely endowed by nature, would have accepted defeat. Not Martha Beck. With a strange perverseness, she began to hit back at life. The fat mother acquired personality from the trials produced by mounting adversity. She started by refusing to accept no as an answer from anyone. This new thrusting quality procured her a position in the Pensacola Crippled Children's Home. She entered it on February 15th, 1946. She threw herself into the work. With her advantage in weight that meant others were displaced. Within six months Martha Beck became superintendent of the home. She had made another success. She was her own boss and boss to a number of other people.

She felt she could relax, which was a not particularly wise decision. Relaxation meant a return to the perusal of those colourfully covered true-romance magazines. Martha Beck had gone twice to love's votive flame, and each time had been badly singed. She had been scared, but not cured. She still believed a man was necessary in her life, even when she was superintendent of the home for crippled children. Her gross body had a capacity for passion that was in direct proportion to its size. The stories she read made her restively aware of that capacity.

Such was approximately the receptive state of her mind when, in one of her magazines, she read an advertisement for Mother Dinene's Friendly Club for Lonely Hearts. Membership cost five dollars. Martha had five dollars, and soon was a member.

Ten days after being enrolled as a Lonely Heart seeking to evade loneliness she received a letter from another Lonely Heart. It was postmarked New York, and was a very flowery epistle, of a kind Martha had never received before in her life. But she had read many penned in the same strain. All of them in those true-romance magazines.

The writer of this extraordinary but hopeful letter was Raymond Fernandez.

With such unlikely strands of weft and woof, Fate had begun to fashion an incredible pattern of human violence.

The correspondents quickly became on cosy terms. A meeting was arranged, and Ray proved most accommodating. He came to visit his pen friend. The meeting took place at the bus terminus where he alighted. It says much for either his presence of mind or his capacity for seeing a deal through that he did not turn tail when confronted by Martha's three hundred pounds of dubious charms, waiting to receive him with open arms. Arms, incidentally, that appeared quite capable of performing their own nutcracker suite on his tinny ribs.

Amazingly Ray took his punishment like a better man than he, in fact, was, and, even more amazingly, found he could enjoy it and enjoy Martha. This incredible pair, brought together after deception and disillusion, were so oddly consorted that each found inexplicable attraction in the other's quality of oddness. The enormous woman, a grotesque caricature of her sex, discovered she could pour affection over the scarred, moth-eaten pate of an obvious liar and shallow-natured deceiver. For his part, the man who had run from a dead woman in a La Linea hotel and who had perfected a technique for preying on other foolish members of the sex, now found himself almost hypnotized by a personality he could not begin to understand, but could only accept.

Just what happened between these strangely paired Lonely Hearts can only be imagined, but it is conceivable that the true development of their peculiar and perverted affection began when Ray made love to her and thereby Martha fell in love with him. Anyway, neither backed down before the advances of the other. There was no pot calling the kettle black. It was diamond cut diamond and no complaints for forty-eight hours. In those two days the couple lived through a queer, concentrated honeymoon. They had met on the common ground of amorous excitement, and their feast of delight was inexpressibly Lucullan while it lasted. Raymond Fernandez was living by the inflexible code of every man of ambition. Business must precede pleasure. Two days were sufficient to inform him beyond hope of contradiction that Martha Beck had no money worthy of his dalliance in the backwoods, away from the bright lights of a city like New York. He liked Martha, was fond of her, she was a swell kiddo, and all the other time-worn exit lines, including urgent business piling up in New York.

Somehow he got away from those vine-tight massive arms, arrived back in New York, and proceeded to apply the *a priori* reasoning process that is the stand-by of confidence tricksters who just haven't enough confidence to overcome the last twinge of conscience. He had nothing to offer Martha, he was better off without her and she without him. They were no good to each other, therefore he didn't like her as much as he had pretended. She was still a good kiddo. But that was all. Period.

He sat down and wrote a letter. He told Martha that absence didn't make the heart grow fonder. Rather otherwise. His feelings had undergone a rapid change. He found he was not really in love with her as he had thought. He knew she would understand.

He bought a stamp and dropped the letter in a post-box.

He was both right and wrong. Right about Martha understanding and wrong about what she would do about it.

When she received the letter Martha Beck was angry. Raymond Fernandez had been something novel in her life, a man she could control while he was with her, a man she could yearn for and whose manhood gave meaning to her yearning, a man she could learn to grow jealous for, a vastly new experience. She realized the letter that had brought tears to her eyes was really a signpost marking a crossroads in her life.

While she hesitated to make up her mind, it was made up for her. Gossips had been at work. After all, a man like Raymond Fernandez and a woman like Martha Beck can't act like honeymooners without observant eyes remarking the fact and slanderous tongues expressing moral outrage.

The governors of the children's home held a meeting, and a resolution was tabled and taken, and within a few hours Martha was no longer superintendent.

She was back where she had started, with two children and a heavy heart as well as a load of hot anger and the desire to travel, this time to New York. So once more she packed her bags, settled her few affairs, and prepared to make a journey that she intended should be one way. At least, for herself. She kept an open mind about the children. After all, New York wasn't Florida.

Her strategy had excellent historical precedent. She wrote no letter. She gave no warning. She collected her bags and her offspring and went.

She also burned her boats behind her.

And when she stood on Ray's doorstep with her gloved finger on the bellpush her courage had been given the necessary shot in the arm to see her through the encounter. When the door opened she announced that she was moving in, and proceeded to do just that.

There is no record of whether Ray surrendered with or without a struggle. But his surrender was complete and absolute. Martha stayed, for all practical purposes as his wife. But the children, with their wide questioning eyes, were not little replicas of Cupid. Instead of aiming love's fiery darts, they were innocently tossing monkey wrenches in the works, from the moment they were installed in the New York apartment, already crowded with three adults, although Mrs Wilson, bemused and troubled by her constantly changing status, did her best to remain from underfoot.

Once having surrendered, Ray was Martha's beamish boy. She started to run him as she had run the children's home, and she began by trying to find somewhere to park her own children. Apparently no one in New York wanted them after clapping eyes on the mother. So they went back to Florida to live with relations of the mother who didn't want them because a man with a scarred bald patch took all her time and attention, day and night.

With the children gone, Martha gave her mind to the problem of Fernandez's income. The large woman desired stability in her life. She also decided that Mrs Wilson must go. She saw to it that, within a very short while, Mrs Wilson was glad to go. Martha was quite enough woman to fill one moderate-sized love nest.

She went to work on Fernandez.

'Just how do you make money, honey?'

Ray Fernandez fumbled his cue and tried to stall, but Martha had a will to match her weight. Fernandez, at close quarters, didn't stand a chance.

'Well, I get it from women – lonely women.'

He looked to see if she was shocked. Martha was far from shocked. She was grinning.

'I'm interested, honey,' she said. 'Maybe we can work together.'

She had suddenly seen an opportunity for hitting back at her own sex, for squaring the overdue account for all the humiliation and misery she had suffered from the years of tender girlhood.

Fernandez gave her a startled look. 'Hey, maybe you've got something there, Martha,' he said, his mouse-quick mind already adapting the suggestion. 'A brother-and-sister act. Yeah, not bad.'

'Better let me in on how you operate,' Martha smiled, 'only don't make it sound too good, Ray. I could get awful jealous.'

So the strange love partnership was put on a working basis. With no qualms, no squeamishness, no show of feminine resentment, a deadly pact was made, and for Martha in 1947 life took on the semblance of a grotesque but intensely exciting charade.

Fernandez, with his thinning hair and sloppy jowls when he tucked his chin down, did not look a real-life Don Juan, but then he did not aim particularly high in choosing his female targets. He contacted correspondents to lonely hearts clubs, and picked his victims with care. He arrived and did his best to dazzle, and before the cheap emotional tinsel had time to tarnish he had pocketed money that was not returned. The proceeds from such confidence trickery did not come enticingly high, but Martha thought a sister act could boost them.

The pair began working with a smooth understanding that quickly became a perfected technique. They chose a lonely-hearted schoolteacher in Pennsylvania for their first victim as a working team. Fernandez made the familiar approach, letters were exchanged, and then the couple arrived at the teacher's home, and Martha became the helpful sister who knew when to make herself scarce and how to explain away some of her alleged brother's shortcomings.

The courtship went according to prearranged plan almost without a hitch. The day arrived for Fernandez to marry his schoolteacher sweetheart. Martha smiled sweetly on the bride and undertook all the arrangements for the honeymoon, which was not the kind the schoolteacher had imagined she would enjoy with her newly wedded mate. Martha went along with the happy couple. She felt she had her own reasons for keeping a wary eye on her bigamous lover who was posing as her brother. Not the least was a jealous determination not to allow Fernandez an opportunity to enjoy the illicit sweets of his stolen marriage. The honeymoon for three was spent with the two women retiring to the same room each night, and the husband retiring to a joyless bed. When the schoolteacher felt like remonstrating at such a preposterous arrangement she was frankly intimidated by Martha's suddenly aggressive manner. She decided that twenty stone of female aggression can be very intimidating. In fact, she became so scared by Martha, and so entirely dominated by her, that she raised no objection when, upon the return of the incredible trio to the Bronx, it was suggested that she place her financial affairs in the hands of her husband and his overwhelming sister. In a short while she was informed that her modest savings had evaporated. Suddenly aghast, and utterly at her wits' end, she came belatedly to her senses. She packed a bag and left.

When the door closed behind her the pattern was set for further such marital adventures by the world's most improbable lovers.

For two years these confidence tricksters worked at their cruel and unrelenting racket, duping the gullible into mock marriages with the alleged brother, and then extracting their personal wealth and making life so generally intolerable that the dupes were glad to decamp. Throughout those two well-nigh unbelievable years a score of female lonely hearts were snared and discarded when dollarless. With unbending insistence, Martha ensured that Fernandez indulged in no amatory adventure with any of his new brides. With her three heavy chins poising her heavily painted face framed with a pile of dark red hair, Martha never relaxed her jealous vigil. Fernandez was kept in strict emotional bounds, and the amazing feature of their rare partnership was his gradual falling deeper in love with her, until eventually she exerted a purely sexual attraction for him that left him cold to all other women. The warm Latin blood was cooled by her purposeful ardour, and the passing of time bound him in closer chains to his outsize inamorata.

As for the women victims of the designing pair, they were conditioned for deception from the moment they joined their various lonely hearts clubs. They were women brought close to despair by solitude and empty lives. Women prepared to go to unusual lengths to acquire the husband that had not appeared in the years of their youth. They were coy and anxious and very, very vulnerable.

They were also creatures capable of feeling shame when it was too late to better their plight. They were that much more vulnerable.

Perhaps it was inevitable that such a ruthless partnership should lead to violence. As a solo practitioner in his lonely hearts racket Ray Fernandez was a despicable vulture preying on women made helpless by emotional entanglements. As Martha's driven partner he was capable of becoming a more fearful bird of prey. Murder became a dark shadow that loomed near with the passing months as custom and expediency drove the relentless lovers from one grotesque excess to another. Martha had taken to big city life with a naturalness that was frightening. In a small town she had been conspicuous and afraid of the unique figure and frame that set her apart from other women. In a city like New York she lost her former sense of being unique and always noticeable.

She bought more fashionable foundation garments and controlled her mounds of flesh. She became more normal as a woman, which unleashed the dark and furtive repressions concealed since childhood. She developed the soul-destroying qualities of a smiling ogress.

Behind the bright lights of a big city she attained a perverted fulfilment of her demanding irrational nature that had to climax in appalling disaster.

The climax was approaching in August 1948.

In that month the incredible lovers were indulging in their latest cruel deception. Keeping to their allotted roles, they had gate-crashed the placid life of a middle-aged widow named Myrtle Young. This whirlwind affair began to fall apart with alarming rapidity when Martha insisted on sharing the new bride's bed. Protestations set Martha on a grim course. Myrtle Young was heavily doped with barbiturates, and seen aboard a bus to Little Rock, in Arkansas. When the bus arrived at its depot, Myrtle Young was in a deep stupor and unable to speak coherently. She was rushed to hospital, but medical care and attention came too late to save her life. As she drew her last breath Martha Beck and Ray Fernandez were driving in her car to call on another likely prospect for their now murderous quick-cash routine. They made several calls in that car, but by Christmas the ghoulish lovers were back among New York's bright lights, their pockets empty, going through fresh lists of women prepared to snatch at romance perhaps for the last time.

They found the name of Mrs Janet Fay. She was sixty-six and a widow, and she lived upstate in Albany, the New York State capital.

'Try her, Ray,' Martha insisted.

Ray Fernandez wrote to Mrs Fay, introducing himself as Charles Martin, a lonely man looking for a sympathetic companion to share his last years. He was now practised and adept at his corny epistolary style of writing. Mrs Fay's searching naïveté was no match for his calculated insidiousness. She wrote back full of encouragement and hope. Even worse for herself, she sent an invitation to this charming letter-writer who promised that he could make her heart less lonely.

With money procured by pawning the last few possessions of Myrtle Young, the pair set off on a fresh deadly adventure in make-believe love. They arrived at Mrs Fay's home burdened with hothouse blooms on December 30th, and if the widow's eyes flickered a few times at the sight of the unexpected bulk of Martha, she nonetheless made Charles Martin's overwhelming sister royally welcome. The year 1948 was about to be supplanted by a New Year, and Mrs Fay had some pet resolutions and hopes for 1949. When Fernandez began his smooth and swift courtship nothing was farther from her whirling mind than the certainty of her death within a few short days.

So bemused was she, so in love with love, that she told no relative of her intended marriage with the meteoric Mr Martin, but allowed herself to be prevailed upon on January 3rd to withdraw from the Albany Savings Bank all her jewellery, cash, and bonds in her name. Her possessions were packed in a trunk provided by Charles Martin's organizing sister. Mrs Fay had no way of telling that the trunk had once belonged to a woman who died in a stupor in a hospital in Little Rock, half a continent away. The lively discussions about the actual wedding ceremony and the first stages of the proposed honeymoon for three passed in a state of only blurred awareness, during which the excited woman signed sundry papers put before her by a smiling Charles Martin. The three left Mrs Fay's home and arrived in a newly rented apartment in the little town of Valley Stream.

The stage was set for further violence.

The cue came a little too soon, before the villains of the piece were quite ready. Mrs Fay wanted to contact her stepdaughter, was dissuaded from writing, and became peevish in a manner suitable to her years. The result was an angry exchange that served as a spark to Martha Beck's now hair-trigger temper. Seizing a hammer, she struck Janet Fay on the head. The skull was cracked like a fractured vase. With chilling presence of mind, the murderess wrapped up the body and stowed it in a cupboard.

'Better put your thinking cap on, Ray,' she told Fernandez. 'We've settled for six thousand bucks and a body. It's the body we've got to dump in a hurry, sweetheart.'

They sat up smoking and drinking and discussing ways and means of disposing of the remains of Janet Fay. Both ways and means seemed clear to Martha when Fernandez remembered that the house of his sister who lived in Astoria, had a large cellar.

Again Martha Beck directed their moves.

First they went back to New York and bought a second-hand trunk in a store in 125th Street, which is in the Negro quarter of Harlem. Returning with it, they stowed the body inside and took off again on their travels, this time to Astoria, where they said they wished to leave a truck for a short while. Fernandez's sister was obliging.

'Sure, you can use the cellar. There's plenty of room for that trunk, and no hurry.'

The obliging sister was not as correct as she imagined in claiming there was no hurry. It was January and temperatures were around freezing, but Martha Beck, the trained nurse, knew that the body was already decomposing. It had to be buried. Besides, New York temperatures could not be trusted, even out in rural Astoria.

Eight days after Janet Fay's skull was broken the scheming pair rented another house. This time at 133, 149th Street, South Ozone Park, in Queen's. They were back among the bright lights of the metropolis. The body was brought there in its trunk, and tipped into a hole in the cellar. The hole was filled with cement that was smoothed over.

Four days passed, and the cement was really hard. The house agent was informed that the property in South Ozone Park had been found unsuitable.

'I can't refund your deposit,' he said firmly.

'Reckon that's our bad luck,' he was told.

A return was made to Valley Stream, where cheques drawn by Mrs Fay before her death were cashed.

'Now,' Martha Beck decided, 'we've got to figure how to get her things from the American Express. We can't go ourselves, it's too risky.'

'We could leave the things,' Fernandez pointed out.

But Martha had grown both rapacious and avaricious. The more she procured by her preying methods, the more she wanted.

'They might be worth plenty, and we've gone to a good deal of trouble. We'd be fools not to collect, Ray. I think we could use that stepdaughter she wanted to write to.'

They debated the matter, and again Martha Beck had her way. A few days later Mrs Mary Spencer received the following typed letter:

Dear Mary,
I am all excited and having the time of my life. I never felt so happy before. I soon will be Mrs Martin, and go to Florida. Mary, I am about to ask you a great favour. I would like you to call on the American Express Agency

and have them ship my trunks and boxes that I have there to me. The address is on the various stickers I am enclosing in the letter.

I would like to sort out many things before I leave for Florida. I am so happy and contented, for Charles is so good and nice to me and also his family. They have done everything to make me feel comfortable and at home. I will now close with my best wishes for you both and love and kisses for the children. I really do miss you all, but I am sure that my prayers are granted to me by sending me this wonderful man.

God bless you all,

Janet J. Fay

Mrs Mary Spencer read this extraordinary letter with genuine amazement and fast-mounting suspicion. First, because she knew that Janet Fay could not type and didn't own a typewriter. Second, because she knew Janet Fay would never sign such a letter in such a formal manner.

She lost no time in approaching the local police.

Even so, the wonderful man of the letter had lost even less in setting out after his next quarry in this fabulous hunt for easy money. Accompanied by the fat woman who had at last found life to be more exciting than those true-romance magazines with the gaudy covers, he was heading for the Middle West and about to bring himself and his suit to the notice of Mrs Delphine Downing of Byron Center, Grand Rapids, another widow anxious that life shouldn't treat her like a rundown shoe. She too invited the strangely assorted pair into her home, made them welcome, introduced them to her small daughter Rainelle, and then made the mistake of walking about the house on tiptoe. If she hadn't done that she might not have lost her life and cost her small daughter hers.

But when she walked into that room where Ray Fernandez was relaxing minus his toupee the circle of violence was finally closed.

When Deputy Sheriff Clarence Randle of Grand Rapids searched the cellar of Mrs Downing's house and found the bodies of mother and daughter he was acting on a hunch, as he stated later. The police had arrived at the request of the New York State authorities. At once, following upon the couple's arrest, a legal problem was presented. Which State was to prosecute for murder? For the grave in the cellar in South Ozone Park had been found and uncovered following upon Mrs Spencer's appeal to the police. In Michigan there was no death penalty for murder. In New York State the electric chair at Sing-Sing was far from being a museum piece. However, the first of the now known murders had been committed in New York. Kent County Prosecutor McMahon waited while extradition formalities were observed. He talked to the prisoners. Martha was sullen, Ray strangely voluble. When questioned about a list of names and addresses found in his pocket he started on a rambling tale that sounded utterly unbelievable to hearers who were aghast at the revelations unfolded.

On March 16th the State of New York finally had custody of the prisoners' persons, and Michigan State waived the right to prosecute for murder before New York. The news broke in mammoth headlines across the United States. Ray Fernandez and Martha Beck were suddenly the centre of a dizzy vortex of wild curiosity. They were flown under armed guard to La Guardia airport, to find ranks of reporters and photographers awaiting their arrival.

Their return to the bright lights had made them front-page news. As entertainers for the readers of the more sensational journals, they were in the big time. The sob sisters really went to town with Martha. 'Overweight Juliet' was one caption over her full figure. 'Obese Ogress' was another. She was introduced to the millions of New Yorkers among whom she had lived for nearly two years as 'Ray's three-hundred-pound lovey-dovey'. The now notorious pair were charged with commiting three murders – those of Janet Fay, Mrs Downing, and the little girl Rainelle. They were suspected from inquiries made by the District Attorney's office of having committed seventeen others. The same office informed avid reporters that there were possibly still more that couldn't be checked.

But this was mass murder with a difference. The difference was the incredible love affair that had fused the personalities of Ray Fernandez and Martha Beck into a team of cruel executioners. The public was agog for facts. Martha and Ray supplied enough to curdle the blood of more timid newspaper readers. They told how the three victims with whose murder they had been charged actually died. Obviously they were being advised legally. Just as obviously a plea of insanity was about to be brought forward.

The backgrounds of the prisoners were raked over for anything relevant or irrelevant that might highlight the general picture of killers falling in love with each other. The strange childhoods of both partners in big city crimes were laid bare. While lawyers indulged in out-of-court legal skirmishes, and while newspapers kept public interest at white-heat, Martha Beck spent the dragging days in her cell reading mystery novels. She had at last graduated from true romances in her required reading to tailor-made murders. She also indulged in frantic bouts of letter-writing, mostly impassioned missives to the man who had ensnared her violent affections through a lonely hearts pen friendship.

Ray Fernandez appeared to pass the days in contemplation. Just what he contemplated he never made known, even to his legal advisers. He read the newspaper assiduously, but fiction did not appeal to him. He wrote some letters. Most of them were addressed to Martha, and were couched in terms of tenderness.

Then in June 1949 the trial of the incredible lovers for the murder of Janet Fay opened in New York before Judge Ferdinand Pecora.

By any court-room standards it threatened to be a bizarre affair, and the threat was fulfilled. For the forty-four days the trial lasted the Bronx County Court-house was packed. From June 9th until July 17th the legal battle continued, with the prisoners offering some of the most appalling detailed evidence ever submitted for a jury's consideration. Both Fernandez and Martha Beck indulged in long descriptions of their riotous intimacy as lovers. In an attempt to convince the jury that both were insane each indulged in obscene word pictures of their mutual love life. Passages went into the court records that could not be printed even by the most sensational of the metropolitan newspapers and journals.

Indeed, there was an overall emphasis on the sexual relationship of the prisoners that nauseated most onlookers and certainly the patient jury suffering as the level of the thermometer rose during those sweltering summer days. Martha staged her own dramatic big moment when called to take the witness stand. She marched forward in vivid green shoes on feet that appeared surprisingly dainty for a person of her gross figure. Her bright dress was of silk, and round her massive throat hung a two-strand necklace that chinked as she swayed forward, too-bright lips curved in a fleshy smile, her lost cheekbones dabbed in with high spots of rouge. Without warning she changed direction, and crossed quickly to Fernandez before blue-shirted guards could prevent her. She reached up and caught his surprised face in her large fat hands and pulled it down towards her. She kissed him on the mouth, and was kissing him when the guards reached her and pulled her away. Fernandez, his face smeared from her lip-rouge, grinned happily, a man on trial for his life who had eyes only for the woman who had brought a storm of passion into their months together.

He was still grinning fatuously when he saw her reach the witness stand, hot and flushed, but bright from a snatched triumph, and heard her shout, 'I love him, I do love him, and I always will!'

Most of her hearers shuddered despite the heat.

The jury sat stone-faced. In that court-room love had become a dirty word.

Finally the last plea had been made and the judge had directed the jury in the matter of insanity and the law. The jury retired, weary but grim. They returned more weary and grimmer. They were asked for their verdict.

'Guilty of murder in the first degree!'

The play-acting, the crudities, and the obscenities had all been offered in vain. The jury that tried Raymond Fernandez and Martha Beck remained convinced they were sane at the time they brought about Janet Fay's death.

The incredible lovers, silent and drained, were led away. They appeared in court together a few days later to hear Judge Pecora sentence them. They were both to be electrocuted.

Then began another long waiting period while lawyers waged a new battle of appeals.

Months passed, in which Martha lost her new-found taste for thrillers. She began writing verse. She addressed several to the man who had shared her violent hey-day of passion and murder. One she entitled *Memo to Ray*. She penned it in the death cell when the last appeal had failed and the incredible lovers knew they must die. It ran:

> Remember, sweetheart, the night that you and I
> Side by side were sitting,
> Watching o'er the moonlit sky.
> Fleecy clouds were flitting,
> How close our hands were linked then,
> When, my darling, when will they be linked again?
> What to me the starlight still
> Or the moonbeam's splendour,
> If I do not feel the thrill
> Of your fingers tender?

Not stuff for future ages to include in an anthology of romantic verse, perhaps, but when Ray Fernandez read it he burst into tears. He picked up a pencil and scribbled a hurried note which was taken to her. The two scrawled lines proclaimed ecstatically:

> I would like to shout my love for you
> to the world.

They were executed on the night of March 8th, 1951, within twelve minutes of each other. Death-chamber etiquette cynically reversed normal social convention. It was the woman who followed the man. When Martha Beck squeezed her hefty thighs into Sing-Sing's oaken chair of death and looked around the green-painted chamber for her last glimpse of things mortal, there was a smile curving her mouth. It was still in place when a switch was thrown and electricity poured through her gross body in a blazing torrent, dimming the lights of Sing-Sing.

Max Pemberton

THE DOUBLE LIFE OF EDITH THOMPSON

This celebrated trial opened at the Central Criminal Court, London, on the sixth day of December 1922.

The charge was that of murder, and it was preferred against a youth of twenty years of age, named Edward Francis Bywaters, and a woman of twenty-eight years of age, Edith Jessie Thompson, who was the wife of the murdered man. Bywaters was the admitted lover of the woman Thompson.

At the outset the public interest in the case had not been considerable. The majority thought it a mere sordid story of murder and adultery, related in a dreary suburb, and concerning people of little importance in the great world of affairs. This view was, in some measure, changed by the tongue of rumour which was loosed after the police-court proceedings; and so did the volume of gossip increase that the actual opening of the trial at the Central Criminal Court discovered an audience which included many of our foremost writers and not a few of our public men.

These people had heard that Edith Jessie Thompson was a woman of such remarkable force of character and such strange personal charm that the case was likely to become as famous as any the Courts had heard for many years – and so they came to hear it, and listened patiently to the recital of a drama which might have come from the pen of a great writer rather than from the lips of a prosecuting counsel for the Treasury.

Briefly stated, the case against the woman and her lover was this:

1

On the night of October 3rd–4th, a shipping clerk named Percy Thompson had taken his wife to the Criterion Theatre, and returned with her afterwards by train to the suburb of Ilford, where the couple lived. They reached the local station about midnight and set off to walk to Kensington Gardens, where their own house stood; but as they were going down a long and dreary thoroughfare named the Belgrave Road, a man came out of the darkness and stabbed Percy Thompson viciously in the neck. Immediately afterwards the agitated wife appealed to some passers-by for help, and then sought medical aid. When, however, they returned to Percy Thompson's side, he was dead.

Upon these facts the Crown charged Edith Jessie Thompson and Frederick Bywaters with murder; preferring also against the woman the further counts: (1) That she did solicit and endeavour to persuade and did propose to Frederick Bywaters to murder Percy Thompson; (2) That she did unlawfully solicit and incite Frederick Bywaters unlawfully to conspire with her to murder Percy Thompson; (3) That she did administer to and cause to be taken by Percy Thompson certain poison or other destructive thing unknown with intent to murder the said Percy Thompson; (4) That she did administer a destructive thing with intent to murder; (5) That she did administer to and cause to be taken a certain destructive thing, namely, broken glass, with intent to murder the said Percy Thompson.

Such was the case which came before Mr Justice Shearman on the sixth day of December in the year 1922. The importance of it was marked by the appearance of the Solicitor-General with Mr Travers Humphreys and Mr Roland Oliver for the Crown; while for Frederick Bywaters, Mr Cecil Whiteley, K.C., had Mr Huntly Jenkins and Mr Myles Elliott with him; and for Edith Thompson, Sir Henry Curtis Bennett, K.C., had Mr Walter Frampton and Mr Ivor Snell.

The trial opened with a protest, Mr Cecil Whiteley rising to submit that the two prisoners should not be tried together; and when this was overruled, Sir Henry Curtis Bennett protested in his turn against the use of certain letters which Edith Thompson had written to Frederick Bywaters. Again the learned counsel failed to find support, and so the case proceeded and a story most remarkable was unfolded.

2

Who were the people concerned in this most amazing story of passion and murder?

To begin with, there was Percy Thompson, thirty-two years of age, a shipping clerk to a city firm, with a very modest income and a scheme of life unlikely to attract a woman of passionate temperament or one who had dreamed dreams of a larger world than that of Ilford and its suburban gloom. A good, honest, plain-dealing man, no doubt, who was shockingly done by, but a difficult man, it may be, in his domestic relations, and most justly jealous of his wife's known intrigues and of those which were suspected but unknown.

Percy Thompson had married Edith Graydon in the year 1915. She was four years his junior and had been employed for twelve months by the firm of Carlton & White, wholesale milliners, of Aldersgate Street. Her maiden name was Edith Graydon, and the fact that she was an exceedingly capable business woman, who earned a larger salary than her husband, seems to have fomented domestic jealousy from the outset.

In the year 1920 this ill-matched couple went to live at Kensington Gardens, Ilford, and in the month of June 1921 they spent a holiday at Shanklin in the Isle of Wight. Thither the young man, Frederick Bywaters, accompanied them, and there the guilty woman first confessed her love for the youth who was to be her undoing.

He was a finely built young man – the prison doctor declared that he had rarely seen a finer – and the fact that he was eight years younger than Edith Thompson but added fuel to the fire of her passion.

Frank of face, with sturdy limbs, a fresh complexion and a high-pitched voice, this youth would have been physically remarkable in any trade or profession; and when we hear that his ship was the *Morea*, we think of him at once as a sturdy sailor, though, as a matter of fact, he was only a laundry steward, and served the P. & O. Company in that capacity at the date of the murder.

Bywaters, it appeared, had lived for a while with the Graydons, Edith Thompson's people, at Manor Park, and thus the intimacy with Edith Graydon had come about. When she was married he renewed his acquaintance with her upon one of the brief vacations his sea life permitted, and so went to the Isle of Wight in June 1921, in the company of her and her husband. From this moment it was evident that the whole tenor of their lives was changed. The happy relations existing hitherto between Thompson and his wife were to exist no longer – and we cannot doubt for a moment that Bywaters was the cause, and that the advances he made to the woman – or she to him – were the whole causes of the disaster.

They returned to London and, for a little while, Bywaters continued to lodge with the Thompsons at their house in Kensington Gardens, Ilford. If Percy Thompson had suspected nothing at Shanklin, it is quite evident that his suspicions were aroused at home, and as early as the month of August a violent quarrel ensued, and the young man was ordered to leave the house. His ship sailed in September, returning in the autumn and leaving again in November. The intervening weeks saw the beginning of as remarkable a correspondence as the annals of secret and guilty love have recorded. A new Madame Bovary is now revealed to us, and we are confronted by a complex study of femininity which Gustave Flaubert would have been proud to create.

Edith Jessie Thompson, book-keeper to a milliner, the housewife of a shabby suburban villa, going laboriously to and fro between her suburb and Aldersgate Street: what sort of a woman was she?

One great writer, Mr Filson Young, whose book upon this crime must stand for a masterpiece, described her in words which cannot be bettered. 'There were,' he says, 'people present at her trial who are connoisseurs in women and scholars of their character, and who are able to recognise behind the most sordid disguises the presence of that something which lifts a woman out of whatever class she may naturally belong to and sets her in a class apart – the class of influencing, compelling, driving, beckoning women who have power over men, and, through them, over the world.'

Undoubtedly she was this – but she was more. Those who saw her at the Central Criminal Court – of whom I was one –

perceived in her such frequent and amazing changes of mood and of manner that we imagined the whole story of her life could be read in them. Sometimes we would say that she was sobbing, and the play of her shoulders and her wonderful neck would seem to support the assumption; but a moment later, she would look up swiftly when some word or charge arrested her attention, and we would see a face sunny with a smile or eyes which blazed indignation or denial.

Never, I suppose, had that Court caged one who presented so difficult a problem to the artist. Sometimes the verdict would be that she was beautiful – or, again, that she was merely pretty. Then fatigue or fear would operate, and all her beauty would disappear as in a flash, and a hard, unwinning expression take its place. No two drawings of her show the same woman: the photographers do not agree – she is the wife, the mistress, the theatrical star, but no two portraits are alike – and the enigma remains, so that we, impressed by her dominating passion rather than by her personality, think of the mistress before remembering the woman.

3

The Solicitor-General named June 27th in the year 1921 as a date of great moment in the story of these three lives, 'because, in Mrs Thompson's letters, it was mentioned as a date which marked a crisis or change in the relations between her and Bywaters.' There followed the quarrel with her husband, and then that 'passionate and ardent correspondence between these two persons, which showed that they were engaged or intended to engage in an intrigue.' Mrs Thompson continued to live with her husband, but henceforth she was to meet Frederick Bywaters secretly whenever he returned from a voyage, and to write him at length and extravagantly while he was away from home.

No doubt the young lover responded in his turn, and we may imagine that his letters were not less ardent and passionate than her own – but, with two unimportant exceptions, these letters had been destroyed, so that we shall never know their nature nor the provocation they afforded the woman.

Schooled in worldly wisdom, Edith Thompson knew well the danger of her written word, and while she burned the amorous evidences of her guilt, Frederick Bywaters appears to have kept all that had been written to him, and so the world was to hear more intimately, perhaps, of this intrigue than of any in the story of crime.

'All these letters,' said Sir Thomas Inskip, 'were found in the possession of Bywaters by the police, and taken from his pocket or from his rooms on the day or day after the murder – or found in a "ditty" box on the ship. There is one letter which I wish to read. It bears no date . . . it appears to have been written to Bywaters when he was some distance from the United Kingdom . . . after the running of the November Handicap of 1921, and the internal evidence in the letter shows that it was written before Christmas. In that letter there appears the following:

> "It is the man who has no rights who generally comforts the woman who has no wrongs. This is also right: darlint, isn't it? as things are, but, darlint, it's not always going to be, is it? You will have the right soon, won't you? Say yes." '

The Attorney-General naturally dwelt solemnly upon this striking passage, and those who listened to him soon became aware of his object. He was going to prove, as it were, out of Edith Thompson's own mouth, the creation of a purpose, not only to terminate the 'rights' of Percy Thompson, but to do so if necessary by the deliberate taking of life. In quick succession, he had quotations from this remarkable correspondence, and each seemed to progress in gravity towards that final deduction which must be overwhelming. Thus an early letter says:

> 'The time goes slowly enough in all conscience – I don't seem to care who spends the money as long as it enables me to dance through the hours. . . . You'll probably say I'm careless and I admit I am, but I don't care – do you?'

And again thus:

> 'The only one I have is the "Dear Edie" one written to 41, which I am going to keep. It may be useful, who

knows. . . . I've surrendered to him unconditionally now – do you understand me? I think it the best way to disarm any suspicion; in fact, he has several times asked me if I am happy now, and I've said "yes, quite," but you know that's not the truth, don't you?'

Even a more characteristic letter is this:

'Darlint, – You must do something this time – I'm not really impatient – but opportunities come and go by – they have to – because I'm helpless and I think and think and think – perhaps – it will never come again. . . . On Wednesday we had words – in bed – Oh, you know, darlint – over that same old subject, and he said – It was all through you I'd altered. . . . About 2 a.m. he woke me up and asked for water, as he felt ill. I got it for him and asked him what the matter was, and this is what he told me – whether it's the truth I don't know or whether he did it to frighten me, anyway it didn't. He said – someone he knows in town (not the man I previously told you about) had given him a prescription for a draught for insomnia and he'd had it made up and taken it, and it made him ill. He certainly looked ill and his eyes were glassy. I've hunted for the said prescription everywhere and can't find it, and asked what he had done with it and he said the chemist kept it. I told Avis about the incident, only I told her as if it frightened and worried me, as I thought perhaps it might be useful at some future time that I had told somebody. What do you think, darlint?'

Sir Thomas Inskip described this passage as 'perhaps dark, but it was the first light thrown in court upon what the prosecution meant by a "conspiracy to murder" '; from this moment onward interest in the case quickened rapidly. Was it possible that this remarkable woman, passionately in love with a youth of nineteen years of age, had deliberately resolved at that time to poison Percy Thompson that she might be quit of him? The prosecution said 'yes,' and said it emphatically. Letter after letter appeared to bear witness to the allegation. She begins to send her 'darlint' gruesome cuttings from the newspapers which specialise in crime. 'Bella Donna,' Mr Hichens' creation, the courtesan who married respectability and poisoned at the bidding of her Egyptian lover – 'Bella Donna' is discussed intimately. We hear of newspaper extracts concerning 'Poison chocolates for University chief'; 'Deadly Powder posted to Oxford Chancellor'; 'Ground Glass in Box'; 'Scotland Yard called in to probe "Serious Outrage" '; 'Girl's Death Riddle'; 'Tales of London Life'; 'Visit to a Chinese Restaurant' – all these figure and with them phrases upon which, it would seem, but one construction can be placed.

Let us consider these extraordinary documents a little more closely and in the order in which the Solicitor-General unfolded them.

> 'I suppose it isn't possible for you to send it to me – not at all possible; I do so chafe at wasting time, darlint.'
>
> 'I ask you again to think out all the plans and methods for me. I wait and wait so anxiously now – for the time when we'll be with each other, even though it is only once – for "one little hour." '

Edith Thompson wrote this next letter on March 31st, the day Bywaters sailed:

> 'After to-night I am going to die . . . not really . . . but put on the mask again, darlint, until the 26th May – doesn't it seem years and years away? It does to me, and I'll hope and hope all the time that I'll never have to wear the mask any more after this time. . . . This time really will be the last you will go away – like things are, won't it? We said it before, darlint, I know, and we failed . . . but there will be no failure next time, darlint, there mustn't be – I'm telling you – if things are the same again then I am going with you – wherever it is – if it's to sea – I am coming, too, and if it is to nowhere – I'm also coming, darlint. You'll never leave me behind again, never, unless things are different.'

'Don't keep this piece. About the marconigram – do you mean one saying "Yes" or "No," because I shan't send it, darlint? I'm not going to try any more until you come back. I made up my mind about this last Thursday. He was telling his mother, etc., the circumstances of my "Sunday morning escapade," and he puts great stress on the fact of the tea tasting bitter, "as if something had been put in it," he says. Now I think whatever else I try it in again will still taste bitter – he will recognise it and be more suspicious, and if the quantity is still not successful it will injure any chance I may have of trying when you come home. Do you understand? I thought a lot about what you said of Dan. Darlint, don't trust him – I don't mean don't tell him anything, because I know you never would – what I mean is, don't let him be suspicious of you regarding that – because if we were successful in the action – darling, circumstances may afterwards make us want many friends – or helpers, and we must have no enemies – or even people that know a little too much. Remember the saying, "A little knowledge is a dangerous thing." Darlint, we'll have no one to help us in the world now, and we mustn't make enemies unnecessarily. He says – to his people – he fought and fought with himself to keep conscious. "I'll never die, except naturally, – I'm like a cat with nine lives," he said, and detailed to them an occasion when he was young and nearly suffocated by gas fumes. I wish we had not got electric light – it would be easy. I'm going to try the glass again occasionally – when it is safe. I've got an electric globe this time.'

'I used the "light bulb" three times, but the third time – he found a piece – so I have given it up – until you come home.

'I don't think we're failures in other things and we mustn't be in this. We mustn't give in as we said. No, we shall have to wait if we fail again, darlint. Fate can't always turn against us, and if it is we must fight it – you and I are strong now. We must be stronger. We must learn to be patient. . . . You said it was enough for an elephant.

Perhaps it was. But you don't allow for the taste making only a small quantity to be taken. It sounded like a reproach. Was it meant to be? Darlint, I tried hard – you won't know how hard – because you weren't there to see and I can't tell you – but I did – I do want you to believe I did for both of us. . . . I was buoyed up with the hope of the "light bulb" and I used a lot – big pieces, too, not powdered – and it has no effect – I quite expected to be able to send that cable – but no – nothing has happened from it, and now your letter tells me about the bitter taste again. Oh, darlint, I do feel so down and unhappy. Wouldn't the stuff make small pills coated together with soap and dipped in liquorice powder – like Beecham's – try while you're away. Our Boy had to have his thumb operated on because he had a piece of glass in it – that's what made me try that method again – but I suppose, as you say, he is not normal. I know I feel I shall never get him to take a sufficient quantity of anything bitter. No, I haven't forgotten the key I told you before. . . . If ever we are lucky enough to be happy, darling, I'll love you such a lot. I always show you how much I love you for all that you do for me. . . . All that lying and scheming and subterfuge to obtain one little hour in each day – when by right of nature and our love we should be together for all the twenty-four in every day.'

'It must be remembered that digitalin is a cumulative poison and that the same dose harmless if taken once, yet frequently repeated, becomes deadly.'

'I'd like you to read *Bella Donna*; you may learn something from it to help us. Then you can read *The Fruitful Vine*.'

'Darlingest boy, I'm trying very hard – very, very hard to B.B.* I know my pal wants me to. On Thursday – he was on the ottoman at the foot of the bed, and said he

---

*Mr Filson Young suggests that this probably means 'be brave'.

was dying and wanted to – he had another heart attack – thro' me. Darlint, I had to laugh at this, because I knew it couldn't be a heart attack. When he saw this had no effect on me, he got up and stormed. I said exactly what you told me to, and he replied that he knew that's what I wanted and he wasn't going to give it to me – it would make things far too easy for both of you (meaning you and me).'

'Then we were pals – this year we seem no further advanced. Why should you not send me something? You still have your own way always. If I do not mind the risk, why should you?'

'From then onwards everything has gone well with our lives. Darling, I should not mind if I could feel some day I could make up to you for some of the unhappiness I have cost you – I feel it shall come right, but there is no conviction in it. Why cannot we see into the future?'

'Darlingest boy, I don't quite understand you about "pals." You say, "Can we be pals only, Peidi? It will make it easier." Do you mean for always? Because if you do, no, no, a thousand times. We can't be "pals" only for always, darlint; it's impossible physically and mentally. . . . It must be still "the hope of all" or "the finish of all." If you still only mean for a certain time and you think it best, darlint, it shall be so – I don't see how it will be easier myself. . . . You sound very despondent when you say about "Time passes and with it some of the pain – Fate ordained our lot to be hard." Does some of the pain you feel pass with time? Perhaps it does – things seem so much easier to forget with a man – his environment is always different – but with a woman it's always the same. Darlint, my pain gets less and less bearable – it hurts more and more every day, every hour really. . . . Yes, darlint, you are jealous of him – but I want you to be – he has the right by law to all that you have the right to by nature and love – yes, darlint, be jealous, so much that you will do something desperate.'

'Darlingest lover of mine, thank you, thank you, oh, thank you a thousand times for Friday – it was lovely – always lovely to go out with you. And then Saturday – yes, I did feel happy. . . . All Saturday evening I was thinking about you. . . . I tried so hard to find a way out of to-night, darlingest, but he was suspicious and still is – I suppose we must make a study of this deceit for some time longer. I hate it. . . . Don't forget what we talked about in the tea-room. I'll still risk and try if you will – we only have three and three-quarter years left, darlingest.'

Edith Thompson, then, is trying to find a 'way out'. Passion – the passion of the amorous woman for the boy of fine physical gifts – is evident in every line that she writes. She has won, and greatly she desires to keep her lover.

Whether his letters did or did not incite her to a criminal act that the offending husband might be removed, we shall never know; but certainly she is willing enough in words, though of deeds there is no evidence. All that the prosecution deduced from these letters is denied by the medical evidence. No trace of poison whatever was found in the body of the unfortunate Percy Thompson. The 'ground glass' she was supposed to have administered to him left no trace upon the organs concerned, and yet doctors could say it would have been impossible to have administered it without trace. There is not a jot or tittle of evidence to prove that the deceased ever swallowed tea which tasted bitter, or that his wife administered it. This plot to poison resolves itself in fact into a plot to hold and to keep – a plot to fire the imagination of a youth by tales of sacrifice – the plot of a desperate woman who saw a lover about to slip from her arms, and would risk all – in words – that she might still embrace him.

We shall consider this aspect of the case again at a later stage. The letters carry us to a situation upon which we must now dwell.

4

Edith Thompson rejoiced in the possession of Frederick Bywaters as a lover, but their opportunities for gratifying their passion were few. In the year 1922, the young man returned to London on January 6th, and sailed again on January 20th; he was in England on May 25th, but left it on June 9th; he returned on September 23rd, but never again set foot on any ship. His brief home-comings were as paradise to the woman. They would meet as they could. Some of their meeting-places we shall never know, but they lunched and had tea together, and even made love in the shadow of that suburban house where the doomed man awaited her. And always they talked of the time when the husband would no longer have 'rights' and they could pass halcyon days in each other's company. Why, then, did she not walk away quietly from Kensington Gardens and set up a new home of her own? Why not, as one of the great counsel in the case asked me but recently, why not go, say, to Ealing or Kew and live with her lover, a life which few need have known or questioned? The answer, unfortunately, is sordid, and has little relation to romance.

Wildly as Edith Thompson adored her young lover, she did not appear ready to make any sacrifices for him. Part of the furniture at Kensington Gardens was her own and she earned good wages in Aldersgate Street. If she had gone away with Frederick Bywaters, undoubtedly she would have lost her job and Percy Thompson would have kept the furniture. Suburbia and the terrible fear of losing her lover constantly oppressed her mind. Her circumstances were as pitiful as those of Madame Bovary – and suicide was no way out for her, a lover of life and passion and dreams.

Often must one pause, in considering this strange woman, to let imagination have its head and to ask what would have befallen her in other spheres. Think of her as a mere humble servant of a theatre and consider what opportunities would have been hers among the rich men who haunt the *coulisses* of the playhouse. She was not a moral woman – and she was ambitious beyond her station. As Mr Filson Young has said, riches undoubtedly would have become her portion; we should have seen her at the night clubs and the great hotels – her pictures would have been in the illustrated papers, and she might have achieved a marriage which the town would have applauded but the peerage rebuked. All this would have been possible to Edith

Thompson in the vicinity of Shaftesbury Avenue. It was wholly impossible at Kensington Gardens, Ilford. There she would remain because of the house, the furniture and the tongues which would clack. We may even doubt if she had any desire to elope with Frederick Bywaters at all.

She did not desire to elope with him, and yet she had a passionate longing to be with him. When Percy Thompson remained unaware of what was going on, the course was clear for the lovers; but, unhappily for himself, his suspicions appear at length to have been aroused, and when Bywaters left the ship *Morea* on September 23rd, the woman at once warned him that there was danger.

Already she had received an anonymous letter in which it was suggested to her that she would be wise not to see her lover during his approaching stay in London; but this clearly whetted her appetite, and we find her waiting impatiently for him to come ashore, and by the 25th day of September they have already met. Henceforth, however, the intrigue is to march with difficulty. They fear being watched. Percy Thompson is suspicious of the woman's every movement. There is an appointment for October 2nd, and they meet. The next afternoon finds them at a Fuller's tea-shop, and that is the last hour of their secrecy they are ever to enjoy.

What happened at that fateful meeting, we shall never know. She may have talked again of all their months of intrigue and desire, may have deplored her 'failures' and spoken of some new attempt. Or, on the other hand, he may have pleaded with feminine design for that flight together which she had no intention of making and for that separation from her husband which her courage could not face. The prosecution naturally suggested to the jury that Percy Thompson's death was actually planned at that humble rendezvous. I do not believe that it was so, for I am in possession of Bywater's confession, made a few hours before his death; but the suggestion was fair and it had to be considered. If it be true, then the subsequent acts are complex and to be understood with difficulty; if it be untrue, our task is easy, and we can say that the murder was merely a sudden and brutal attack which disappointed lust had provoked and drink had made possible.

Bywaters asked Edith Thompson to go out with him on the night of October 3rd and she refused, fearing her husband. The pair separated, apparently in some anger, and she returned to her office and subsequently went to the Criterion Theatre with Percy Thompson, as she had said that she would do. Bywaters, for his part, appears to have wandered about for some time and then to have gone to the Graydons' house, where he learned that Edith would be returning to her home about midnight, and, having got the information, he quitted these people just at eleven o'clock, according to the prosecution, and when next heard of is arrested (on the evening of October 4th) and taken immediately to Ilford Police Station.

Yet in the meantime, a foul murder has been committed, and Percy Thompson lies dead in his own house, stabbed brutally in the head and neck by an assassin then unknown, but speedily to be discovered.

He had arrived with his wife at Ilford Station just about midnight, and the pair had set out to walk home down the lonely Belgrave Road, when suddenly a man had leaped upon him violently, given him many blows, and vanished in the darkness. Such was the end of the romance of Frederick Bywaters and his mistress – such the terrible climax of this terrible story.

Let us hear the witness who had the first intimation of the crime:

Says Dora Finch Pittard:

'A few minutes before midnight on October 3rd I arrived with friends at Ilford and proceeded to walk home by Belgrave Road. When between De Vere Gardens and Endsleigh Gardens I saw a woman running towards me – the prisoner, Mrs Thompson. She cried out: "Oh, my God! Will you help me? My husband is ill, he is bleeding." I asked her where he was, and she said he was on the pavement. I took Mrs Thompson to the house of Dr Maudsley at the corner of Courtland Avenue, and then I went back to Kensington Gardens, Mrs Thompson being just in front of me. Finding a man lying on the pavement, I asked Mrs Thompson what had happened to her husband, and she said: "Oh, don't ask me, I don't know. Somebody flew past, and when I turned to speak to him, blood was pouring out of his mouth." Mrs Thompson was very agitated and incoherent.'

Says Percy Edward Clevely:

'I live at 62 Mayfair Avenue, Ilford. I was one of the party which included the last witness, Miss Pittard. While walking through Belgrave Road, we met the prisoner, Mrs Thompson, who seemed to come out of the darkness, as it were. She spoke about her husband having fallen down, that he was ill, and she wanted help, and she asked where we could find a doctor. We went to Dr Maudsley's house, and on returning, we found the deceased lying on the pavement, with his back propped up against the wall. I asked Mrs Thompson how it happened and she said she could not say – "Something brushed past," or "flew past" or words to that effect, "and he fell down." '

John Webber, examined by Mr Roland Oliver, testifies:

'I am a sales manager and I live at 59 De Vere Gardens, Ilford. About 12.30 in the morning of October 4th, just as I was about to retire to bed, I heard a woman's voice saying: "Oh, don't; oh, don't," in a most piteous manner. On hearing that, I went out into the street and I saw two ladies and a gentleman coming towards me in the direction of Dr Maudsley's house. One of the ladies was running in front of the other two. After they had passed me I saw a match being struck. I went up to the place and found a man sitting against the wall. Mrs Thompson was there alone with him, and I asked her if the man had had a fall, but she said she did not know. I asked her if I could be of assistance to her and she said: "Don't touch him, don't touch him; a lady and a gentleman have gone off for a doctor." After that Dr Maudsley came with Miss Pittard and Mr Clevely. I helped the doctor to undress the man. I heard the doctor ask if he had been ill, and where they had come from. She told him that he had not been ill and that they had come from the Criterion Theatre.'

Cross-examined by Sir H. Curtis Bennett:

'I have no doubt whatever that the voice which said, "Oh, don't; oh, don't," was the voice of Mrs Thompson.'

The doctor naturally was the next witness, and he told how he had discovered the dead man on the pavement:

'I struck a match and made an examination of the man. I first examined his pulse and found that he was dead. I should think about five or eight minutes would elapse from the time I was first called until I actually got to the body. When I examined the man, I should say he had been dead somewhere about ten minutes. Mrs Thompson was in a confused condition, hysterical and agitated. . . . When I told her that her husband was dead, she said: "Why did you not come sooner and save him?"'

So here was the man dead upon the pavement, and here was the end of this amazing romance. Edith Jessie Thompson need seek a 'way out' no more. Lust and brutality had found it for her.

Of course, the police were soon upon the scene, and at three o'clock that morning the woman was examined by Sergeant Grimes of the K division. She protested that she could not say how her husband had been killed. 'I only know that he suddenly dropped down and screamed out "Oh!"' Later on the Sergeant asked her if she had been carrying a knife in her handbag and she replied emphatically: 'No!' the same answer being given to the question: 'And did you notice anyone as you came along the Belgrave Road?' Unhappy woman!

Just think what might have happened if she had kept her head at that critical instant and had said: 'A strange little man with a hump on his back and a squint in his eye had come up and asked my husband for his money, and when my husband refused to give him any, he stabbed him.'

Who, as a great criminologist asked me the other day, who would then have heard of Bywaters or the letters?

Happily for the cause of justice, she had no such courage. They arrested her next day, and after one statement, which was a lie, she began to babble of Frederick Bywaters and so swiftly put the police on his track. 'Oh, oh, God!' she cried, 'what can I do? Why did he do it? I did not want him to do it. When we got to Endsleigh Gardens a man rushed out from the gardens and knocked me away and pushed me away from my husband. I was dazed for a moment. When I recovered, I saw my husband scuffling with a man. The man whom I knew as Freddy Bywaters was running away. He was wearing a blue overcoat and a grey hat. I knew it was him although I did not see his face.'

Of course, Bywaters was arrested directly she had named him in the affair, was, in fact, taken at the Graydon house, where he had gone to talk about the murder; and he also began with a lying statement, accusing the dead man of great cruelty towards his wife, and declaring that he had left their house originally because the woman had been thrown across the room by her husband. The rest was the merest pretence – that he had visited the couple occasionally when he came home from sea, but that he was as innocent as a child where the murder was concerned. This attitude, of course, could not be maintained. The woman had confessed, and that was the end of it; and we find him making a second statement on the following day, and its terms settled the matter.

'I wish to make a voluntary statement. Mrs Edith Thompson was not aware of my movements on Tuesday night, 3rd October. I left Manor Park at 11 p.m. and proceeded to Ilford. I waited for Mrs Thompson and her husband. When near Endsleigh Gardens I pushed her to one side, also pushing him farther up the street. I said to him, "You have got to separate from your wife." He said, "No." I said, "You will have to." We struggled. I took my knife from my pocket and we fought, and he got the worst of it. . . . The reason I fought with Thompson was that he never acted like a man to his wife. He always seemed several degrees lower than a snake. I loved her and I could not see her go on leading that life. I did not intend to kill him. . . . I gave him the opportunity of standing up to me as a man, but he wouldn't. I have had the knife for some time; it was a sheath knife. I threw it down a drain when I was running through Endsleigh Gardens.'

Such was his statement, emphasising, as we know, merely the substance of the truth, but richly decorated with fabrication. He did not argue with Percy Thompson – he did not stand up to him in fair fight. So much he confessed upon the very eve of his execution. Rather he leaped out from the darkness, stabbed his enemy viciously in the neck and then disappeared in a flash. That he said himself, and he should know. Had he said it in the witness-box he might have saved the woman's life.

Here I would observe that I have had this very knife in my hands, and that Percy Thompson's blood was upon it when I had it. The people who sold it described it as a hunting knife – one carried in a sheath and commonly worn by seamen, to whom a long knife is a necessity. It was keen and long, and we can readily understand that a man stabbed in the neck with it, as Percy Thompson was, would not have many minutes to live. Indeed, he seems to have died almost immediately, as has been said – and because he died, Mr Cecil Whiteley and Sir Henry Curtis Bennett were faced with as hard a task as must have confronted them in all their long careers.

Firstly, of course, there was that terrible ordeal of putting the man and the woman into the box. Some have criticised Sir Henry for letting Mrs Thomspon appear as a witness at all; but this is to confess complete ignorance of her character, and as Mr Cecil Whiteley himself declared to me – 'she absolutely insisted and nothing short of a miracle could have kept her out.'

But for such insistence we see quite plainly that Sir Henry might have challenged the prosecution to prove her complicity. He might have said: 'We took no part whatever in this murder; we did not conspire with nor incite the prisoner to commit it – it is for you to bring it home to us if you can.'

I do not say that such a course would have saved her, but undoubtedly it would have spared her the terrible questions which the cross-examination put to her.

Those amazing letters – how Bywaters must have regretted that he did not do with hers as she wisely had done with his, and put them in the fire!

'It would be so easy, darlint – if I had things – I do hope I shall.'

What things, then, and for what purpose?

Reluctantly the admission is dragged from her that Bywaters had been sending her something 'to injure her husband,' but firmly and calmly she swears that nothing had been given. She is many figures by turn but nothing long – pathetic, courageous, pleading, emphatic – but never hysterical, as her critics have said. And the picture of her changes to the eye most curiously, so that you see her young and very beautiful – or again, haggard and careworn, and you say that a man who knew her in one rôle might absolutely fail to recognise her in another.

After all, the task was colossal enough, and even this great actress was not wholly equal to it. Had she been free to tell the truth, she might have given answers to some of the questions which would have astonished the court. What, for instance, if she had confessed that many of the references to 'ground glass' and other poisons did not concern Percy Thompson at all, but were remedies to be taken by her for a purpose which was nefarious. She might have done so and with truth – though her counsel was most wisely against the admission. 'We could not have put it before the world in such a guise,' one of them said to me, and I am sure that he is right. In my view her defence was masterly, and that of Frederick Bywaters not less so. All that could be done was done, and with an eloquence worthy of those who did it.

Hopeless as the position obviously was, both man and woman struggled with it to the bitter end. They tried vainly enough to explain away the damning phrases. Their 'disappointments' did not refer to Percy Thompson's death, but to his unwillingness to get a divorce. Their refusal to wait any longer meant that eventually they would go to Australia together and so cut the Gordian knot. But neither Judge nor jury was impressed, and it was evident at an early stage that Mr Justice Shearman took the gravest view. When he came to sum up, he declared that it was an ordinary charge of a wife and an adulterer murdering a husband; but all who had heard it had long been of a different opinion, and many feel that in this respect his description of the case was not wholly accurate.

As this wonderful drama unfolded, there were many speculations as to what would be its outcome.

Counsel for the defence did not believe for a moment that Edith Thompson would be convicted of murder in the first degree. They thought that she, found guilty of the conspiracy, would be given twelve years' penal servitude. This is the sentence she should have received – for there is no longer a doubt that she should not have been hanged.

Not, mind you, that it was necessary for her to be present at the actual moment of the crime to convict her and sentence her to the scaffold. If it really was proved that, because of her incitements, Frederick Bywaters struck Percy Thompson down, then she was guilty. But we cannot believe that this was so. Wisely did Sir Henry Curtis Bennett refer in his great speech to the atmosphere of a play or an opera.

'You have got to get into the atmosphere of this case. This

is no ordinary case you are trying. These are not ordinary people that you are trying. This is not an ordinary charge of murder. This is not an ordinary charge against ordinary people. It is very difficult to get into the atmosphere of a play or opera, but you have to do it in this case. Am I right or wrong in saying that this woman is one of the most extraordinary personalities that you or I have ever met? Bywaters truly described her, did he not, as a woman who lived a sort of life I don't suppose any of you live in – an extraordinary life of make-believe. She reads a book and then imagines herself one of the characters of the book. She is always living an extraordinary life of novels. She reads a book, and although the man to whom she is writing is at the other end of the wide world – in Bombay, Australia, the Suez Canal – she wants his views regarding the characters in the books she has just read. You have read her letters. Have you ever read, mixed up with criticisms of books, more beautiful language of love? Such things have been very seldom put by pen upon paper. This is the woman you have to deal with, not some ordinary woman.'

Truly she had lived in an atmosphere that was wholly false and glittered with strange lights. She sought to hold her lover by her melodrama, and was willing to pose as a poisoner in his sight if thereby she might win and hold him. Not incitements were the letters, but embroidered lies, and it is just to imagine that they had no more to do with the actual murder than the newsboy who sold the papers which recorded the crime. Unhappily for her, a jury could understand neither the melodrama nor the hidden meaning of her words. The Judge would accept no subtler views. Did she, in truth, know that Frederick Bywaters meant to murder her husband? Few people now believe that she did.

'I am not guilty – oh, my God, I am not guilty.'

Her last words at the Old Bailey rang out terribly in Court, and they must still ring o' nights in the ears of some.

5

A few hours before he died, Frederick Bywaters made a statement which seems to tell the whole truth about this terrible case. He then declared that he was blind drunk when he committed the murder. He said that he was determined that Edith Thompson should go out with him that night, and that he pleaded with her to go when they were at the tea-shop together during the afternoon. Most unexpectedly she refused, saying that she was going to the theatre with her husband, and she refused to be turned from that purpose. He left her and got drunk, and then went to the Graydons', where he learned that she was at the Criterion, and this angered him the more, so that he got more drunk when he left their house and finally resolved to go to Ilford Station and wait for her arrival. He had himself successfully followed the pair down the Belgrave Road. Suddenly, he declared, Percy Thompson put his arm round his wife's waist, made a gesture of affection and was not resisted. The act and its significance drove the drunken man to a state of fury. He leaped upon his victim, and there and then struck him down. Mrs Thompson knew nothing of his being there nor of his purpose. 'They are hanging an innocent woman,' he protested, and his protest rang true.

Yet they hanged her on January 9th, 1923, at Holloway Prison, and Bywaters upon the same morning at Pentonville. Of these executions, Mr Filson Young says in an eloquent passage:

'He went to his death with firmness and assurance. She was taken to hers in a state of collapse and, I hope, of merciful oblivion. For, on the most sober consideration of the case, her execution seems to have been without other than merely legal justification, and to have been the result of a kind of frozen moral inertia which seized those whose business and responsibility it should have been to avoid an act that, though technically justifiable on legal grounds, was, in the considered judgment of public opinion, as essentially unjust as it was inexpedient.'

Miriam Allen DeFord

SUPERMAN'S CRIME

Murder without motive is very rare. Murder by a near-genius, whose act can be traced not to any demonstrable insanity, but to a profound physical and emotional abnormality, is rarer still. In 1924 such a murder struck Chicago and became a world-wide sensation.

This celebrated case had still further anomalies. It was the deed of two young boys, acting together; and in view of all the evidence it can be said categorically that the crime would never have been committed by either of them acting independently; it was the combination of their peculiar personalities and their reaction on each other that brought it about. It is known as the Loeb–Leopold case.

In 1900 the youngest child of Nathan F. Leopold, a millionaire business man, was born in Chicago and named for his father – though to his family he was always known as 'Babe.'

The boy was not very old before any competent physician could have seen that there was something very wrong with his physical make-up. In every way he was precocious – but precocious as a forced plant is, which grows awry, develops brilliant premature blossoms, and from root to leaf-tip is subtly malformed. Nathan Leopold's adrenal, pineal, and thymus glands were all diseased – either insufficiently developed or too early involuted; while his thyroid gland was overactive. He grew up an undersized, round-shouldered boy, with coarse hair and skin and bulging eyes. Sexually he was fully developed at an age when most boys are just beginning to feel the first stirrings of puberty. Like any other intelligent child, he realized very well his deficiencies and peculiarities, compared himself painfully to others, and suffered. Human beings thus forced into an inferiority complex may succumb to it and end in shrinking abjectness; or they may react by what is called over-compensation. Young Leopold's was the latter way. He became touchy, sensitive, easily offended, a permanent chip attached to his drooping shoulder. And he built up a comforting picture of himself as superior to all of humankind – a Superman who could do no wrong. His extraordinary mind helped him to put over the picture; for Nathan Leopold was far more than just a brilliant student. He was widely read in literature and philosophy – Friedrich Nietzsche and his theory of the Superman became his guiding principle; he was an inspired amateur ornithologist and botanist whose work was taken seriously by professionals; he spoke nine languages fluently. In his ordinary studies he did so well that at eighteen he received his B.Ph. degree from the University of Chicago – the youngest graduate in its history – and then went on to its law school, where he equally distinguished himself.

All this might have built up a not altogether unknown figure – the child prodigy who makes up for weaknesses and defects by exaggerated distinctions and abilities, and who probably ends as an honoured and a bit out-dated professor. This boy ended as a convicted murderer.

Why? There are many answers; but one which is glaringly obvious is the idiotic nature of his upbringing. If his well-meaning parents had deliberately set out to make a monster of their child, they could not have succeeded better.

Here was a boy who needed above all things to be made to feel one with the rest of humanity – different, perhaps, but still essentially akin to his fellow beings. Instead, he learned from his earliest childhood that his family's possession of great wealth gave him special privileges and immunities; the laws that govern others did not govern him. Did he want to kill birds in the park or fish out of season? Very well: his father would secure a special permit for him or pay his fines and get him off. Was there anything at all he wanted? Here it was: $125 a month allowance; a car of his own; $3000 for a trip to Europe before he entered the Harvard Law School. The one thing never told him was that he owed any duties or obligations to anyone.

All this might only have turned him into a hard and selfish creature; but far worse developments occurred. From the beginning, Leopold's disordered glandular system doomed him to sexual aberration. He was shy, he was afraid of girls, his daydreams were all of someone stronger and bigger whom he could worship, whose cruelty would be his joy. As Irving Stone put it, this boy who boasted of being a Nietzschean Superman actually yearned to become 'a superwoman, a female slave . . . to some big, handsome, powerful king.' He was to find his king, but not until he had been thoroughly warped into an unchangeable pattern.

In early childhood he was put completely under the charge of a governess straight out of horror fiction. She obsessed him, she fostered the rank growth of his Uranian tendency, and being herself a pervert, she took delight in practising on the child, and in teaching him to practise on her, forms of abnormal sex play that only Kinsey can describe in print.

Then, when at last his parents noticed that Babe did not seem to have the normal boy's attitude towards girls, they devised a marvellous scheme to cure him. They deliberately sent him - under the care of the same governess - as the only boy pupil in a school for girls!

Finally, as if to make sure that nothing was lacking for his ruin, his mother died when he was an adolescent. She had been the one exception to his horror of the female - she was a 'saint,' a 'Madonna.' Her death 'proved' that there was no God.

Somehow this boy - who had become almost a classic case history of the growth of a psychopathic personality - might still have adjusted himself superficially to the demands of normal society, except for one thing. At the age of fourteen he met the personification of his dream of the god-king to whom he could be a worshipping slave.

This other boy, a year younger, was Richard A. Loeb, known as 'Dickie,' son of Albert H. Loeb, vice-president of Sears, Roebuck and Company. In his own way, Dickie was as abnormal as Babe, but on the surface they were very different. Where Leopold's intellect was of the first order, Loeb was merely a clever lad who learned easily without trying; he in turn became the youngest graduate of the University of Michigan, and was ready to enter law school at seventeen. He too had been reared to think of himself as outside the restrictions that bound those of lesser wealth, and he had been even more pampered, if that were possible – his allowance was twice the size of Leopold's, for example. But where Leopold worked his rearing into a fantasy of the Superman and the Superman's only god, the god of pure strength, Loeb had become merely callous and arrogant.

In two other aspects he was very different from Leopold, and these differences were the seed of the evil plant that grew from their association. Loeb was tall, handsome, a good athlete, with a ready smile and charming manners. To be sure, he also had his physical abnormalities – a stutter, a tic, a tendency to sudden fainting which resembled the *petit mal* of epilepsy, a suicidal trend. But these were not apparent, as were Leopold's shortness and ugliness. Outwardly he was exactly the master of Leopold's swooning dreams.

The other differences between them were even more fatal. For Dickie Loeb was, if such a thing exists, a congenital criminal. Subconsciously he sought the catharsis of indirect participation by reading of crime and playing the detective – even as you and I, the readers and writer of this book. But there was too much of it in him, and it overflowed. Where Leopold dreamed of a god to worship, Loeb dreamed of a perfect crime to commit. As Dr William J. Healy said at their trial, 'each supplemented the other's abnormal needs in a most unique way.' And as Dr William Alanson White put it, Leopold would never have committed the crime alone; he had no basic criminal tendencies as Loeb had: but Loeb 'would never have gone as far as he did without Leopold to give him the final push.'

When these two potential monsters met, at thirteen and fourteen, Leopold instantly fell in love with Loeb, and begged him for a pederastic relation. Loeb was rather repelled by the idea (though his ending proved that he was at least bisexual if not exclusively homosexual), but he agreed – on one condition. This was that Leopold should sign with him a formal compact, agreeing in exchange for sexual favours, to enter into a career of crime with his lover.

For four years both sides of the compact were kept – interrupted, however, by violent quarrels, by threats of murder on both sides and threats of suicide on Loeb's. Loeb was obsessed by the glories of crime; he who seemed so frank, honest, and lovable was actually an incorrigible thief, who lied and cheated as if by instinct. Kleptomania has a deep underground connection with sexual aberrance, and it was the form that Loeb's sexual disturbance naturally took. So he and Leopold, under Dickie's leadership always, committed petty thefts, devised a system of cheating at bridge, set small fires and turned in false alarms, perpetrated acts of vandalism. They were caught sometimes, but they were never taken seriously, never punished or stopped.

In Loeb's mind all this was the merest apprenticeship. He longed to commit, and get away with, the perfect crime. Leopold, no criminal at heart, nevertheless found the commission of such a crime quite consonant with his Nietzschean philosophy. 'The Superman,' he wrote to Loeb, 'is not liable for anything he may do, except for the one crime that it is possible for him to commit – to make a mistake.'

In 1924 the four-year relationship was about to be broken up. Leopold was going to Europe on a vacation trip, and from there to Harvard. Loeb began to cast about in his mind for a 'new pal' who would be his accomplice when he and Babe parted. But first, here was the final opportunity for them to reach the criminal heights together – to carry away with them the memory of having accomplished the ultimate, the supreme, the never suspected felony.

The whole thing was considered and planned like a scientific experiment – which, indeed, in some sort they felt it to be. No hatred, no revenge, was involved – even profit was not the motive, though they certainly intended to profit financially by it. After long discussion they decided that the apex in crime was kidnapping, murder, and the collection of ransom. An essential feature was that the ransom was to be collected *after* the murder, while the victim's family was still being assured that he was alive. Carefully, they worked out every detail. They made their arrangements for weeks in advance. In fact, they may be said to have begun them the previous November, when they attended a football game at Ann Arbor, and Loeb stole a portable Underwood typewriter from his fraternity house – together with some gold pins, watches, and money, just to keep his hand in. This was the typewriter on which the ransom notes were written. The police stupidity in insisting at first that these notes had been written on a Corona - the only possible explanation being that they thought all portables had the same type - is matched only by some of the other official antics before Leopold and Loeb confessed, such as reliance on the visions of a clairvoyant and the frantic hunt for a mythical red-haired woman.

They did not want to use Leopold's own car, for obvious reasons. Deviously they set about renting one. First they took a room at the Hotel Morrison under the name of Morton D. Ballard. Then Leopold, as Ballard, 'a salesman from Peoria,' went to the Rent-A-Car agency and applied to its president, a man named Jacobs, for the hire of a sedan. As reference he gave one Louis Mason, with an address and a telephone number. Mason was Dickie Loeb. He was waiting at the number and gave 'Ballard' a fine recommendation. Leopold then paid a $50 deposit, took the car out for two or three hours to establish credit, and was all set to pick it up when it was needed.

Meanwhile they had provided also for the disposition of the proposed ransom. They opened bank accounts, not in their own banks, under the names of Ballard and Mason. The money was to be paid in currency and would probably have been deposited gradually in these accounts.

Next, every afternoon at three o'clock, from April to the week of May 15th, the two of them boarded a Michigan Central train, buying tickets to Michigan City. Standing in the observation car Loeb, the athlete, practised throwing off packages of the right dimensions and weight at the spot selected by Leopold (who knew this territory well from his ornithological and botanical trips).

By May 20th the boys were almost ready. They took out the rented car and after lunch they went to a nearby hardware store, at 43rd Street and Cottage Avenue, and bought a chisel, some rope, and hydrochloric acid. (There had been some discussion whether hydrochloric or sulphuric acid was better for destroying the identity of their victim, and they finally agreed on hydrochloric.) The first plan was to garrot the chosen victim, each of them holding one end of the rope so that each would be equally guilty. The chisel was a second choice, but proved to be the correct one.

From a medicine chest in Leopold's house, the next afternoon, May 21st, they got adhesive tape with which to bind the chisel to make it easier to hold. At Leopold's home they also collected a lap-robe, some cloth rags to use as a gag, and hip boots, since the place selected to hide the corpse was in a swamp. Each boy carried a loaded pistol in case of emergency. Now everything was prepared. The ransom notes were already written – all but the name on them.

The one thing they had *not* arranged in advance was the victim.

The only important requisite was that he must be a boy, small and weak enough for them to overpower easily, since neither Leopold nor Loeb had much physical courage. The victim must also possess a wealthy father, able and willing to pay out $10,000, the sum the boys had fixed upon as proper ransom.

They talked over possibilities but could find nobody who exactly fitted their qualifications. The two discussed Loeb's young brother Tommy but decided it would be difficult for Dickie to collect ransom from his own family without being caught. Next they thought of Billy Deutsch, a grandson of the famous philanthropist Julius Rosenwald, president of Sears, Roebuck; but they dropped him because Loeb's father was vice-president of the firm, and it 'would hurt the business.' Then they played with the idea of taking on their close friend Dick Rubel, with whom they had lunch three times a week, but vetoed him because his father was a notorious tightwad.

Finally they decided to cruise around the Harvard Preparatory School (Loeb's own former school), across the street from Leopold's home, and see what could be found. Some boys were playing outside and they quickly settled on one of the right size whom they knew by sight, Johnnie Levison. But the pair were not sure of his address, so they drove away to look it up in the phone book. When they returned they couldn't find him. They got Leopold's spyglasses, continued hunting for Johnnie, located him, and started to follow him home, but he went up an alley and disappeared.

Both got out of the car and scouted around. Leopold reported some boys near by on Ellis Avenue, so they drove there. The first one sighted was Bobbie Franks, just fourteen, a distant relative of Loeb's. Leopold scarcely knew him by sight, but Loeb had often played tennis with Bobbie. Later Babe called him 'a nice little boy,' but apparently Dickie didn't like him much. When, in the early days of the police hunt, he was excitedly 'helping' detectives and reporters to search for Bobbie's murderer, he blurted out; 'If I were going to pick out a boy to kidnap or murder, that's just the kind of cocky little son-of-a-bitch I would pick.' But Bobbie wasn't picked because Dickie disliked him; any other boy who met the specifications would have done just as well. Robert Franks was small, his father was a millionaire retired box manufacturer, Jacob Franks; so he fitted excellently.

When they spotted Bobbie, Loeb called him over to the car and invited him for a ride. Bobbie declined; he was about to go home, and he didn't know Leopold. Dickie asked him to get in for a minute to talk about a new tennis racket. Unsuspecting, Bobbie climbed in.

After Leopold and Loeb had confessed, there was at first but one discrepancy in their stories. Loeb insisted that he had been driving the car; that Leopold had sat behind and hit Bobbie Franks over the head with the chisel. He refused to demonstrate the murder method unless he could sit in the driver's seat of their rented car, parked in the yard of the police station. Leopold, disgusted, called Loeb 'only a weakling, after all,' and said (which was the truth, as Loeb himself acknowledged later) that it had been he who had driven the car and Loeb who had done the actual killing.

In broad daylight, on a crowded street, the rope strangulation had been out of the question. Loeb struck Bobbie from behind four times and the boy fell to the floor of the car, streaming with blood from the gashes in his head. The murderers stuffed his mouth with rags they had brought – it was a needless gesture as he became unconscious immediately – and let him lie there and slowly bleed to death.

Meanwhile they were driving around aimlessly, waiting for it to grow dark enough to hide the body. Once they stopped for a slight snack, leaving the corpse in the auto. So that his family wouldn't worry about him, Leopold also phoned his home, saying he would be back late. Later they went to a restaurant and ate a hearty dinner.

When darkness came at last, the two killers drove to 118th Street and the Panhandle tracks, where a concrete culvert, or drain pipe, opened from a swamp not far from the highway. At one time they had thought of throwing the body into Lake Michigan, and had brought along some bricks from a building going up near the Harvard Preparatory School with which to weight it. Now the bricks weren't needed so they threw them away. Bobbie's shoes, stockings, and trousers were removed in the car, he was wrapped in the lap-robe, and carried out to the edge of the swamp. There they stripped him completely and Loeb poured the acid on his face and body. Loeb carried the clothes back to the car while Leopold changed into hip boots, after taking off his coat to give himself more freedom of movement, and stuffed the body into the drain pipe with his foot. They had been carrying it around so long that *rigor mortis* had set in, so it was a hard job. Their belief was that the corpse would not be discovered for a long time, probably not until after it had been reduced to an unidentifiable skeleton. In the darkness neither noticed that one naked foot protruded.

The job done, they drove to Leopold's house, leaving the car parked next door to a large apartment house. Bobbie's blood had seeped through the lap-robe and the upholstery was spotted with blood. They hid the lap-robe temporarily in the yard, burned some of the clothing in the furnace, and addressed the already typed ransom letter.

Then they started out again. They drove to a country spot in nearby northern Indiana, and buried Bobbie's shoes, belt-buckle and class-pin – everything which had metal in it. When they got back to the city, Leopold telephoned the Franks's home. He asked for the father, but got Bobbie's worried mother instead; the family had been trying to learn where Bobbie was ever since he had failed to return in time for dinner at half-past six.

'Your boy has been kidnapped,' the strange voice told her calmly. 'He is safe and unharmed.' He added the usual threat that if the police were informed the boy would be killed at once, and told the parents they would receive a ransom letter the next day.

The distracted father, when he arrived to hear this news, communicated at once with his attorney. By his advice, Mr Franks did tell the police, but secured their promise to avoid any publicity for the present. The next morning the ransom note came by special delivery. It was signed 'George Johnson.' It directed Mr Franks to prepare $10,000 - $2,000 in $20 bills, $8,000 in 50's, all old, unmarked money - and to put it in a small cigar box or a heavy cardboard box, wrapped in white paper sealed with sealing wax. The kidnapper would phone further instructions after one p.m.

In the meantime, Leopold and Loeb had been very busy. There was still much to do. They had concluded the previous evening at Leopold's house, playing cards till midnight, when Babe drove Dickie home. Now, this morning, they drove the rented car into Leopold's garage and set to work trying to wash the blood spots off the upholstery. The chauffeur, a man named Englund, noticed them, and was told they had spilled red wine in the car. They took the hidden lap-robe to a vacant lot in the outskirts of the city and burned it. Next, they drove to Jackson Park and Loeb twisted the keys off the typewriter. They threw the keys in one lagoon, the rest of the machine in another.

Next, they went to the Illinois Central station and Loeb boarded the Michigan Central train they had taken so often in the past few weeks. In the telegram slot of the stationery desk of the observation car he placed another letter, written long beforehand as the ransom note had been, but now addressed in ink to Jacob Franks. On the outside was written: 'Should anyone else find this note, please leave it alone. The letter is very important.'

It contained Franks's instructions for delivering the ransom money. He was to wait until the train passed 'the first LARGE red brick factory on the east side of the track, with a black water tower with CHAMPION printed on it. Wait till you have completely passed the south end of the factory, count five, and then immediately throw the package as far east as you can.' This letter was found, when the train had reached New Haven, by Andy Russo, a yard electrician.

Loeb got off the train at 63rd Street, where he rejoined Leopold. Leopold then telephoned Jacob Franks, saying he was 'George Johnson,' and told Franks to take a taxi that was being sent to his house and to go to a drugstore on East 63rd Street, where he would be told by telephone what to do next. Franks was told that if he had already disobeyed orders and informed the police, then he must keep these further developments from them or his son would be killed. He must be alone, have the money with him, and see to it that the public phone was kept clear.

Leopold then called the Yellow Cab Company and ordered a taxi sent to the Franks's home. The two youths drove about until they felt Franks had had time to reach the drugstore, then Leopold phoned there and asked for Franks. He had not arrived. Leopold phoned three times without results. That worried them, for there was now barely time for Franks to catch the train.

It was at this moment that they saw newspaper extras announcing that Bobbie's body had been found and identified.

A railroad maintenance man had seen the protruding foot. He notified the police, who got in touch with Jacob Franks. Franks, with a pathetic belief in the word of the kidnapper who had phoned and written him, refused to agree that this might be Bobbie's corpse but he did send his brother-in-law to view the body. Five minutes before the taxi arrived at the Franks's door, the brother-in-law had reported his identification.

The city, which was inured to gang massacres but not to atrocious murders of children, was in an uproar. Jacob Franks was a rich and prominent business man, one of a group of millionaires of German Jewish descent – many of them related by blood or marriage – living in the exclusive Kenwood district. These people had much influence, and they spurred the hunt. Arrests were made wholesale. The usual psychopaths 'confessed'. The clairvoyant came forward and her tips were followed. Some of the innocent people picked up and questioned (including two teachers at the Harvard Preparatory School) were ruined for life by the notoriety.

Leopold sat tight and said nothing, but Loeb became feverishly active. He carried around clippings about the case, he could talk of nothing else. Franks, in his bewilderment and grief, had forgotten the address of the drugstore to which he had been directed to go; it was Dickie who suggested questioning all drugstores on 63rd Street until they found the one – as they did – that had received a phone call asking for Jacob Franks.

There were few useful clues. Somebody found the bricks, somebody else found the bloodstained taped chisel. The police made their absurd error of deciding the notes were typed on a Corona and arrested a typewriter repair man who had been carrying one around near the school. Bobbie's clothing had disappeared. There was no success in tracing the phone calls, which had all been made from public booths. The officials continued to arrest people almost at random.

And then, near the culvert where the body had been found, a pair of horn-rimmed glasses were picked up. By May 30th they had been traced to Almer Coe and Company. Mr Coe and his associate, Jacob Weinstein, said that they had sold only three pairs with these unusual rims. One had gone to a lawyer who was now in Europe. A second had been sold to a woman who, when interviewed by the police, was wearing them. The third had been purchased by Nathan F. Leopold, Jr.

Leopold readily admitted that the glasses were his – or that they could be his, if he wasn't sure his own were at his home. He seldom wore or carried them, he said. At the request of Police Captain Wolff, he searched his room for them but found only the case. Then Leopold said he must have dropped them from his coat-pocket during one of his ornithological trips, many of which had been made in that general neighbourhood. He recalled having stumbled once or twice and the loss must have happened then. But when by request he put his glasses in his pocket and then stumbled deliberately, they did not fall from his coat pocket. When he took off his coat and lifted it by the tail, they did. What really must have happened was that when he called to Loeb to carry his coat back to the car, while he was changing back from his boots to shoes, the glasses fell without either of them noticing.

Asked what he had been doing on Wednesday, May 21st, Leopold said he had been driving with Loeb in his own car and that in the evening they had taken two girls for a ride in Lincoln Park. Loeb, questioned a day later, said he couldn't remember what he had done. This was by previous arrangement; if they were questioned within a week or so of the crime, they were to give the prepared alibi; if later, they were to say they had forgotten Wednesday's events.

Rather apologetically, State's Attorney Robert E. Crowe took both youths into custody and held them for further questioning. Crowe said this was being done 'merely out of prudence,' and the boys' fathers agreed, confident that their sons could easily clear themselves of any suspicion. Crowe held them as his personal prisoners in the Hotel LaSalle, instead of taking them to the Cook County jail.

Soon each became snarled in contradictions. The chauffeur, Englund, revealed that Leopold's car had been in the garage for repairs all day on the twenty-first. Other discrepancies piled up until first Loeb and then Leopold made full confessions.

The news that the boys had confessed came as a terrific shock to their families. Loeb's father, already an invalid, died two months after his son was sentenced. Very probably his death was largely caused by his grief and shame. So long as he lived he never again spoke Dickie's name or allowed it to be mentioned in his presence. Loeb's mother refused to visit him in jail until Clarence Darrow persuaded her to come for one unsatisfactory interview. Leopold's father was equally shaken and horrified. These parents had reared their sons to feel that their immense wealth gave them immunity from the obligations and standards of society, yet saw no connection between such an upbringing and the crime.

Both families did rally to the defence so far as legal help was concerned. While the two were only being held 'out of prudence' for questioning, the services of Loeb's first cousins, Walter and Benjamin C. Bachrach, both well-known attorneys, were thought sufficient. But when they confessed and were indicted on two charges of kidnapping and murder, there was only one man who could possibly save them from execution. That man was Clarence Darrow.

Darrow was probably the most famous and the best criminal defence lawyer in America. He was the champion of the underdog and he had saved 102 accused murderers from the gallows. He was a convinced opponent of the death penalty, and his avowed object was 'while the state was trying Loeb and Leopold, to try capital punishment.' Leopold himself wrote that Darrow's advocacy was 'more than bravery; it is heroism.'

For the news that Darrow was to be the chief defence attorney loosed a tremendous wave of popular fury. Darrow was accused of having sold out – he who had always defended the poor and defenceless. It was prophesied that he would have the boys declared insane; then, after a few comfortable years in some luxurious private asylum, their families would secure their freedom by bribery. The rumour was that Darrow was to receive $1,000,000 for his defence. As a matter of fact, no sum was agreed upon in advance; Darrow waited seven months after the trial for his fee, with all reminders unanswered. Finally he was paid $30,000, with the remark that 'the world is full of eminent lawyers who would have paid a fortune for the chance to distinguish themselves in this case.' This from the same man who had literally thrown himself on his knees to beg Darrow to undertake the defence!

There was only one bright aspect to this sorry story. There was no opportunity (as would have been only too easy, in the inflamed state of popular opinion) to inject the issue of anti-Semitism into the case. The victim as well as everybody else concerned in it (except Loeb's mother) was Jewish.

Darrow decided to plead his clients guilty to both charges. He knew he had no chance whatever before a jury; he was also preventing bringing up of the charges separately and so risking a capital sentence of one charge if not on the other.

The judge on whom rested the whole of this dreadful responsibility was John R. Caverly, Chief Justice of the Criminal Court of Cook County, who had long been a judge of the circuit and municipal courts and had helped to establish the juvenile court in Chicago. The defendants pleaded guilty on July 21st, 1924. Two days later the trial began, with the prosecution in the hands of Crowe and his assistants, Thomas Marshall and Joseph B. Savage. Darrow's chief associates were the Bachrach brothers.

The trial lasted thirty-three days. Darrow's concluding speech and the final speech of the chief prosecutor took up three days apiece. Crowe had to ask for frequent recesses, in the Chicago summer weather, to change his sweat-soaked clothing and have an alcohol rub.

The Chicago papers and those of the whole nation – and outside it – ran thousands of columns on the case. The courtroom was packed daily, and crowds were turned away. Judge Caverly was the recipient of hundreds of threatening letters (as was Darrow), in which Leopold and Loeb were called unspeakable names, the mildest of which were 'rattlesnakes' and 'mad dogs.' Charges that Darrow had made sure of a 'friendly judge' infuriated Caverly, who called them 'a cowardly and dastardly assault upon the integrity of this court.'

Against all this, Clarence Darrow stood alone, pleading for reason and justice and mercy against the unthinking rage of a public bent on vengeance.

The judge agreed to listen to evidence in mitigation of the crime. The defence tried hard to prevent the presentation of evidence on details of the killing, but the prosecution got around that by claiming that these details demonstrated the 'state of mind' of the defendants. Darrow and his associates did not cross-examine any of the state's witnesses and the only lay witnesses they called were a dozen or so of the boys' schoolmates, to testify to their abnormality of mind. The defendants were not, Darrow alleged, technically 'insane,' but they were demonstrably 'mentally diseased.'

Both sides brought in a battery of psychiatric aces; of these, the real stars were those who testified for the defence. Darrow's experts included an endocrinologist, and it was easy for him to show how much both of the defendants, and Leopold especially, were suffering from abnormalities of the endocrine glands. It was not the minds of the pair, it was their bodies and their 'moral sense' that were corrupted. Loeb and Leopold were moral imbeciles – what is called nowadays psychopathic personalities.

The fact shown most clearly by the painstaking researches of the psychiatrists called by Darrow was that, inherently, Leopold had no criminal bent. He followed blindly wherever his lord and master led him, but he had little of Loeb's cold cruelty. When little Bobbie Franks slumped down in the car, it was Leopold who cried: 'Oh, God, I didn't know it would be like this!' But Loeb, when he chanced to pass the Franks home as his victim's coffin was being borne out of the house by 'small white-faced boys,' merely felt, for a brief moment, 'a little bit uncomfortable.'

But in the eyes of the prosecution there could be no mitigation. Crowe exclaimed that if Darrow won, 'a greater blow had been struck to our institutions than by a hundred, aye, a thousand murders! . . . There is nothing wrong with them mentally. The only fault is the trouble with their moral sense, and *that is not a defence in a criminal case*.' (Italics mine.)

To Darrow, it took 'something more than brains to make a human being who can adjust himself to life.' He was fighting not for the lives of two miserable, maladjusted boys, but for the triumph of reason and mercy over the barbarity of 'a life for a life.' In his great concluding speech, a classic of legal pleading, he said:

'I know the future is with me, and what I stand for here; not merely for the lives of these two unfortunate lads, but for all boys and all girls; for all the young; as far as possible, for all the old. I am pleading for life, understanding, charity, kindness, and the infinite mercy that considers all.'

If Judge Caverly ordered Leopold and Loeb to hang, Darrow cried, he would be turning his face towards the past, 'making it harder for every other boy who in ignorance and darkness must grope his way through the mazes which only childhood knows. . . . I am pleading for the future; I am pleading for a time when hatred and cruelty will not control the hearts of men, when we can learn by reason and judgment and understanding and faith that all life is worth living and that mercy is the highest attribute of man. . . . If I can succeed, my greatest reward and my greatest hope will be that I have done something for the tens of thousands of other boys, for the countless unfortunates who must tread the same road in blind childhood . . . something to help human understanding, to temper justice with mercy, to overcome hate with love.'

Judge Caverly took until October 10th to pronounce sentence. Then he condemned both defendants to life imprisonment on the murder charge, and to ninety-nine years on the kidnapping charge, 'not because they are abnormal or because they pleaded guilty, but solely because they are under age.' He recommended that neither of them should ever be paroled. And he added: 'To the offenders, particularly for the type they are, the prolonged suffering of years of confinement may well be the severer form of retribution and expiation.'

The judge made it plain that he did not consider this case a test for others involving psychopaths, and that he felt himself bound only by the legal precedent that boys in their teens were not ordinarily sentenced to execution. He did say that the psychiatric evidence presented by the defence was 'a contribution to the study of criminology.' He was eminently fair. Apparently he was uninfluenced by Darrow's arguments. He was not lenient and he did not recommend leniency. His insistence of lifelong imprisonment for both defendants was sufficient demonstration of his viewpoint.

Loeb and Leopold were both sent to the Northern Illinois Penitentiary, at Stateville (usually called Joliet because it is near that city). Little was heard of them until February, 1936. Then Loeb was killed by another convict, James Day.

Leopold and Loeb had not been kept apart in prison. Leopold had been a teacher in the prison school and a nurse in the prison hospital. In 1933 he and Loeb were allowed together to inaugurate a correspondence school for inmates. Day, a bantamweight prizefighter in for larceny, was given a clerical job in this school, of which Loeb was registrar. Loeb made homosexual advances to him; Day spurned him and Loeb was persistent. The prison wing was being remodeled, and in the confusion some inmates were using an officers' shower-room in violation of rules. Loeb, armed with a razor he had stolen from the barber shop, cornered Day in this room. Desperate, Day kicked Loeb in the groin, then grabbed the razor from him and in a frenzy slashed him fifty-six times. Loeb, as blood-covered as had been little Bobbie Franks on that day nearly twelve years before, managed to get the door opened and staggered naked into the corridor, where he collapsed.

His mother, by permission of Warden James Ragen, rushed the family physician to the prison. Leopold stood by Loeb's bed in the prison hospital, and heard him whisper, 'I think I'm going to make it.' But his jugular vein had been severed, and he died soon after. A hearse with its plates covered was sent for his body, and police kept out the curious crowds at the funeral parlour and the cemetery. There were wild rumours that the whole thing was a fake; that the killing had been an invention and that the Loeb family had plotted a successful escape. But that was nonsense; Dickie Loeb was dead. Day was tried for murder and acquitted on the ground of self-defence.

So now only Nathan Leopold was left. He had been a model prisoner. He kept up his studies in half a dozen fields, eventually securing a Ph.D. for a thesis on ornithology. He continued to carry on the prison correspondence school after Loeb's death. In 1924 Darrow had said that both boys should be 'permanently isolated from society.' But later in his defence he remarked that he was not without hope that 'when life and age have changed their bodies and emotions . . . at the next stage of life, at forty-five or so,' they might be fit to be free. Leopold at forty-six, in his own words, had been 'an irresponsible youth, but [was] now a new man.'

By Illinois law, a life prisoner is eligible for parole after twenty years. A prisoner sentenced to a specific term of years is eligible after a third of his sentence has expired. According to this, on the 99-year kidnapping sentence, Leopold could not apply for parole until 1957. In 1949 he petitioned for a reduction of this sentence. The Parole Board turned him down.

But during World War II, Leopold was one of the volunteers at Joliet who permitted themselves to be inoculated with experimental sera in studies of the treatment of malaria, and he became seriously ill as a result. These volunteers had all been promised reduction of their sentences. So on September 22, 1949 the board reduced his kidnapping sentence to 85 years, making him eligible for parole at the end of 1952. Adlai Stevenson, then governor of Illinois, approved the ruling. Darrow had died in 1938 and could not be consulted.

From 1953 on, the board kept refusing his application. Early in 1958 his autobiography, *Life Plus 99 Years*, was published and became almost a best seller. Royalties from it went to support a foundation to aid emotionally disturbed, retarded, and delinquent children, under the direction of his new lawyer, Elmer Gertz.

Finally, after five years, his fourth application for parole was granted. 'I am a broken old man,' he said. (He was fifty-two; he had diabetes and a bad heart.) 'I want a chance to find redemption for myself and to help others.'

He was released on March 13th, 1958, and went to Puerto Rico, where he became a laboratory technician at the Church of the Brethren Hospital in Castaner, and enrolled in the department of social work at the University of Puerto Rico.

In January 1961 Leopold asked that he be discharged from parole to enable him to become a teacher, and also to make it possible for him to marry. The board refused him a full discharge (they finally granted it in March 1963), but they did give permission for his marriage to a widow, Trudi Feldman Garcia deQuevedo, who ran a flower shop in Santurce. They also agreed that he might teach if the Puerto Rico authorities approved. A month after his marriage in February he was appointed a lecturer at the university, under a special dispensation by Governor Luis Munoz Marin.

He taught mathematics in night school while he worked for his M.A. in social work; his thesis was on alcoholism and its relation to criminality. Now he is director of a research project for the Puerto Rican Department of Health, which is studying parasites. In 1963 he came back to Chicago for the first time since 1924, to attend a national convention on tropical diseases and hygiene. At the same time he is working on a book which will deal with 'the relation between penal methods and parole administration as they affect readjustment of the paroled prisoner.'

The whole course of Nathan Leopold's later life goes to verify the judgment that his extremely high mental endowment was accompanied by an equally extreme psychic disturbance which was finally outgrown. Whether Richard Loeb, with a rather less brilliant mind and a still more marked emotional disorder, would ever have been able to rehabilitate himself as Leopold has done, is exceedingly doubtful.

Rupert Furneaux

THE AMATEUR GANGSTERS

It started as a boy and girl pick-up in wartime London. It ended with the gallows for one, and a last minute reprieve and a long term of imprisonment for the other. They met on October 3, 1944. 'Hi, there,' called the American paratrooper. 'Hello,' replied the little Welsh dancer. The scene of the encounter: a café in Hammersmith, London. Almost at once the conversation turned on crime. 'I want to do something dangerous,' exclaimed the girl, 'like being a gun-moll, as girls do in the States.' Within a few minutes she was riding in the American's truck, and he was saying, 'Well, lady, you are doing something dangerous now. You are riding in a stolen truck with a deserter from the American army'. He told 'Georgina Grayson', the name she gave him, that he was Karl Hulten, 'Ricky' as he called himself, and that back home he was a Chicago gangster, boasting, 'I moved around with the slickest outfit in the Middle West'.

Up to that moment Hulten had never committed a crime. Back home in Boston he was a blameless bank clerk. Within the next three days Hulten and Elizabeth Maud Jones, to give her true name, assaulted three girls, leaving one for dead, and shot a hire care driver. Individually they might have remained blameless citizens. By some odd quirk of nature their association turned them into amateur gangsters, and now their names are as inseparably linked in infamy as are those of the other terrible criminal 'shooting' partnerships, Kennedy and Browne, and Craig and Bentley.

Within an hour of their meeting, Hulten and Jones knocked a girl off her bicycle and robbed her. Hulten tells the story:

'It must have been about 0100 hours Wednesday morning when we were coming into a little village near Reading. We passed a girl on a bicycle who was riding in the opposite direction. I went a short distance and turned the truck round.

I drove past the girl on the bicycle and stopped the truck. I got out of the truck and stood beside it next to the road. When the girl on the bicycle went by I pushed her over. She fell off her bicycle and ran away. I saw her pocket book hanging on the handlebars of the bicycle. I took the pocket book and threw it up to Georgina before I got back into the truck. I did not see the girl again. We drove back towards Hammersmith. While we were driving along, Georgina searched the pocket book with her torch. I don't recall how much money was in the pocket book, but I think it was five or six shillings. There were also some clothing coupons but I don't know how many. Georgina kept the money and the coupons. The next morning I took the coupons and gave them to a man who sold them for me. As I recall he gave me £1 for them. Georgina kept the money.'

That was the partnership's first night's work – Yield 26s. 0d.

Next night they were out again. Hulten told Jones they would rob a pub, but when it came to the point he was scared and they drove off. Passing Marble Arch, Georgina suggested, according to Hulten, that they rob a taxi driver. She pointed out a taxi and he drove behind it until it stopped. Jumping from the truck, he held up the driver with a gun and demanded his money, but he said he hadn't any, so they drove back towards Marble Arch. Going up the Edgware Road, Georgina again, according to Hulten, exclaimed, 'There's a girl; stop'. They stopped and on learning that the girl was going to Paddington to catch a train to Bristol, they offered her a lift to Reading. She agreed. They drove to Windsor, again Hulten tells the story:

'I stopped the truck off the road. I told the girls we had a flat tyre. We all got out. I told Georgina to get the girl's back to me. She said "All right". Georgina gave the girl a cigarette and lit one for herself. Georgina told me she thought the girl was wise. I told Georgina to get up in the back of the truck and see if she could get some blocks. When she was in the truck I hit the girl over the head with an iron bar. She did not fall down. I grabbed her round the neck and we went down on the ground. She fell on her stomach and I knelt on her back with my left leg on the ground and my right leg on the middle of her back. I had a head-lock on her neck. The girl was moving her right arm around and I told Georgina to hold her arm.

Georgina knelt on her right arm and went through her coat pockets. She found about five shillings. By this time the girl had ceased struggling. I picked up her shoulders and Georgina picked up her feet. We carried her over and dumped her about three feet from the edge of the stream. I threw the iron pipe into the stream.'

With their 5s. 0d. 'take' Hulten and Jones drove to the house where she lodged and they spent the night there. As far as they knew, the girl they had thrown into the Thames was dead.

On Friday evening the unholy partnership was out again. Sometime just before midnight, Hulten said, 'Come on, let's go and get a cab', meaning to rob the driver.

Hulten and Jones are now standing in a doorway in Hammersmith; this time she tells the story: 'A grey Ford car approached us very slowly like a taxi-cab: it was coming from the direction of Hammersmith Broadway. I yelled "taxi" and it stopped. Ricky thought it was a naval car and he stopped in the doorway while I went over to speak to the driver. I said, "Are you a taxi?" and he replied, "Private hire. Where do you want to go?" I replied, "Wait a minute" and went back to Ricky. I told him it was a private car and he asked how many there were in it. I told him only the driver, so we went across to the car and Ricky asked the driver to take us to the top of King Street.'

When they got there Hulten told the driver to carry on into the Great West Road, and to drive slowly, and after about 300 yards he ordered the driver to stop, telling him, 'We will get out here'. Georgina heard a click and saw an automatic pistol in Hulten's hand. Let her tell the story of the murder that brought her to the edge of the scaffold:

'Heath (the car driver) leaned over from his seat towards the middle of the car with the obvious intention of opening the nearside back door for me to get out. Ricky was sitting to my right, and as Heath leaned over I saw a flash and heard a bang. I was surprised that there was not a loud bang because Ricky had told me it would make a big noise when it went off. I was deafened in my right ear by the bang. Heath moaned slightly and turned a little towards his front. Ricky said to him: "Move over, or I'll give you another dose of the same." I saw that he still had the automatic in his hand. Heath seemed to understand what Ricky said because he moved further over to the left-hand side of the front seat until his shoulder was almost touching the near side door. I heard him breathing heavily and his head slumped on his chest. The next thing I realised was that Ricky was in the driving seat and the car was moving.

'As we went over the bridge nearby Ricky told me to tear down the back window blind to see if anyone was following us. I tore the right corner down, and looked out and told Ricky no one was following. Ricky then told me to go through Heath's pockets. I leaned over and heard him breathing in short gasps. Ricky told me to look for his wallet in the breast pocket of his jacket. I felt in that pocket but didn't find the wallet – I found it instead in the left pocket of his overcoat. It was a small suede folding wallet with a photograph inside and four £1 notes in it. I put the wallet in the back seat. Then I removed from his pockets a white book and papers. Among these were his identity card from which I learned his name and address, a cheque book with a blue cover, a driving licence, a blue card, some petrol coupons, and some photographs and letters. I also put this stuff on the seat by my side. From his trouser pockets I took a big brown fountain-pen, a silver pencil, a long silver cigarette case which had a funny sliding action to open, and an expensive cigarette lighter with a snap-down action. I put all those in my pocket.

'Ricky drove on until he turned off the main road on to a sort of common. He drove on the grass and stopped two or three yards from a ditch. He got out and dragged Heath's body from the car and rolled it into the ditch. He said there was blood on his hands, and I gave him Heath's handkerchief to wipe it off. He then told me to pick up the papers and get into the front seat quickly. He told me to be careful of fingerprints at the same time.'

Hulten drove the car back to Fulham, parked it and walked home with Georgina who asked, 'He's dead, isn't he?' Hulten replied, 'Yes,' and she told him, 'That's cold-blooded murder, then – how could you do it?' Hulten replied, 'People in my profession haven't time to think what they do.' Having examined Heath's possessions, Jones and Hulten went to bed. Next morning they sold Heath's wrist watch for £5 and his fountain-pen and pencil for 8s. 0d. They made £10 5s. 0d. from their night's work. Jones's statement that they expected a bigger bang from the gun shows that she knew that Hulten was carrying a gun and meant to use it.

The body of the hire car driver was found early on the morning of Saturday, October 7, and it was identified as that of George Heath of Ewell, Surrey, who drove a Ford car registration number RD 8955.

On the evening of Monday the 9th a policeman spotted the car outside a house in the Fulham Palace Road. Flying squad cars were alerted and positioned to intercept the Ford should anyone try to drive it away. Three-quarters of an hour went by and then a young American Army officer came from the house and got into the car. A policeman walked over to him and asked, 'Is this your car, sir?' When he did not answer, the police officer shouted and the other policemen rushed up, seized the officer and searched him. In his pocket they found an automatic pistol, loaded, cocked and with its safety catch off. He was taken to Hammersmith Police Station, where he gave his name as 'Second Lieutenant Richard John Allen, 501st Parachute Infantry Regiment, United States Army'.

As the United States of America (Visiting Forces) Act of 1942, whereby an American arrested had to be handed over to his own authorities, was still in force, the American Army Criminal Investigation Department was called in, and Private Karl Gustav Hulten, as he now admitted his identity, was questioned by Lieutenant de Mott. He agreed he was a deserter, and he declared he had found the Ford car abandoned near Newbury in Berkshire, on the previous afternoon. On the night of Friday, October 6, he said he had been sleeping in a truck at Newbury. Later he changed his story to say that he had stolen the car from a car park at Hammersmith, and that he had spent Friday night with a girl he knew as 'Georgina Grayson'. He said, 'I do not know George Heath and I have never seen him. I swear I did not shoot him.'

Traced by the police, Georgina told them her real name was Elizabeth Jones. She stated she was Welsh, eighteen years old and married, 'but I do not live with my husband'. She said that on the night of the murder she had been to a cinema with Hulten. He left her for two to three hours, returning at 11.30 p.m. when they spent the night in her room. Jones was not detained. Next morning she spoke to a War Reserve policeman, a casual acquaintance, who remarked how ill she was looking. She said she had made a statement to the police about Heath's murder, adding, 'If you had seen somebody do what I have seen done, you wouldn't be able to sleep at night.' When this significant remark was reported to Inspector Tansill at Hammersmith, Jones was again interviewed. She confessed she had lied previously, and admitted, 'I was in the car when Heath was shot. I didn't do it,' and she told the story of the shooting.

Questioned again, Hulten agreed that Jones's confession was substantially true, but he declared that he had shot Heath accidentally. According to him it had happened like this: 'When the car stopped I was holding my loaded and cocked pistol in front of my chest. When the car stopped I looked over towards Georgina. As I was looking towards the front again, I pulled the trigger. Heath raised up and reached over the back seat to open the rear door. When I pulled the trigger I intended to pull the trigger and fire the pistol. I intended to fire it through the car, but I did not expect George Heath to raise up to open the door as I did it.' He said, too, that if it had not been for Jones wanting to stop the car, he wouldn't have shot Heath.

With the disappearance of the American troops to Europe, the Visiting Forces Act was revoked and Jones and Hulten stood trial for Heath's murder at the Old Bailey in January 1945.

Against Hulten the evidence was overwhelming. He had been found in possession of the stolen car; his pistol was proved to be the murder weapon; he had sold some of Heath's possessions. His defence of accidental shooting, even if true, could not mitigate his crime for he had killed Heath during the course of a felony, robbery. Against Elizabeth Jones the case was equally strong. She had admitted that she knew her companion in crime had a gun and intended to use it. Now she contended she was in terror of Hulten and that he had threatened to shoot her. She admitted to being seven months over the age of eighteen, a question the grim significance of which could hardly have escaped her, for eighteen years is the limit for hanging. She said she did not tell the police the true facts at first because she did not think it concerned her, or 'that I would be drawn into it'. Asked, 'It was your hands or fingers that took the wrist watch off the dead man's body?' she replied, 'Yes.' 'And it was your hands that went through his pockets?' the prosecution counsel went on inexorably. Again came the answer, 'Yes.' 'And then you went to the cinema?' 'But I was still frightened' was all she could say.

Neither Hulten nor Jones could have been in much doubt that the jury's verdict would be against them. But there was another shock to come. Later in the proceedings the prosecution brought a girl into court, the girl they had left for dead on the river bank. Did they know the girl? prosecution counsel enquired.

The jury needed only three-quarters of an hour to find both prisoners guilty, adding in Jones's case a strong recommendation to mercy, a recommendation they may have wished to withdraw when the judge informed them, after sentence of death had been pronounced, that Jones and Hulten's statements to the police showed that they had assaulted and nearly killed at least one girl.

Would Jones hang? That was now the question. If she was reprieved, would the life of her American partner be saved too? Popular opinion demanded that both should hang, and such was probably the intention of the Home Secretary until Ernest Bevin, the Socialist Minister of Labour, intervened. He declared that Jones's crime was due to her upbringing in the bad old capitalist world of a Welsh mining town, and he urged the Home Secretary to grant a reprieve.

On March 6, two days before she was due to be hanged, and after she had been weighed by a silent gentleman in a bowler hat, Jones was reprieved. Hulten was hanged on March 8. Elizabeth Jones has since been released and has disappeared into the obscurity from which she came.

The name of their victim, George Heath, was soon forgotten, as are the names of most murder victims. But we remember the names of Jones and Hulten, as two peculiarly callous killers who shot and killed an inoffensive car driver for the sake of a few pounds. Jones, one feels, was fortunate to escape a fate she richly deserved. She was in it up to her neck. If the Home

Secretary did indeed take note of Ernest Bevin's plea for mercy, she must be one of the few murderers in England to owe her life to 'political' considerations.

Lew Louderback

CLYDE, BONNIE, BUCK AND THE BOYS

'Machine Gun Kelly!' Clyde Barrow sneered the day he read of his capture in Memphis. 'I've forgotten more about a Tommy gun than that phony creep ever knew.'

It was probably true. The pint-sized Texan with the weak chin and the soft hazel eyes had no equal for sheer gunmanship. Guns were more than just the tools of his trade. They were objects of beauty to him, almost of veneration.

Ray Hamilton, who ran his mouth a lot after he was captured, told how Clyde was always fussing with his extensive collection of weapons, modifying them, oiling them, polishing them, holding them up to the light admiringly.

Clyde was the most heavily armed outlaw of the thirties. His arsenal included several submachine guns, a half dozen automatic rifles, and a bewildering variety of shotguns, automatics, and revolvers. When he ran low on ammunition or needed more guns, he backed his car up to a National Guard Armoury and filled it - at gunpoint.

His aim was deadly. Target practice was a daily ritual with him. Anybody who rode with him had to be good, too. He drilled them until they were. His diminutive blonde travelling companion, Bonnie Parker, was said to be able to shoot the pips out of a playing card at twenty paces. Clyde himself could slice the card sideways, shoot the head off a dove in flight.

The speed of his draw was equally phenomenal. He carried a sawed-off shotgun in a zippered compartment in his right trouser leg, and was proud of the fact that he could draw it almost as fast he could his pistol. His gunfighting attitude was Billy the Kid's: 'It's a game for two - and I get there first.'

The Barrow gang robbed and killed in five states before the law finally caught up with them. They never made a big score, never, to anyone's knowledge, tried for one. Their favourite targets were gas stations, luncheonettes, variety stores, plus an occasional small-town bank. Their biggest haul was $1,500.

They moved across the countryside aimlessly, heading anywhere - sometimes even in circles - to avoid their final destination. They had no political or legal connections, never had enough money to buy their way into established underworld retreats like Hot Springs and St Paul, and were unwanted in such places anyway.

They were outlaws even to the rest of the criminal world. Most big-time heist men would have turned them in on sight. To them Barrow and his crowd were 'kill-crazy punks' who were ruining the business for everyone else.

Yet today Clyde and his sweetheart, Bonnie, have the bigtime reputations, while the big-leaguers of their day - the Harvey Baileys, the Eddie Bentzes and Frank Nashes - are largely forgotten.

It's partly the work of the film: its appeal, particularly to the young, came from its portrayal of Clyde Barrow and his moll as a pair of displaced kids on the run, barrelling along from crime to crime in a restless search for their place in the sun. As the screen Bonnie puts it: 'When we started, I thought we were going somewhere, but we're just going.'

Barrow and his girl are presented in the film as sad, murderous, dumb kids - confused neurotics rather than the old Hollywood 'mad dog' stereotype. What they do is crazy and terrible but it's never that far removed, from the secret desires of a debilitated, apathetic population trapped in the economic decay of the Depression.

The film's period flavour - the cheesebox sedans, the moneyless banks, the hopelessness on every face - underscores this message. So do scenes of the gang in repose - listening to Eddie Cantor on the radio, playing checkers, taking endless pictures of themselves with a Kodak. They're just folks and, like the rest of us, disorganized, confused, frustrated.

So far, so good. This is what the real Bonnie and Clyde were probably like. Even the neurotic sensualities that plagued the two star-crossed lovers are there. Granted, their sexual hang-ups have been changed a bit, but at least they're present. They would have been glossed over completely in a standard Hollywood 'shoot-'em-up.'

Biographically the film sticks close to the facts. The screenwriters have left out some things and have shifted others around to tighten the plot, but many of the scenes, particularly the action ones, re-create in faithful detail exactly what happened.

Where the film and reality go their separate ways, however, is in the suggestion that Bonnie and Clyde were Robin Hood figures to the poor people of the Southwest. That is simply not true. Other outlaws - Dillinger, Pretty Boy Floyd, even the Barkers - robbed the wealthy and left the poor alone. But not Bonnie and Clyde. They preyed on their fellow poor and they killed them when they got in their way. The Barrow gang was universally feared, and most of all by those likeliest to encounter them - the poverty-stricken farm folk of the Dust Bowl.

It's been argued that Bonnie and Clyde don't really deserve a place in American folklore because of this. Maybe they don't, but the argument is academic. The two of them are already there, enshrined beside Billy the Kid and Jesse James, and no amount of debunking is going to dislodge them now.

It isn't just the film's doing. It began in their own lifetime with the discovery of a handful of snapshots and one of Bonnie's poems, 'The Story of Suicide Sal.' The photos and the verses gave people an intimate, keyhole view of what it must have been like during those two years of driving, killing and hiding.

It struck a nerve. The poetry was bad, little more than doggerel, really. The emotions expressed were often trite and sentimental. But there was the thrill of its having been composed in the heat of action. And there was something else, too - a strangely detached, abstracted view that Bonnie had of Clyde and herself and of their crazy, pathetic ride to nowhere.

The real Clyde was born on a farm near Telice, Texas, on March 24, 1909. He was one of eight children. His father, Henry, was a tenant farmer. Clyde was farmed out to relatives when he was five, living first in Dallas, then in Corsicana and Houston. He was in trouble right from the start. At age nine he was committed to the Harris County School for Boys as an 'incorrigible truant, thief, and runaway.' He served three years.

He was released to his parents after Henry Barrow finally gave up the land for good and moved to Dallas, finding work in a gas station.

Clyde's first serious brush with the law involved cars. He loved them, tinkered with them, stripped them down, drove them fast. Speed intoxicated him. He never voluntarily stopped for anything, including red lights. The police started chasing him, but Clyde just drove faster. 'It's easier to run than explain,' he told his older brother, Ivan Marvin ('Buck') Barrow.

What he needed, he stole. Clyde had a feeling for music, so he swiped a saxophone. It went everywhere with him. Clyde had a date with a girl in San Antonio. His roadster burned out that same day. So he rented a car and kept it. He was arrested and charged with auto theft. His parents dug up the money, and he was released.

Buck, meanwhile, had been getting into trouble on his own. He had started out peddling hot turkeys, had graduated to stealing cars, and was now doing it professionally, turning the vehicles he clipped over to a hot car ring for a cut of the resale price. Clyde wanted to work with him, but Buck didn't want his kid brother in the racket. He advised him to go straight.

Clyde did – to Houston. His travelling companions were two West Dallas toughs, Frank Clause and Raymond Hamilton. Clause was a small-time sneak thief. Hamilton, the descendant of one of the Southwest's most noted outlaw families, had never seriously considered any life other than crime.

The three of them gravitated to Houston's Fifth Ward, a section so tough that oilman Glenn McCarthy would later recall that '. . . the cops were afraid of the people, and there was almost always a dead man somewhere in the street in the morning.' There they enrolled in the Root Square Gang, a finishing school for burglars. Soon Clyde was hard at work with the others, learning how to break and enter, strip cars, and roll drunks.

Graduation day saw him holding up a Ford Bend gambling spa with a rusty 'Saturday Night Special' that wouldn't even fire. It didn't matter, though. Before housemen could figure the odds, Clyde had lifted a couple of long-barrelled .38s from two off-duty deputies. That gave him the winning hand – a pair of sixes.

The gang returned to Dallas, where an impressed brother Buck and a youth named 'Dapper Dan' Black joined them. After pulling a string of robberies in the Dallas area, the group headed across the line into Oklahoma, where Hamilton had kinfolk.

They hit a whole flock of grocery stores and gas stations in the Choctaw country, high-tailing it from town to town along the back country roads. Clyde was the wheelman and a damned good one. He could manoeuvre their sedan along the rutted roads at eighty-five and better, bucking through the gulches between the clay cuts and the trees, sucking the dust out of the cornfields into their wake, boiling it up into a thick white cloud that choked the pursuing posses.

At Henreyetta, Oklahoma, the gang stole a new car and started back to Dallas, pulling holdups and burglaries along the way.

In Denton, Texas, they stuck up a gas station and when they couldn't open a small safe, they heaved it into the car. Outside of Lewisville a police car jumped them. Clyde was driving. He floor-boarded her. The police started shooting. Bullets shattered the rear window, slammed into the metal door stanchions. Buck pitched forward. 'I'm hit,' he grunted as he clutched at his right shoulder.

Clyde had her up to ninety when he came to a right-angle turn with no road signs to warn him. He stood on the brakes, but it was too late. The car careened across a ditch and ploughed into the chaparral, both axles snapping. The men leaped out and started running. All except Buck escaped.

The next morning the police came for Clyde. Everybody in Dallas knew that the two brothers were working together. Clyde made a deal – the only one, it's said, of his career. He sold Clause and Black out on a burglary charge. Buck drew a five-year jolt at the Eastham prison farm. Clause and Black got suspended sentences.

Clyde went back to work with Ray Hamilton, pulling a series of jobs in the Waco area. He was arrested three more times for investigation of burglary and car theft. None of it stuck. He was only five feet, six and three-quarters inches tall and had the face of a choirboy. People simply couldn't believe that a boy like that would do anything bad.

Clyde met Bonnie Parker in January 1930. He was twenty-one, she was nineteen. They met through Ray Hamilton, who had been her husband's friend and was now hers. The husband, Roy Thornton, was chopping cotton at Eastham and would be at it for the next twenty-nine years. Bonnie had his name tattooed on her right thigh, along with two hearts, but that was the limit of her devotion. At the time she met Clyde, she was working as a waitress in Dallas and was juggling dates with several men on the side.

She was a tiny girl, less than five feet tall and weighing only ninety pounds. She had boyishly flat flanks, an angular body, and an almost pretty face that was spoiled by an overly hard mouth. She had come to Dallas from Cement City, one of those arid, innocent North Texas towns where nothing happens in even the best of times. Before that there had been another town, Rowena, where she had been born, the daughter of a bricklayer, and where nothing had happened, either.

Bonnie wanted desperately to make something happen that winter of 1930. She wasn't sure just what or how. All she knew was that she was 'bored crapless' and had been most of her life. Then Clyde came along – an unimpressive little squirt who parted his hair in the middle, had long eyelashes, small delicate hands, and a slightly effeminate manner.

In the film version Clyde was pretty explicit as to what he was offering: excitement and fame. It's doubtful that the real Clyde offered Bonnie anything of the sort. Or that he even thought of himself in those terms.

Clyde Barrow, in 1930, was essentially a burglar and a car thief. He had yet to fire his gun in anger or desperation. All that would come later. After Eastham.

Bonnie saw some quality in him. What it was, we will never know. They started keeping company. They were together the night the law came for Clyde – 'mooning on the sofa,' according to one of the arresting officers.

It seemed that Clyde had forgotten to wear gloves on a couple of jobs in Waco. And if that didn't stick, Chief of Police Hollis Barron had him nailed on five car thefts, too.

Clyde pleaded guilty, and a McClellan County judge sentenced him to two years on each count. The court allowed the sentences to run concurrently, but that didn't cheer Clyde up any. He dreaded prison. He had a claustrophobic horror of locks and bars, a hangover from those early years he'd spent in the Harris County School.

Then, on March 2, 1930, his brother Buck came busting out of Eastham like a bull through a corral fence.

Inspired, Clyde began to make plans of his own. His cellmate in the Waco jail, William Turner, told him he had a gun hidden away in his house, a .38 Colt with a slim Bisley handle that would fit through the bars. Clyde sent Bonnie to get it. She came back with it taped to the inside of her thigh and managed to slip it to him without the guard noticing.

That night, when the jailer brought them their supper, Clyde pressed the barrel into his neck. 'Open up,' he said. 'Fast.'

Clyde and Turner went barrelling out. Bonnie had a car hidden behind the K. C. dance hall. She wanted to go with them. Turner nixed the idea, and since the gun was his, the play was, too, and Clyde backed him on it.

The two of them raced to Abilene, then to Wichita Falls, where they switched to a stolen Graham coupe. It was a good car, with new tyres, and they burned up the roads with it. When it ran out of gas, they abandoned it and hopped a freight. Railroad dicks grabbed them a few days later at Middleton, Ohio, and sent them back to Texas in handcuffs.

This time the law didn't kid around. Clyde was sent to replace his brother in the cotton fields of Eastham.

Back in the thirties Eastham was known among cons as the 'Burnin' Hell' of the Texas prison system. Sadism was the order of the day there. Men were beaten by wardens, by trustees, by one another. In the fields whippings were regular and almost maniacally brutal. The men were underfed and dressed in tatters. They slept on bunks, jammed one against the other, in barracks that stank of excrement.

The slightest infraction of the rules meant a hitch in the 'barrel cavalry.' This was a roughhewn pickle barrel mounted on a sawhorse in the blazing sun. Prisoners were made to straddle the barrel for hours at a time. Even the strongest eventually collapsed. Some of the weaker ones died or 'lost it' (went insane).

Clyde's sentence had been beefed up since his escape try. It no longer ran concurrently. He was in now for the full fourteen years.

In desperation he chopped two toes off his right foot with an axe. He hoped it would get him transferred to the 'Walls' at Huntsville. It didn't. It didn't even get him out of the cotton fields. The guard captain reassigned him to a hoe squad as soon as his foot stopped bleeding.

At Eastham Clyde was involved in murder – his first. He and some other cons had been sentenced to the 'barrel cavalry' for gambling. They all knew who had fingered them – the barrack stoolie, Ed Crowder.

When the punishment period was over, they trapped Crowder in a secluded section of the prison yard. Clyde had a length of lead pipe. The others had homemade knives.

There were no repercussions. At Eastham one more death was hardly noticed.

Clyde had served twenty months of his sentence when Buck Barrow surrendered outside the walls of Huntville. His mother, Mrs Cumie Barrow, had talked him into it. 'I'll go back, do my time,' he told her, 'so long as it's not at Eastham.'

Mrs Barrow went to Austin now, where she managed to secure a personal meeting with Governor Ross Sterling. She made an impassioned plea for both her sons. The Governor promised to review their cases.

A month later Clyde was granted a parole.

It came too late, though. Eastham had done its work. He 'hit the ground' on February 2, 1932, and he hit it running. It would take almost two hundred rounds of ammunition to finally stop him twenty-six months later.

Bonnie described the change in him in 'The Story of Bonnie and Clyde':

> They class them as cold-blooded killers,
> They say they are heartless and mean,
> But I say this with pride,
> That I once knew Clyde
> When he was honest and upright and clean.

But the law fooled around,
Kept tracking him down,
And locking him up in a cell,
Till he said to me,
'I will never be free,
'So I will meet a few of them in hell.'

This road was so dimly lighted
There were no highway signs to guide,
But they made up their minds
If the roads were all blind
They wouldn't give up till they died . . .

Bonnie was exaggerating, of course. She had never known Clyde when he was 'honest and upright and clean.' No one had. But at the same time she was right. Clyde had gone into Eastham a burglar and a car thief who avoided gunplay. He came out the most dangerous Texan since Wes Hardin.

In March he and Bonnie went on the road together for the first time. It was a false start, though. The car was hot, and the law jumped them outside Mabank. There was a wild chase along U.S. 175. Clyde skidded the car off the highway and onto a backcountry road, where it immediately got bogged down in the mud. Clyde, Bonnie, and the kid who'd been riding with them took to the fields. Bonnie lost her shoes and was caught.

She sat for three months in the jail at Kaufman, Texas. The jailer's wife had advised her mother not to make bail. The theory was that a session in the pokey would cool Bonnie's ardour for Clyde.

To an extent it did. She was deeply hurt that he never tried to spring her. The experience probably contributed to her later poem, 'The Story of Suicide Sal.'

While Bonnie sat brooding, Clyde was busy robbing. He had teamed up with his old buddy, Ray Hamilton, once again. On March 25 the two of them hit the Sims Oil Company in Dallas and escaped with several hundred dollars.

Hamilton was a small, wiry youth, smaller even than Clyde. He walked with the swaying strut of a rooster about to crow. He was talkative, quick to anger, and as jumpy, a friend once said, 'as a stud horse in a box stall.' He had a cruel streak in him that verged at times on the sadistic. All in all, bad news, particularly for someone standing across a gun from him.

On the night of April 30 that was John N. Bucher, a 65-year-old jeweller and service station operator in Hillsboro, Texas. Bucher's wife had just opened the safe so that he could give Hamilton and his companion change of a ten. Both youths suddenly whipped out guns. 'We'll take it all, old man,' snapped Hamilton. Bucher's hand darted towards the drawer where he kept his gun. They blasted him. Then, after scooping just forty dollars out of the safe, they ran for the car. A third youth was waiting behind the wheel, the motor running.

Later Mrs Bucher identified her husband's killers from mug shots: Clyde Barrow and Ray Hamilton.

Clyde's relatives denied it. His mother claimed that Clyde had told her he was the wheelman on that job, that he'd been waiting out in the car when the shooting had taken place.

Maybe so. But it didn't matter now. The chase was on. Governor Sterling offered a $250 reward for Bucher's killers, a lot of money in the Depression. Dallas newspapers, meanwhile, went ahead and convicted Clyde. He was described as 'the killer of John Bucher,' even though he had only been charged with the crime.

The third member of the old 'Root Square' trio now joined Hamilton and Barrow. Frank Clause had apparently forgiven Clyde for fingering him after the Denton job. The three of them hit several gas stations in the Lufkin area in early May, then sped back to Dallas to knock over a liquor store on May 12. The take: a spectacular $76.

In June the Kaufman Grand Jury met and no-billed Bonnie. She returned home and told her mother that she was finished with Clyde.

The gang was in Oklahoma now. Dallas had gotten too hot. They were staying with some of Hamilton's relatives near Tishomingo. Clause had been replaced by a local gunsel.

On the night of August 5, as the three men were cruising through the Choctaw country around Atoka, they passed a barn dance. Hamilton, who was driving, sniffed the air. 'Poontang,' he said, grinning, and whipped the car into the parking area.

Clyde didn't want to stop. Neither did the other man. Hamilton ignored them. He was a billygoat who had to have his daily exercise. Clyde got into an argument with him. Their voices became loud.

Atoka sheriff, C. G. Maxwell, and his deputy, Eugene Moore, heard the commotion and approached. They thought the three of them were farm boys who had come out of the hills to attend the Stringtown dance. 'What's going on here?' drawled Maxwell. 'You boys been drinking?'

Clyde and Hamilton whirled, saw the stars on their shirtfronts and opened fire. They emptied their .45s, then reached into the car for replacement weapons.

Deputy Moore was killed instantly. The sheriff staggered back against a car, fumbling for his pistol, but he was dropped by a second barrage of bullets before he could reach it.

Several men came running out of the dance. They leaped for cover as Clyde leaned out the car window and swept the front of the building with a raking fire from a Browning automatic rifle. Hamilton threw the car into reverse and floorboarded her. The machine hung there a second, wheels spinning in the gravel: then it shot out of the lot like a cork out of a bottle.

Hamilton spun the wheel hard left. With a clash of gears, the car roared off into the darkness.

The road was slick from a recent rain, though, and a few minutes later they went slithering off the shoulder into a ditch. Cursing, the three men climbed out and looked around. A farmhouse lay a hundred yards down the road. As they approached it Clyde spotted the silhouette of his favourite car, a Ford V-8, in the front yard. They knocked on the door and asked the farmer who answered if he would help get them out of the ditch.

The farmer nodded and climbed into his V-8. Clyde, Hamilton, and the third man piled into the seat behind him. 'Never mind pulling us out,' said Clyde, as he pressed the muzzle of the BAR into his neck. 'Just start driving.'

The farmer drove too hard. The engine soon began to sputter and clank. It had thrown a rod. Another car came along. Clyde flagged it down and asked the driver if he wanted to trade. He said he didn't. But he traded anyway and was glad to do so.

They drove the new car to Clayton, fifty miles east of Stringtown. There Clyde spotted a brand new V-8 parked on a side street. He couldn't pass it up. He jumped the switch on it, and the gang piled in. With Clyde behind the wheel now, they roared out of town, heading through the Kiamichi mountains towards the Arkansas line.

Several days later Bonnie received a phone call. 'Pack your clothes,' said Clyde. 'Then turn on the radio. When you hear the Neuhoff Company has been robbed, be ready to leave.'

That same afternoon, August 12, the bulletin came over the radio: two men identified as Clyde Barrow and Raymond Hamilton had just held up the Neuhoff Packing Company offices in downtown Dallas. The two, sought for the recent murder of an Atoka County sheriff and his deputy, were heavily armed. They had escaped with approximately $1,100 and at last report were driving west towards Fort Worth at high speed.

Bonnie got ready. The Parker home was on the Fort Worth Turnpike, not far from Arcadia Park. She kissed her mother good-bye and told her that she had a ride to Wichita Falls. A new cafe had just opened there, and she thought she might be able to find work.

A car honked, and Bonnie ran out to meet it. Mrs Emma Parker glanced out the window. The car was a dusty V-8 sedan with Oklahoma plates. As it pulled away Mrs Parker caught a glimpse of the two men sitting in the front seat with Bonnie. One of them looked an awful lot like Clyde Barrow.

In the car there was backslapping and laughter. It was a happy reunion. For all three of them. They decided to honeymoon in New Mexico, where Bonnie had an aunt. Clyde drove the whole distance with lead in his foot.

Bonnie's aunt gave them a big welcome when they pulled into Carlsbad the next morning. It was certainly nice of the two young men to have brought her niece all the way from Dallas for a visit. 'Glad to be of service, ma'am,' said Clyde, grinning. 'I'll just get our things from the car.'

He turned – and stopped short. A tall man wearing a gun belt was looking over their car. 'Howdy,' said the man. He came sauntering up the walk, and Clyde saw the silver star on his shirtfront.

Clyde and Hamilton had left their guns under the car seat. Because of that, Sheriff Joe Johns lived to tell the story to his grandchildren. 'I was just passing' – the sheriff smiled amiably – 'an' I saw the out-of-state plates an' wondered who was visitin' Missus –'

He felt a sudden pressure between his shoulder blades and turned. A tiny, freckle-faced blonde in a dark blue beret was holding a shotgun on him. 'Don't move, damn you!' she snapped.

Clyde leaped forward, snatched the sheriff's pistol out of his holster, and prodded him in the belly with it. 'Get in the car,' he snarled.

The aunt stood watching from the porch, eyes wide with disbelief. Bonnie had sighted the sheriff through the window, had raced to her uncle's room, grabbed his shotgun, and skinned out the back door to sneak up behind him – all in thirty seconds flat.

The four of them were in the car now. It roared away in a cloud of dust. The aunt went back into the house and had herself a good case of hysterics.

The trio drove the sheriff all the way to San Antonio. It was a nonstop trip with Clyde, as usual, keeping the needle hovering between ninety and a hundred.

Hamilton didn't want to release him. 'We either got to kill him or keep him with us,' he kept saying. But Clyde overruled him. They couldn't take him with them, and as for killing – that was out. Clyde never killed a hostage. It was a quixotic quirk of his. He would kill in the heat of action and never think twice about it. But a hostage was different. A hostage presented no immediate threat, and Clyde, to his credit, killed only when threatened.

After dropping the sheriff off along the highway between Beckman and San Antonio, the gang drove east towards the Gulf.

In Victoria Clyde spotted a new V-8. Naturally he had to have it. He and Bonnie clouted it, and Hamilton followed them in the other car. The theft had been seen, though, and reported to the local sheriff. He got on the phone to Wharton, describing the two cars that were headed their way.

There was only one bridge across the Colorado River, a narrow trestlelike affair on U.S. 59 just outside Wharton. A dozen armed officers hurriedly took up position at either end of it.

The two cars came roaring along the highway. The Wharton sheriff tried to flag them down, then jumped for his life as Clyde opened up with a pistol, shooting around the edge of his windshield. The other officers returned the fire. A deadly fusillade tore into the two cars as they roared onto the bridge.

The men at the other end got ready, zeroing in on the first car. Suddenly Clyde spotted them. He threw the V-8 into second gear, cocked the wheel and hit the accelerator, bringing the rear end skidding around in a perfect 180-degree arc. It was the famous 'bootlegger's turn,' flawlessly executed.

He went roaring back across the bridge with a dozen pistol, rifles, and shotguns spitting hell at him. Bonnie stuck her twelve-gauge out the window and let the ambushers have it. Hamilton, still right behind them, was driving with one hand, shooting with the other.

It was Bonnie's first taste of combat, the first time she had heard the angry buzz of bullets around her head or felt the thud of buckshot ripping into glass and metal. It didn't bother her a bit. She handled herself with an easygoing skill that won the instant admiration of both men. 'That Bonnie,' Clyde said later, as they licked their wounds in an empty field near Yoakum, Texas, 'she's sure full of piss and vinegar.'

They hid out in an abandoned farmhouse at Grand Prairie for the next few weeks. From here Clyde and Hamilton raided the National Guard Armoury at Fort Worth, returning with boxes full of sub-machine guns, automatic rifles, shotguns, and extra ammunition. The Wharton ambush had taught them the importance of firepower.

From here, too, they pushed off against the Abilene State Bank on October 8, 1932. Bonnie was the wheelman on that job, Hamilton the centre fielder. Clyde took the cages. It was their biggest haul so far – $1,400.

They headed north and east from Abilene, intending to swing up into the Choctaw country. At Sherman, in the Red River Valley, they stopped for food and supplies. Bonnie and Hamilton waited in the car while Clyde entered a small general store. Casually he looked around. He saw only two attendants working amid the jumble of dried sausages, meal, flour, and fly swatters – Homer Glaze, at the cash register, and Howard Hall, behind the meat counter.

After Clyde had ordered everything on his shopping list, he showed Glaze the .45 he was carrying. 'Open the register,' he said. Glaze's pupils shifted slightly. Clyde swung around just as the butcher leaped towards him, a meat cleaver in his hand. Three of the four shots he squeezed off found their mark. Clyde scooped $50 out of the till, grabbed his groceries, and ran. The butcher was dead on arrival at the Dennison Hospital.

The trio worked their way north, riding the back country roads by night, sleeping in the car or beside it. They lived on sandwiches and on coffee, which they brewed over an open fire. On the rare occasions when they slept in a bed, it was in remote tourist cabins or fishing resorts where there were no telephones, newspapers, or radios.

They were famous now. Newspapers in the Southwest called Clyde the 'Texas Rattlesnake.' Bonnie hadn't been identified by name as yet; she was simply his 'quick-shooting woman accomplice.' They had a good description of her, though, and they kept running it in the papers and on the radio.

So the gang stayed off the main roads as they moved north that fall, heading through the Ozarks to Illinois, and up through Indiana to the North Woods of Michigan. The car was the focal point of their lives. They relaxed only when they were in it or near it. The gas tank was kept full, the motor tuned to perfection. Their belongings were in the trunk, their arsenal on the back seat, together with a four day supply of food, a first-aid kit, Clyde's saxophone, and a five-gallon jug of drinking water.

The outdoor life didn't appeal much to Ray Hamilton, though. He began to get restless. Finally, in late October, he announced his decision: he was going to strike out on his own. 'All right,' said Clyde. 'But you'll get caught, and I'll have to get you out. You ain't smart like I am.'

Hamilton returned to Texas, where he recruited his former girl friend's brother, Gene O'Dare. The two of them hit the Carmine State Bank at LaGrange on November 9, and then, with a gunsel named Les Stewart in centre field, the Cedar Hill

State Bank in Dallas on the 25th. The take from that job was $1,800, more than Hamilton had ever made with Bonnie and Clyde. Who was smart now?

Clyde pulled only one job during the same period – a minor one. With Bonnie behind the wheel, he took the Oronogo, Missouri, bank for a few hundred dollars on November 15. Then, because Bonnie was homesick, the two of them returned to Dallas and hid out with relatives.

While there, they shopped for Hamilton's replacement. They found him just down the street from Henry Barrow's filling station. He was a seventeen-year-old car thief named William Daniel Jones. Most people called him either 'W.D.' or 'Deacon,' a tribute to his guileless appearance.

In the film his name became 'C. W. Moss,' and he was supposedly picked for his mechanical skills. Actually, he didn't have any. Nor much criminal experience, either. But he had other attributes: vacant, blue-eyed good looks, an almost overbearing innocence.

'Want to take a ride with us?' Clyde was said to have asked him. 'I'm Clyde Barrow and this is Bonnie Parker. We rob banks.'

Awed beyond belief, the seventeen-year-old climbed into their V-8 and was swept off into thirteen months of 'living hell,' during which he was shot at, unnaturally assaulted by both of them, kept in chains, and forced, while fleeing from police, to fire a submachine gun.

That's W. D.'s story at any rate – the one he told police when he was finally picked up. His remarkable 28-page confession is a goldmine of information about Bonnie and Clyde and the way they lived while on the run. Most of it has an authentic ring to it, particular the parts about their sex lives. W. D. was an innocent at heart, a Panhandle fundamentalist who believed that fleshly sins deserved fleshly punishment. His profound shock at some of the stuff that went on is apparent in every line of the confession.

The three of them left Dallas on December 22 and headed south.

Ray Hamilton was back in town – in police custody, just as Clyde had prophesied. Hamilton had gone tomcatting all over the country with the Cedar Hill loot and had naturally been collared. Now he was busy running his mouth for the benefit of police and press.

Clyde, Bonnie, and young Jones drifted quietly south. As they drove through Temple, Texas, on the afternoon of December 23, Clyde spotted a new V-8 parked along a quiet, residential street. He turned to W. D. 'Go get it, boy.'

Jones trotted over to the Ford obediently, climbed in, and started fussing with the ignition wires. A minute passed. Two minutes. Nothing happened. Sighing, Clyde got out of the car and walked over. 'Not that way,' he said. 'This way.' But Jones was nervous now and lost the contact after the motor had turned over once with a loud growl.

That brought the Ford's owner, Doyle Johnson, charging out of his house. He'd been in the middle of dinner and was still wiping gravy off his chin. 'Hey! That's my car!' he shouted. 'What are you fellows doing?'

Clyde whirled, drew, and fired in one motion. Johnson dropped to his knees, a surprised look on his face. He clutched at his stomach and slowly toppled forward, dead.

Bonnie had the other car in motion, doors open. Clyde tumbled in, cursing, pushing W. D. ahead of him. Bonnie slammed the accelerator to the floor, and the car vanished around the corner, tyres squealing like pigs being slaughtered.

In Dallas, meanwhile, a jury listened to the evidence against Ray Hamilton and decided that he needed to do some time in the cotton fields of Eastham. They thought two hundred and sixty-three years would be about right. Hamilton was returned to the Hill Country Jail to await transfer. While there, he hit the panic button.

Clyde had a pretty extensive communications network set up by now. He could be contacted, or make contacts, through strategically located 'drops' in Texas, Oklahoma, and Louisiana.

Hamilton's message reached him in late December. It was short and to the point: 'Get me out.' Clyde decided that it might be a good idea. It would stop that nonstop mouth of his, at any rate. He made arrangements to visit Ray's sister in Dallas, Mrs Lillie McBride. She would be the go-between.

The McBride house was already under surveillance, though.

Odell Chandless and Les Stewart had robbed the Grapevine Bank on December 31. Texas Rangers had nabbed Stewart, and he'd told them that Chandless was supposed to visit Mrs McBride on the night of January 6.

That was the night that Clyde decided to come calling.

The house was packed with Rangers and Tarrant County sheriffs and deputies, all heavily armed.

Clyde cruised past the darkened house twice. Instinct told him something was wrong. He had W. D. park directly in front. 'Keep the motor running,' he told him. He slipped a sawed-off twelve-gauge into the zippered compartment of his pants leg and told Bonnie to cover him. As he moved through the shadows and up onto the porch, Bonnie trained a .30-.30 Winchester on the front of the house.

Inside, Ranger J. F. Vannoy heard Clyde's footsteps. He tapped Ray Hamilton's 18-year-old sister on the shoulder and signalled her to go to the door and open it.

As she started forward Clyde suddenly cut loose. He hadn't heard anything, hadn't seen anyone. It was just a sudden 'feeling' he had. His automatic shotgun blasted out a second-storey window. Tarrant County Deputy F. T. Bradberry dropped to the floor, cut by flying glass.

Vannoy and his men opened up from inside now, firing blindly through doors and windows. As they did, Deputy Malcolm Davis raced around from the back of the house. He saw Clyde starting down the steps. He leaped onto the porch, gun in hand. 'Hold on there!' he shouted. Clyde spun towards him. His twelve-gauge roared. The load of buckshot caught Davis in the chest, catapulting him backwards to the ground, killing him instantly.

Bonnie opened up with the Winchester as Clyde ran for the car. The withering fire from her .30-.30 kept Vannoy and his men inside the house until the car was in motion. W. D. had them halfway down the block and pushing seventy by the time the first officers reached the street and opened fire.

Dallas County was immediately sealed off by roadblocks. Rangers and city police armed with riot guns began raiding every known gangster haunt. Clyde, Bonnie, and W. D. Jones were far away, though, roaring through the red clay cuts of Oklahoma.

Back in Texas things were looking up for Clyde's older brother, Buck. Mrs Miriam A. ('Ma') Ferguson had replaced Ross Sterling as governor in January. 'Ma' was famous for granting pardons. She had issued more than two thousand of them during her first term in office back in the twenties.

Buck's wife, Blanche, mother of three children and about to give birth to a fourth, saw her chance. She hitchhiked to the state capital with the kids and made a tearful, in-person plea. 'Ma' was so moved that she granted Buck Barrow a full pardon. He walked out of Huntsville on March 20, 1933 a free man.

He hung around Dallas until Blanche gave birth. Then both of them suddenly vanished, leaving all four kids behind. Mrs Cumie Barrow told police that Buck had gotten a letter from Clyde and was on his way to see him to try and talk him into going straight.

She must have got the message wrong, because Buck's next public appearance was in a jewellery store stickup in Neosho, Missouri. A few days later he and his brother popped up again, not to surrender, but to get themselves some new guns out of a federal armoury in Springfield, Missouri. Three days after that they appeared once again, using their new arsenal to kick in a loan office in Kansas City.

Then they went to ground, renting a garage apartment in Freeman's Grove Addition, a suburb of Joplin, in early April.

Clyde didn't like the idea. He preferred to be in, or near, his car, with open country on all sides of him. But Blanche was still kind of 'delicate.' So he let himself be talked into it.

The five of them took life easy for a while, sleeping late, playing cards, admiring the Kodak snapshots they had taken of each other.

The Texas licence plates were noticed, though, and a delivery boy got to wondering why the women never let him into the apartment with his packages. Both reports reached the ears of Sergeant G. B. Kahler of the Missouri Highway Patrol. He figured it for a bootleg liquor operation and decided to raid. He rounded up a highway patrolman, a Newton County constable, and two Joplin police detectives, and on the afternoon of April 13, the five men drove out to Freeman's Grove Addition in a couple of unmarked cars.

It was around 4 p.m. Clyde and W. D. Jones were standing in the garage, checking over their Marmon sedan. Blanche was upstairs cooking. Buck was sitting in his undershirt reading a newspaper. Bonnie was hard at work on her first poem, 'The Story of Suicide Sal.'

Clyde spotted the two cars coming up Oak Ridge Drive and got one of his sudden 'feelings.' He leaped into the garage, pulled W. D. in behind him, and slammed the doors.

Sergeant Kahler brought his car to a stop a few yards beyond the driveway. The second vehicle swung in, blocking the gang's escape route. The garage doors opened a crack, and a blast from a shotgun sprayed the car with lead. Newton County Constable Wes Harryman leaped out with his pistol drawn. He managed to squeeze off one shot before his head was practically torn from his body by a second blast.

Detective Harry L. McGinnis sprinted forward, firing his pistol. Suddenly his right arm was ripped off at the elbow. Buckshot showered his face and head. He dropped to the pavement, dying.

Upstairs Buck had grabbed his submachine gun. Bonnie ran into the bedroom and snatched up two pistols. Blanche just stood there, hands over her ears, screaming. It was her first taste of combat.

Detective Thomas DeGraff had taken cover behind the car. He fired into the garage as Sergeant Kahler and Patrolman W. E. Grammer moved to the left, trying to outflank the gang.

Suddenly W. D. Jones came running out of the garage, spraying the car with fire from a Browning automatic rifle. DeGraff was forced to retreat around the east side of the building.

Jones leaped over the two bodies and struggled with the hand brake on the police car. Kahler fired at him. Jones clutched at his head and staggered back into the garage.

Buck Barrow came charging out next, spraying machinegun fire in all directions. He ran to the police car, released the brake, and gave it a push. The car coasted down the driveway, slowly gathering speed, then shot across the street, bounced over the kerb, and smashed into a red oak tree.

Blanche, still screaming at the top of her lungs, burst out of the building and went racing down the driveway into the street.

At that moment the garage doors suddenly swung open, and the Marmon sedan roared out, gears clashing. Kahler saw three men and a woman in it. As the lawmen peppered the car with bullets, it swung left, chasing Blanche. It slowed down as it reached her, and Kahler saw a man lean out and pull her inside. Then it roared off in a whirl of red dust.

Kahler sent Patrolman Grammer for help. An ambulance came. It was too late, though. Harryman and McGinnis were both dead. Reinforcements arrived shortly after that. Half of them were sent after the Marmon. The rest made their way cautiously into the upstairs apartment.

There they found an arsenal of rifles, machine guns, and BAR's. And snapshots. One of Bonnie holding a shotgun on Clyde. Another showing Bonnie with one foot up on a car bumper, puffing on a cigar. And on the dining room table they found Bonnie's unfinished poem:

THE STORY OF SUICIDE SAL
By 'Bonnie' Parker

We, each of us, have a good alibi
    For being down here in the joint;
But few of them are really justified.
    If you get right down to the point.

You have heard of a woman's glory
    Being spent on a downright cur.
Still you can't always judge the story
    As true being told by her.

As long as I stayed on the island
    And heard confidence tales from the gals,
There was one interesting and truthful,
    It was the story of Suicide Sal.

Now Sal was a girl of rare beauty,
    Tho' her features were somewhat tough,
She never once faltered from duty,
    To play on the up and up.

> Sal told me this tale on the evening
>   Before she was turned out free,
> And I'll do my best to relate it,
>   Just as she told it to me.
>
> I was born on a ranch in Wyoming,
>   Not treated like Helen of Troy,
> Was taught that rods were rulers,
>   And ranked with greasy cowboys . . .

The press went to work on the legend. The 'Battle of Joplin' shared the front page with the Japanese siege of Peking. The snapshot of Bonnie with the cigar appeared alongside Amelia Earhart's photograph in one of the more prestigious newsweeklies. Excerpts from 'Suicide Sal' ran in practically every paper in the country.

The gang didn't learn about their new fame immediately. They were holed up in the swamps of Lincoln Parish, Louisiana, too hot to even venture out for feed, let alone a newspaper.

W. D.'s head wound was more painful than serious. They were able to treat it with their own first-aid supplies. In his confession Jones said that he ran away from the gang at this point, stole a car, and fled home to Dallas, but that Clyde and Bonnie had forced him to return.

The Barrow gang struck next in Indiana. The Lucerne State Bank. A small take but plenty of fireworks: two women bystanders wounded by machine gun fire. Eight days later, on May 16, they swooped into the First State Bank of Okabena, Minnesota. A redheaded woman stayed at the wheel of a dark green V-8 sedan. The townspeople opened fire from the sidewalks as the man came barrelling out with their $1,500 take. Bullets thudded into the car as it pulled away. The gang shattered the car windows and fired back, with BAR's and shotguns. 'The battle raged furiously,' according to one account, 'but it was impossible to face the outlaw barrage and live. Slowly the defenders fell back to the shelter of buildings, and the bandits escaped.'

Bonnie was homesick. Clyde wanted to see his family, too. Buck said it was too risky. So he and Blanche were dropped off at a hideout in the Arkansas Ozarks, while Bonnie, Clyde, and W. D. ran the gauntlet into Dallas.

They met their families at an abandoned stone quarry off the Fort Worth Turnpike. There was time just for a few quick embraces, inquiries about each other's health, and a hurriedly gobbled picnic of cold chicken and homemade apple pie. Then the running started again.

Clyde raced north through the Texas Panhandle, the speedometer needle shivering, as usual, between 90 and 100 mph. They were to meet Buck outside Erick, Oklahoma, late that night.

Clyde didn't see that the bridge over the Salt Fort River north of Wellington was out. The car sailed off the edge, flipped over, and burst into flames on the dry river bed below. Bonnie was pinned beneath the wreckage. Clyde and W. D. were thrown clear.

Two farmers who had heard the crash came running. Bonnie was screaming, begging Clyde to shoot her so that she wouldn't burn to death. The farmers, Steve Pritchard and Lonzo Carter, helped Clyde and W. D. pull her free. She was badly burned. Her arms were seared to the shoulders. The lower part of her face was white with blisters. Her whole right leg was a mass of cooked flesh.

'This woman needs a doctor,' said Pritchard.

'No doctor,' said Clyde. 'Where do you live?' Pritchard pointed, and Clyde said, 'All right, carry her up there.'

The two farmers looked at the automatic rifles the men were holding and did as they were told. At the farmhouse Mrs Pritchard made up a paste of baking soda and spread it on the burns. Bonnie was writhing and moaning, obviously in terrible pain.

'I'm going back for the rest of the guns,' Clyde said abruptly. He turned to W. D. 'Keep them covered.'

W. D. had been unnerved by the whole business, though. He was careless, and Lonzo Carter got away. The farmer ran through the darkness to a neighbouring house and telephoned Sheriff George Corry at Wellington. Corry picked up City Marshal Paul Hardy and the two of them sped towards the Pritchard farmhouse.

Clyde returned with the guns and W. D. told him that Carter had probably called the law. Moments later, there was a knock at the door. Clyde whirled, snatched up his shotgun and fired.

A woman screamed. He swung the door open. There stood Pritchard's daughter-in-law, her right hand shot off. Clyde herded her inside with the others. 'Get down on the floor, all of you,' he commanded tersely. 'Don't let me hear a sound out of you.' He and W. D. carried Bonnie out of the house and into the underbrush. They made her comfortable on a bed of leaves, then waited there beside her, guns ready.

Sheriff Corry's car pulled up a few minutes later. He and Marshal Hardy got out and cautiously approached the farm-house with drawn weapons. Clyde and W. D. stepped out of the darkness, shotguns aimed at their heads. 'Back into the car,' ordered Clyde. He forced the two of them to hold Bonnie on their laps in the back seat while W. D. covered them from the front.

Clyde drove west to Pampa at high speed, then north towards Erick, relaxing only when he had crossed the state line. 'You're in a fine pickle,' he shouted over his shoulder at the two men. 'I'm Clyde Barrow. Guess what that means for you?'

The officers swallowed heavily, but Clyde was just kidding around. When they reached Buck Barrow's car and Buck asked if they were going to kill them, Clyde shook his head. 'Naw,' he chuckled, 'I've had them with me so long I'm beginning to like them.'

The officers were left bound to an oak tree with barbed wire. They managed to get loose a few hours later and limped into town to tell their story to a breathless world. 'One thing's sure,' said Sheriff Corry. 'The woman's burned bad. She'll die if they don't get her to a doctor.'

The gang knew that. They took Bonnie to an isolated tourist cabin near Fort Smith, Arkansas, and Clyde brought a doctor out to see her, explaining that his wife had been burned by an oil stove explosion at their campsite. The doctor treated her but said that she would either have to be taken to a hospital or have round-the-clock nursing. Clyde settled for the nursing. For a week he never left her bedside, day or night.

Bonnie kept begging for her mother in her delirium. So Clyde left Buck in charge and ran the gauntlet into Dallas once again. He refused to bring Mrs Parker back, though. She would be recognized by the police. He settled instead on Bonnie's younger sister, Billie Jean.

Meanwhile, the medical bills continued to pile up, eating into the gang's slim reserves. By mid-June they were broke. Leaving W. D. in charge of the thee women, Clyde and Buck drove forth to scare up some cash.

They knocked over the Alma State Bank on June 22, then raced north to hit a Piggly Wiggly store in Fayetteville. On their way back to Forth Smith on U.S. 71 they had to pass through Alma once again. A description of their car had been phoned ahead to Alma's marshal, H. D. Humphrey. He realized that it was the same car that had been used in the bank job – a '33 Ford V-8 with Indiana plates.

He and his deputy, A. M. Salyars, jumped into their patrol car and headed north to intercept them. Two miles outside Alma they saw a car approaching. They slowed down. So did the other car. The driver waved. It was Webber Wilson, night manager of a nearby garage, on his way to work. Wilson stopped his car and leaned out the window, about to say something.

At that instant Humphrey saw the second car. It was approaching at better than 90 mph. 'Better not stop,' he shouted to Wilson. 'That fellow will run you over.' Humphrey started forward, saw that it was the V-8 they were looking for, and jammed on the brakes.

The second car went ploughing into Wilson's. Metal shrieked. Flames burst with a roar from both cars. Humphrey was sure that no one could have survived the wreck. But to his surprise he saw Wilson crawl free and the Barrow brothers, too. He and Salyars leaped out, guns drawn. 'Get them up!' they shouted, racing towards the wreckage.

Buck and Clyde took shelter behind the open doors. There was a quick burst of shots as one of them opened up with a Browning. Humphrey and Salyars fired back. Then a shotgun roared, and the marshal seemed to trip over his own feet and go sprawling face down on the highway.

Salyars kept firing until he was out of ammunition. Then he ran behind the corner of a farmhouse and reloaded. Buck and

Clyde came charging out. Clyde stopped and leaned over Humphrey as his brother ran towards the police car. 'I ought to finish you right now,' he snarled.

'Go ahead,' the marshal groaned. 'I think you've already finished me.' (He had, Humphrey died of his wounds four days later.)

Clyde ran on, leaping into the police sedan. It roared off, passing the terrified occupants of cars in the opposite lane. Deputy Salyars peppered it with shots but to no avail. It quickly vanished into the darkness.

Buck and Clyde drove to Van Buren. There they forced a Fort Smith couple to surrender their car. Clyde took a wrong turn a few minutes later, though, and got on a dead end road that petered out at the top of Mount Vista. Quickly a half dozen posses closed in on them.

The Barrows took to the brush, making their way on foot to a cabin in the Ozarks just north of Winslow. Clyde kicked in the door and ordered Mrs John Rogers to hand over the keys to the ancient jalopy standing out in the yard. She refused. Clyde whipped out his shotgun. She still refused. The posses were so close now that the two men could actually hear them hallooing.

Buck picked up a trace chain and began to beat her with it. She still wouldn't give them the keys. Clyde tried to jump the switch meanwhile, but he wasn't familiar with a Pierce-Arrow's innards and had to give up. 'Okay,' he snarled, 'we'll fix it so nobody can use it!' With Buck's help he gave the car a shove towards a nearby cliff. The woman leaped to her feet and ran after it. Clyde levelled his shotgun at her. 'Don't touch it!' he yelled.

Mrs Rogers ignored him. She leapt onto the running board and gave the steering wheel a twist that sent the car careening into a tree.

The Barrows had finally met their match: a hill woman who refused to be separated from her car.

Cussing wildly, the two of them fled into the woods behind the cabin. Mrs Rogers heard a great trampling behind her. She swung around. Possemen came streaming out from among the trees at the far end of the clearing. 'They went thataway!' she shouted. 'They're only seconds ahead of you!'

They were sure they had them now. Extra men were poured into the area with instructions to shoot first, then ask. Scouts went ahead of the main body to guard against ambush. Everyone regarded a major battle as imminent. Sheriff A. H. Maxey of Crawford County rushed men up State 59 to get ahead of the outlaws and throw out a net. The Barrows slipped through like minnows through a whale net.

They made it back to the Fort Smith tourist cabin and pulled out that same night. Bonnie's sister, Billie Jean, was sent home to Dallas; the others headed across the line into Oklahoma.

When the doctor stopped by the next morning and found them gone, he got suspicious and called the police. There could be no doubt from his description – he had been treating Bonnie Parker. 'They won't get far,' he said. 'She's an extremely sick woman. She shouldn't have been moved.'

The gang surfaced next at Enid, Oklahoma, where they stole Dr Julian Fields's car in order to get his medicine kit. Within the hour they knocked over the National Guard Armoury, too, escaping with fifty Army automatics and armloads of ammunition.

Fort Dodge, Iowa, was next. On July 18 three men and two women in a Ford sedan robbed three filling stations in quick succession. One of the women, a redhead, had bandages on her face and arms. It was obviously the Barrow gang.

At ten o'clock that same night the five of them pulled up in front of the Red Crown Cabin Camp at the junction of U.S. 71 and State 59, six miles southeast of Platte City, Missouri. They rented a double brick cabin separated by two garages and paid the attendant, Delbert Crabtree, in small change. After backing the car into one of the garages and closing the doors, the group split up – three into the left-hand cabin, two into the right. A little later the bandaged redhead bought five sandwiches and five beers from Crabtree. Again she paid in small change. The next day the cabin rental was renewed, and the redhead bought five chicken dinners. The bill came to ten dollars and something. She paid it with nickles, dimes, and quarters.

Crabtree told his boss. His boss phoned the Missouri Highway Patrol. The lawmen listened to the description of the five, plus the fact that they paid for everything in silver, and realized that it was the group who had hit the Fort Dodge filling stations – and that spelled Barrows. They called Kansas City for reinforcements.

The extra men and equipment arrived shortly before midnight – sheriff's deputies, constables, and city police armed with shotguns, machine guns, automatic rifles, even an armoured car mounted with searchlights. The small army moved quietly into position, confident that the gang was asleep.

Actually, every move they made was being watched.

W. D. Jones had gone into Platte City earlier that night to buy bandages and salve for Bonnie. While there, he had overheard a man in the drugstore mention 'all the officers out at the highway junction.'

Jones had alerted the gang, and they were now crouched in Buck's darkened cabin, watching as the armoured car drove up and two helmeted figures set machine guns up behind steel shields. Suddenly the searchlights blazed on. There was a knock at the door. 'Officers,' a voice announced. 'We want to talk to you.'

'As soon as we get dressed,' said Bonnie. Then, as W. D. slipped through the inside door connecting the cabin with the garage and got behind the wheel of the car, she added, 'The men are on the other side.'

'You had better come out,' called the lawman.

The Barrow brothers were in position now: one at the window, one at the inside door. 'Let the bastards have it!' yelled Clyde.

There was a sustained roar of gunfire. Bullets rattled off the steel shields as the machine gunners swung into action. Armour-piercing rounds sliced through the armoured car as if it were paper. Deputy George Highfill crumpled, shot through both legs, but still shooting as he fell. Sheriff Holt Coffey went down, a bullet in his neck. His son, Clarence, pitched to the ground. Bullets had smashed his right arm, punctured his cheek.

A shotgun blast short-circuited the armoured car's horn. It began a steady blast. The rest of the men thought it was a signal to charge and came rushing forward into the murderous cross fire.

A fragment of glass jammed the mechanism of one of the machine guns. 'Let's get out of here,' yelled Deputy James

Thorpe, realizing that they were sitting ducks. He and Highfill managed to throw the armoured car into reverse. They backed away from the garage doors as bullets continued to buzz around their heads like angry hornets.

Buck Barrow came charging out of the right-hand cabin now, a blazing automatic in each hand. Bonnie and Blanche were behind him, holding up mattresses as shields.

The posse directed its fire at the trio. As they did, a motor roared into life inside the garage. A man suddenly swung open the doors and hopped on the running board of the car that came shooting out. It was Clyde Barrow, hanging on with one hand and laying down a deadly barrage of sub-machine gun fire with the other. W. D. was behind the car's wheel, a cap pulled low over his face.

Bonnie and Blanche dropped their mattresses and began firing pistols as they ran towards the car. The officers returned their fire. Suddenly Buck staggered, shot through the temple. Blanche and Bonnie leaped to support him. They pulled him into the car, Blanche screaming that she'd been hit.

The car roared forward into a withering cross fire. Its windows dissolved into milky opalescence. The metal door frames seemed to actually shiver under the impact of dozens of rounds, a woman inside the car screamed in terrible, agonized pain. The vehicle swung onto the highway, careened wildly from side to side for a moment, then straightened out and disappeared in the direction of Platte City.

Though seriously wounded, Sheriff Coffey dragged himself to a telephone. Roadblocks were immediately set up on all major highways.

The gang had already swung east, though, and was travelling along backcountry roads. About halfway between Platte City and Hoover they stopped and took stock. Buck was in the most critical shape; a bullet had entered his right temple and had exited from his left. Clyde had a scalp wound. Bonnie had a bullet burn along the ribs. Blanche's eyes had been cut by bullet-showered glass; she could only see vague, shadowy shapes and was in terrible pain. W. D. alone had come through unscathed.

At this point any other gang would have retreated to a city

where the fix was on. Crooked lawyers would have arranged hideouts; underworld surgeons would have treated their wounds. But the Barrows, with around $200 in nickels and dimes in their pockets, had only one alternative – keep running.

A vast manhunt was already in progress. The FBI, which had been keeping an eye on the gang since their raid on the Enid armoury, sent agents to all hospitals in a five-state area, warning them to hold anyone with gunshot wounds. WDAF, the radio station of the *Kansas City Star*, broadcast detailed descriptions of the fugitives. A motorist near Mount Ayr, Iowa, just north of the Missouri line, heard one of these broadcasts. A few minutes later he spotted a car parked on a lonely side road. A man lay on the rear seat. Two men and two women were bent over a fire, burning bloody bandages. They leaped into the car and drove off the moment they saw him.

He reported what he had seen and the manhunt shifted to Iowa. Three days later a farmer came across a smouldering campfire and bloody bandages at a deserted amusement park halfway between the towns of Dexter and Redfield.

John Love, a member of the county vigilantes, hid in some nearby bushes and waited. He saw two cars drive up later that afternoon. Three men and two women got out. Love crept away and phoned Sheriff C. A. Knee of Adel. His description of the five matched the Barrows.

Knee called the sheriffs of surrounding counties and also the Iowa National Guard. By evening a good-sized army of officers had assembled at Dexter, its ranks swollen by dozens of local citizens armed with shotguns and squirrel rifles. With all possible escape roads sealed off, the posse moved in. They crept cautiously from tree to tree, slowly encircling the campsite. At dawn they began to tighten the noose.

Bonnie was brewing coffee over an open fire. Blanche was frying eggs. Clyde stood watching them, smoking a cigarette. W. D. Jones sat with Buck on the running board of one of the cars. Buck was clad only in a one-piece suit of underwear. Blanche, who wore riding breeches and boots, had a pair of dark goggles over her injured eyes.

Suddenly Clyde went diving towards his shotgun. He had caught a glimpse of movement in the tree. 'The law's coming!'

he shouted. The coffee spilled into the fire as the others snatched up weapons. It was too late, though. They were surrounded. A murderous fusillade was already pouring into them from all sides.

'Get the car started!' Clyde shouted, as he fired back, trying to cover the others. W. D. ran towards it but was hit by a load of buckshot and fell, momentarily stunned. Still firing, Clyde shoved him into the back seat while Bonnie ran around to the other side and climbed in.

Clyde slid behind the wheel, and the car started forward. A couple of dozen guns roared. The machine was riddled. Clyde lost control of it as a bullet ripped into his arm. The car went ploughing into a tree stump.

The three of them leaped out and ran through withering fire to the second car. As it started up, a thunderous volley smashed into it, dissolving the windows, ripping the tyres to shreds. They scrambled out and plunged off into the woods on foot with half the posse on their heels while the other half stayed to shoot it out with Buck.

Buck and Blanche were trapped behind a tree stump. Both had automatics. The posse surrounded them, called on them to surrender. Buck's answer was a curse as he opened fire. Bullets laced into them from all sides. Buck was hit twice, but kept firing. Blanche huddled closer to him, handing him clips of shells. He jammed them into the gun, emptied it, then loaded up again. He was hit four more times. Blanche began to scream hysterically. Buck's head slumped forward, but he managed somehow to keep firing. Finally Doctor H. W. Keller of Des Moines, a national guardsman, rushed forward and kicked the gun out of his hand.

Blanche struggled with the possemen who seized her, hitting out at them blindly with her fists, spitting and cursing as they tried to drag her away. 'Don't die, Daddy,' she screamed. 'Don't die!'

But there wasn't much else Buck could do. Blood was pouring from his old head wound and also from six new ones – all critical. He was taken to the Kings Daughters Hospital at Perry, where he died five days later.

W. D. and Bonnie, meanwhile, were fighting their way

through the woods towards a creek that skirted the north side of the park. Clyde was right behind them, laying down a covering fire. All three were wounded – Clyde in the arm, Bonnie in the fleshy part of the back, Jones with a shoulder full of buckshot.

Possemen seemed to be lurking behind every bush. No matter which direction the trio headed, they found themselves trapped. 'They fought desperately each step through the woods,' an eyewitness report later stated, 'darting from brush clump to brush clump. They made difficult targets and they were shooting with deadly accuracy.'

They reached the stream and dived in, heading for the cornfield on the opposite side. The possemen halted at the edge of the clearing and took careful aim. Spouts of water rose around the fleeing outlaws. Bonnie screamed and sank out of sight. Clyde tugged at her but couldn't lift her because of his injured arm. W. D. gave him a push up the steep bank, then went back for Bonnie. The posse opened fire as he lifted her into his arms and carried her up the bank. W. D.'s head jerked to one side. The possemen cheered. They were sure they had gotten him. He didn't stop, though, and now the three of them were in the cornfield, and even the bravest member of the posse didn't want to go in after them.

A ring of men was thrown around the field, but it was too late. The three had already dashed out the other side, commandeered a farmer's Plymouth sedan, and fled north in it. An airplane was brought in to aid in the search. Two hundred possemen in cars followed it on the ground. Suddenly, near Guthrie Centre, it dipped low, a signal that the outlaws had been sighted. An armoured car was rushed to the head of the column to shield the possemen. This time they were sure they had them, but they didn't. The Plymouth ran the gamut of their fire and escaped.

They had Blanche, though. And after displaying her to the press, police tried to question her. She was incoherent. The months of running, the gun battles, her blindness, and now Buck's death had finally gotten to her. She subsequently served ten years in the Iowa State Prison for her part in the Dexter battle.

Clyde, Bonnie, and W. D. Jones stayed on the back roads that fall. They treated each other's wounds and lived on food that they stole from the fields.

The Fort Smith doctor had been right. Bonnie should never have been moved. Her burned leg had drawn up. She couldn't walk and was delirious much of the time. She had been a pretty twenty-year-old blonde only sixteen months earlier. Now, at twenty-two, she was scarred and crippled, and looked twice her age.

W. D. split with them some time in October. He made his way back to Texas and was arrested. He didn't seem unhappy about it. While awaiting trial, he dictated his twenty-eight-page confession, then pleaded for a life sentence. At least behind bars he would be safe from Bonnie and Clyde.

In early November the two of them dashed in to Dallas to see their parents. It was a foolhardy venture, but they brought it off, managing to spend almost an hour with them in a field near Grand Prairie. The parents noticed that they both seemed obsessed with thoughts of death. Bonnie even discussed funeral arrangements with her mother. When the two came home for another visit around Thanksgiving, those arrangements almost went into effect.

The Dallas County sheriff, Smoot Schmid, had heard about the last visit and had put tails on both families. When the two mothers drove to a lonely road off the Fort Worth Turnpike on the morning of November 22, Schmid concealed a group of heavily armed deputies in the ditches and woods on each side of the car in which they were sitting.

When Bonnie and Clyde showed up, the deputies let them have it. They blasted with machine guns, rifles, shot-guns, and pistols. They put seventeen holes in their car altogether. Clyde and Bonnie were hit in the legs but managed to drive away.

Clyde was furious that his mother's life had been endangered. He sent a message to Sheriff Schmid through a Dallas newspaper, warning him that if a hair of his mother's head was ever harmed, he would personally kill him.

The audacity of the threat appealed to the underworld. News of it travelled via the grapevine to Eastham, where Ray

Hamilton decided that Clyde might be in the mood to spring him. Hamilton had been boasting that he was going to be sprung ever since they had put him away back in October. On checking into Eastham, he had told Warden B. B. Monzingo: 'I won't be here long. Clyde Barrow won't let me die around no prison farm.' He had said it so many times that even his fellow cons had stopped believing him.

But now Clyde received Hamilton's message and was receptive.

On the morning of January 16, 1934, a party of ninety-five convicts marched through dense fog to the brush-covered river bottom where they had been clearing land. Three mounted guards were in charge of the detail. As the cons got down to work, Ray Hamilton slipped away from his squad and joined Joe Palmer and Henry Methvin. The three edged their way over to a large pile of brush next to a drainage ditch. Quickly they reached in – and came up with the .45 automatics that Clyde had hidden there.

The three guns roared in unison. Major E. M. Crowson was hit in the stomach by a shot from Hamilton's gun and toppled out of his saddle. Joe Palmer hit Guard Olen Bozeman as B. B. Bullard, a new screw, managed to bring up his shotgun. Nine pellets of buckshot slammed into Joe Palmer but didn't stop him. He swung towards Bullard, whose horse was rearing, and fired. The shot went wild as Bullard leaped from his saddle and dived behind a stack of cordwood.

Bozeman's horse bolted, with the wounded guard still clinging to the saddle. An auto horn had begun to blare, meanwhile, somewhere beyond the fence. Hamilton, Methvin, and Palmer asked who wanted to go with them. Convicts Hilton Bybee and J. B. French stepped forward. 'Let's go, then,' shouted Hamilton. The five of them slipped through the drainage ditch and ran towards the road.

Clyde and Bonnie were waiting beside two cars. As the men burst through the trees, they opened up with a submachine gun and a BAR, laying down a heavy barrage of covering fire. But no guards were following them. It had gone even smoother than expected.

Convict J. B. French split a few miles away from Eastham.

He wanted to be on his own. He was recaptured the next day. Hilton Bybee was let out in Amarillo. He lasted a week.

The others hit a bank at Lancaster, Texas, then raced north to Oklahoma. It was like the old days, with Clyde, Bonnie and Hamilton riding together once again. But with a difference. Now there was no refuge anywhere. They were too hot even for Hamilton's relatives. 'Keep going,' they were told. And so they drove north, out of Choctaw country, heading towards the Cookson Hills.

The heavily timbered hills had been a sanctuary for bad-men since the days of Jesse James and Belle Starr. The topography favoured fugitives. It was wild, inaccessible, sinister country, honeycombed with caves and crisscrossed by chasms and gorges – 2,400 square miles of roadless wilderness covered over with scrub oak and blackjack. A fugitive could step twenty feet off the main road – gravel-topped State 82 – and be in Tibet, as far as anyone could tell.

Lawmen didn't enter the hills. It was a waste of time. Not only did the topography favour the outlaws, but so did the hill dwellers. They fed and sheltered fugitives, and even refused to take money from those they liked. But they wouldn't lift a hand to help the Barrow gang. Word had come down from the 'Boss of the Hills,' Pretty Boy Floyd: shun them, starve them out, if necessary lead the law to them. They were too hot for the Cookson Hills; they would ruin it for the other outlaws holed up there.

The Barrows got the message. They packed up. But it was already too late. Their two cars, as hot as their occupants, had been sighted turning off into the hills at Muskogee. It had been the final straw for the already hard-pressed Oklahoma authorities.

On the night of February 17, 1934, 1,000 lawmen, including four companies of Oklahoma National Guardsmen, began surrounding the Cookson country in drizzling rain. For the first time in history a large body of troops would be sent sweeping through the hills in search of outlaws. Their orders: shoot to kill.

At dawn they pushed off. Guardsmen set up Army machine guns at all crossroads. Their instructions were to stop and search every car moving. If they refused to stop, shoot.

It was the biggest manhunt the press had ever had a whack at. Every newspaper in the Southwest sent reporters. Hubert Dail, of *True Detective* Magazine, was lucky enough to hitch a ride with an advance group. 'Every officer was heavily armed,' he reported. 'Each police car carried bright red lights and signs reading: "Stop! Sheriff!" It was a weird scene, the darting cars with their red lights and the big shadowy trucks loaded with guardsmen lumbering along more slowly. A thin snow lay over the Hills and the dirt roads were deep in mud. Even the chill air seemed hostile . . . The officers soon left all trails behind and trudged across the open country. Occasionally the rat-a-tat-tat of machine gun fire reached their ears. It meant that someone out along the road had refused to stop for questioning.'

But all the rat-a-tat-tatting came to naught. Only nineteen people were caught in the dragnet, all of them small-fry. Pretty Boy Floyd got away. The Ford Bradshaw gang escaped. And so did the Barrow outfit.

They headed north once again, hitting banks in Michigan, Iowa, and Indiana before Joe Palmer, who had stomach trouble, left the gang. At Terre Haute, Clyde and Hamilton got into a squabble over Bonnie's share of the loot, and Hamilton bowed out, too.

That left Bonnie and Clyde alone with Henry Methvin, a shy Louisiana farm boy with blond hair and blue eyes. He was W. D. all over again.

Keeping Methvin with them was a mistake. But Bonnie and Clyde would never have time to regret it. They would discover their error and die in the same instant.

Death was all they could think about these days; and the news from home only confirmed the manner in which it would finally come to them.

The Texas Legislature was up in arms. Major E. M. Crowson had died of his wounds following the Eastham Prison Farm delivery, and lawmakers were talking about a 'Wanted Dead' reward for Bonnie and Clyde.

T. H. McGregor, the representative from Austin, pleaded against the pressure. 'You are about to do in cold blood a thing which a mob does in the heat of passion,' he cried.

That brought Congressman George Winningham to his feet. 'I place Barrow and his gang beyond the category of human beings,' he shouted angrily. 'You are talking about according a trial to a beast. I say give him the same chance he gave those he murdered. Shoot him down like the mad dog he is.'

A $2,500 reward was finally settled on, and the words 'or alive' were added to the 'Wanted Dead' posters that would be distributed. It was a victory for the moderates.

Lee Simmons, the general manager of the Texas prison system, didn't think that proclamations or rewards were going to do any good. He had his own ideas on how to get Bonnie and Clyde. He sent for Frank Hamer, a former captain of the Texas Rangers. The fifty-year-old Hamer was an almost legendary figure in Texas. An old-style lawman who always dressed in sombre black, he was reputed to be the fastest draw south of the Red River. The sixty-five desperadoes he had killed in face-to-face encounters made Clyde's fatality list look pretty feeble.

Simmons gave Hamer a free hand, unlimited authority. 'I don't care how long it takes,' he told him. 'I'll back you to the limit.' And then he added, 'I'd be foolish to tell you how to do your job, but the way I look at it, the best thing to do is put them on the spot, know you are right, and shoot everybody in sight.'

On February 10 Hamer set out on his grim assignment. Like Clyde Barrow, he used a Ford V-8 and, like Clyde he lived in it for days at a time. As he travelled through the Southwest Hamer stopped and interviewed anyone who had ever known Bonnie and Clyde. Slowly a picture of his quarry emerged – right down to the cigarettes they smoked, the food they ate, the kind of clothes they wore. A pattern of movement began to emerge, too. The fugitives travelled along a rough circle from Dallas to Joplin, Missouri, then over to Louisiana and back to Dallas.

In late February Hamer missed them by minutes at Texarkana. He was close again at Shreveport, then at a campsite outside Wichita Falls. Then suddenly the trail grew cold.

They had come to rest at the Methvin farm in Bienville Parish, Louisiana.

Bonnie had become obsessed with the idea of writing one

last poem that would explain everything. She would send it to a newspaper and then the world would finally understand that they weren't as bad as they were painted. She sweated for some hours over the opening stanzas:

> You have read the story of Jesse James,
> Of how he lived and died.
> If you still are in need of something to read,
> Here is the story of Bonnie and Clyde.
>
> Now Bonnie and Clyde are the Barrow gang.
> I'm sure you all have read
> How they rob and steal,
> And how those who squeal,
> Are usually found dying or dead.
>
> There are lots of untruths to their write-ups,
> They are not so merciless as that;
> They hate all the laws,
> The stool-pigeons, spotters and rats.

After explaining how Clyde had been 'honest and upright and clean' until the law had started hounding him, she elaborated on how every crime of the period was being attributed to them:

> If a policeman is killed in Dallas
> And they have no clues to guide –
> If they can't find a fiend,
> They just wipe the slate clean,
> And hang it on Bonnie and Clyde.

She also recorded her version of the battles of Joplin and Platte City, concluding:

> If they try to act like citizens,
> And rent them a nice little flat,
> About the third night they are invited to fight.
> By a submachine-gun rat-tat-tat.

There was also a rather shrewd comment on their fame, and what it meant to some people during the Depression:

> A newsboy once said to his buddy:
> 'I wish old Clyde would get jumped;
> 'In these awful hard times,
> 'We'd make a few dimes
> 'If five or six cops would get bumped.'

Before she could finish the poem, the running began once again. State and Federal officers made a vice raid on nearby Ruston in mid-March, heating up all of Bienville and Lincoln Parishes.

Clyde, Bonnie, and young Henry Methvin drove west, crossing the Sabine River at Joaquin, Texas. They hid out in the 'big piney' country for the next few weeks, then made a dash into Dallas on April 1.

It was Easter Sunday. Bonnie had bought a baby rabbit for her sister. At around 2 p.m. they arrived at the rendezvous point, a lonely country lane a hundred yards off the Preston Road near Grapevine, Texas. They tied a ribbon around the rabbit's neck and let it out to play in the grass.

As they stood watching it two motorcycle cops roared past on State 114. The cops glanced at the trio, then swung around and came back. It's thought that the two, State Highway Patrolmen E. B. Wheeler and H. D. Murphy, were just going to ask them to move on.

Clyde watched them rack their cycles at the edge of the dirt lane and start towards them. Casually he reached inside the car for his shotgun.

A lot of newsboys made a lot of extra dimes that night.

The reaction to the double killing was intense. Both officers had been young – in their early twenties. Neither had had a chance to unholster his gun. Clyde was made Texas' Public Enemy Number One.

Captain Hamer wasn't far behind as the trio sped north from Grapevine along backcountry roads. At Tioga he found a campsite. He knew it was theirs from the marks left by rabbit's teeth in some lettuce leaves. There were also stubs of Bonnie's Camels, one of them still warm. Hamer raced on.

The V-8 was found abandoned outside Cannon, Texas. There were no recent auto theft reports in the area, though, so gradually the trail began to cool.

Clyde, Bonnie, and Methvin surfaced five days later outside Commerce, Oklahoma. They were driving a new Plymouth now. As they jounced along a rutted dirt road known locally as The Lost Trail they got mired in the mud. Clyde tried to flag down a farmer, but the man caught a glimpse of the rifles stacked inside their car and sped away. He drove straight in to Commerce and told Police Chief Percy Boyd what he had seen.

Boyd picked up Constable Cal Campbell, and the two men drove out along the road until they spotted the Plymouth. They stopped and got out of their car. As they approached on foot, Clyde Barrow suddenly stepped out from behind the Plymouth. He had a Browning automatic rifle in his hands.

Campbell, a large man with a western-style moustache, was proud of his fast draw. He had his pistol out and was firing it before Clyde could get off a shot. His aim was wild, though. Clyde's wasn't. Campbell dropped, mortally wounded. Chief Boyd had also drawn and fired. He was sent spinning into the mud by a second blast from the BAR.

Barrow ran down the road while Methvin covered the two men. Clyde got a farmer in a truck to pull the Plymouth out of the ditch. Then the chief, who wasn't seriously wounded, was loaded into the back seat, and the four of them drove off.

That night they stopped at Fort Scott, Kansas, and Bonnie bought a newspaper and food, which they ate in the woods. They learned from the paper that Constable Campbell had died. 'I'm sorry I killed the old man,' Clyde told Boyd. 'But I had to. He shouldn't have shot at me.'

They released the police chief near Prescott, Kansas, an hour later. Bonnie's last words to him were that the much-publicized snapshot of her had been a joke. 'Tell the public I don't smoke cigars,' she called out as the car drove away. 'It's the bunk.'

Captain Hamer, as usual, was only a half hour behind them. He had been on their trail forty-five days now. It was a record. 'Clyde Barrow,' he would later tell newsmen, 'was the smartest of them all. He was the most elusive and shrewdest man I ever tracked.'

The FBI was too busy with the Dillinger case to waste much time on the Barrows, but one Special Agent, I. A. Kindell, had been acting as a liaison between local police agencies and the Bureau.

In early April, Kindell discovered the identity of the third gang member, Henry Methvin. He took a trip to Louisiana and turned up another interesting fact – that Clyde and Bonnie often visited Methvin's father, Ivan.

While poking around the Arcadia area, some eighty miles east of the Texas-Louisiana border, Kindell met Frank Hamer, who had also been drawn there by the Methvin angle. The two men went to see the Arcadia sheriff, Henderson Jordan.

He reported that Ivan Methvin had moved recently. At their request, Jordan tracked him down. Methvin was living on a rented farm about halfway between Arcadia and Gibsland. The three men went to see him. Methvin admitted that his son was involved with Bonnie and Clyde. But he refused to help them. 'I've got my boy to think about,' he said.

A few weeks passed, while the lawmen tried to figure out their next move. Then suddenly Ivan Methvin came to seem them. Clyde and Bonnie had returned and had forced him to move once again. The four of them were holed up in an abandoned farmhouse deep in the woods. Methvin was now willing to cooperate with the law – for a price.

Hamer contacted Prison Manager Simmons and named the price. He could put Barrow and his girl on the spot, but it would take a full pardon for Henry Methvin.

Simmons went to Austin and conferred with 'Ma' Ferguson. She agreed to issue the pardon if Methvin's father cooperated. Hamer passed the word on. Methvin was satisfied. He promised to help the lawmen and even suggested a plan.

The gang's routine, in the event they got separated, was to meet at the abandoned house. Methvin said he would tell his son to get lost, and when Clyde and Bonnie appeared at the rendezvous point, they could – well, be captured.

Ivan Methvin took his son aside that same night and told him the plan. Henry said they were going in to Shreveport the next day to do some shopping and that he would vanish at the first opportunity. He did. Clyde and Bonnie waited for him almost an hour. Then, figuring that something must have scared him away, they drove out to the abandoned house and waited.

Ivan Methvin sat watching them, sweat pouring down his face. But they apparently suspected nothing. Finally Bonnie said, 'Maybe he got mixed up and went over to the rented place.'

Clyde said to Methvin, 'You better check on it. We'll meet you on the road between Sailes and Gibsland tomorrow morning at nine.'

As soon as they were gone, Ivan rushed to Sheriff Jordan's house. Jordan phoned Federal Agent Kindell, but his office said he was out of town on an emergency assignment and couldn't be reached. Captain Hamer was in town, though, and came right over. With him was an old Ranger sidekick, M. B. 'Manny' Gault, and two men from Sheriff Schmid's Dallas office, Chief Deputy Bob Alcorn and Deputy Ted Hinton.

After picking up Jordan's deputy, Paul M. Oakley, the six men drove back and forth between Sailes and Gibsland, looking for the best ambush spot. They finally settled on a patch of woods outside Mt Lebanon. The road was narrow at this point and with steep banks on both sides. Clyde wouldn't be able to pull off his famous U-turn.

The men got into position behind the embankment. Captain Hamer and Sheriff Jordan had automatic shotguns. Hinton had a BAR. Gault, Oakley, and Alcorn had Winchester repeaters. All had a perfect field of fire.

Finally, around eight o'clock that morning, May 23, they heard Ivan Methvin's truck approaching. Sheriff Jordan flagged it down. Methvin was told to pull over to the side of the road and to take the truck's right front wheel off, as if he had a flat.

Then the waiting started once again. At nine o'clock several cars passed. The men tensed each time, but the cars sped by without stopping. Then, at nine-fifteen, a Ford V-8 suddenly appeared over the rise and came speeding towards the ambush site.

Clyde was at the wheel. He wore sunglasses and was driving in his socks. Bonnie sat beside him, munching a sandwich. She had on her best dress, a flashy red one that she had bought in Terre Haute a few weeks earlier. Clyde's sawed-off twelve-gauge was propped between them. Their usual armoury was on the back seat – eleven pistols, a revolver, three BAR's, and more than two thousand rounds of ammunition. Bonnie's overnight case was on top of it, together with Clyde's saxophone and some sheets of music.

Bonnie's poem wasn't in the car, though. She had completed it a few weeks earlier and had sent it to the Dallas *Evening Journal* with instructions to publish it after her death. The poem's final verses ran:

> The road gets dimmer and dimmer.
> Sometimes you can hardly see,
> Still it's fight, man to man,
> And do all you can,
> For they know they can never be free.
>
> They don't think they are too tough or desperate,
> They know the law always wins,
> They have been shot at before
> But they do not ignore
> That death is the wages of sin.
>
> From heartbreaks some people suffered,
> From weariness some people have died,
> But take it all in all,
> Our troubles are small,
> Till we get like Bonnie and Clyde.
>
> Some day they will go down together,
> And they will bury them side by side.
> To a few it means grief,
> To the law it's relief,
> But it's death to Bonnie and Clyde.

Clyde saw Ivan Methvin's truck and slowed to a stop beside it. 'Got a flat?' he called out. Methvin nodded nervously. 'Did you find Henry?'

Methvin shook his head, then turned suddenly to Bonnie and asked her for a drink of water.

'Sure,' she said, and reached for the thermos. Methvin dived behind his truck.

'Put 'em up, Clyde. You're covered!' Sheriff Jordan bellowed.

Clyde shifted into first, grabbed his shotgun, and swung the door open – all in one movement. Bonnie already had her pistol out.

The ambush party opened fire. Six powerful weapons poured nonstop streams of lead into the car. Bonnie and Clyde's bodies danced like puppets on a string. Clyde's jacket was literally torn from his body. He sagged against the wheel. His foot slipped off the clutch pedal. The car rolled forward against the embankment and there it bounced to a stop.

'Be careful, they may not be dead,' Ranger Gault shouted as Captain Hamer cautiously approached the car.

One hundred and sixty-seven slugs had ripped into the vehicle, all of them breast-high on the two occupants. Yet there was still doubt in the lawmen's minds as to whether Bonnie and Clyde were actually dead. Such was the power of their legend.

The crowds got at the bodies immediately. They tore away scraps of their clothing and snipped off locks of their hair. They gathered up the empty cartridges and bits of broken glass.

The car was towed into Arcadia with the bodies still in it.

Photographs taken at the funeral parlour show the two bodies lying riddled and leaking on adjoining stone slabs, the tools of their trade piled on their chests, as crowds file past, gaping, hungry for one last thrill.

Captain Hamer's job was over. He had finally taken them – after 102 days of tracking. 'There isn't much to it,' he told the chief of the Texas Highway Patrol over the telephone. 'They just drove into the wrong place. Both of them died with their guns in their hands, but they didn't have a chance to use them.'

The news was flashed around the world. In New York City the *Herald Tribune* observed solemnly that 'society is glad that Louisiana rubbed them both out.'

They were not buried side by side as Bonnie had predicted

in her poem. Clyde was buried beside his brother Buck in West Dallas Cemetery. Bonnie was lowered into the ground at Fish Trap Cemetery several miles away while a quartet sang 'Beautiful Isle of Somewhere.' Her body was later moved to Crown Hill Memorial Park.

The authorities were busy, meanwhile, rounding up the remnants of the gang. Ray Hamilton and Joe Palmer were caught and sentenced to death for killing Major Crowson during the Eastham bust-out. They made a spectacular escape from the Huntsville death house in July 1934 but were later recaptured and electrocuted.

Henry Methvin got his pardon from Texas, but Oklahoma officers were waiting for him. He was taken to that state and sentenced to death for the murder of Constable Cal Campbell. The sentence was later commuted, and he was paroled in 1942. A train ran over him in Sulphur, Louisiana, six years later.

Mrs Cumie Barrow and many other relatives of Bonnie and Clyde served prison terms ranging from a few days to years for having given 'aid and comfort' to the pair while they were fugitives.

And that was supposed to be the end of it. Time would pass and people would forget. Instead the legend grew. Around Grand Prairie and the West Dallas viaduct it got more elaborate with every passing year.

There were the poems, and there was Clyde, who had carried Bonnie with him when she was crippled and no longer pretty, and there was Bonnie herself tough and hard-mouthed, a killer, yet capable of caring for him in some furious, half-crazy way.

After Bonnie was buried at Crown Hill Cemetery, her family had a plaque put over her grave. There were some verses on it. Not Bonnie's, just those standard lines that used to come with a certain price headstone back in the Depression. They read:

> As the flowers are all made sweeter
> By the sunshine and the dew,
> So this old world is made brighter
> By the lives of folks like you.

George A. Birmingham

IN THE INTERESTS OF SCIENCE

The murderer who hopes to escape detection must arrange for the disposal of the body of his victim; and this, fortunately for society, is a very difficult thing to do. The poisoner tries to avoid the difficulty by leaving it to be supposed that his victim has died a natural death. The body is then, after some signing of certificates, buried in the usual way. But sometimes doctors will not sign certificates without post-mortem examinations. Then there cannot be a funeral. Sometimes, even after the funeral, suspicious persons insist on making inquiries. Then the body is dug up again and an examination takes place. These are the risks which the poisoner runs. The murderer by violence is in a still more difficult position. If he has stabbed, shot or battered his victim to death, he cannot hope for a quiet funeral without inquiry. He must dispose of the body. Many methods have been tried and none of them can be regarded as satisfactory, from the point of view of the murderer. An exceedingly gruesome book might be written about the burnings of bodies, their burial under floors and in other unauthorized places, the sinking of them in water, the packing of them in trunks, and so forth. The result of a careful study of these methods would, I think, lead to a conviction that the disposal of a dead body - in a manner safe for the murderer - is very nearly impossible.

Yet Burke and Hare, owing to the peculiar conditions of their times, not only succeeded in disposing of the bodies of sixteen victims in the course of nine months, but did it without leading anyone to suspect that murder had been committed at all. Or, perhaps it is not possible to give Dr Knox and his assistants so complete a coat of whitewash as that. It is safer to say: without leading the police or the coroners or society in general to suspect that murder had been done. Their method, fortunately, can never be adopted again.

Edinburgh has been famous for its medical school for perhaps 400 years. Since 1705 there has been a regularly appointed, officially recognized professor of anatomy. For a century and a quarter the office was hereditary in the Monro family. An Alexander Monro was succeeded by Alexander Monro, his son, and he by another Alexander, grandson of the original professor. Perhaps the family genius began to wear thin in the third generation. Perhaps the demand for instruction in this particular subject increased. At all events the third Alexander Monro found his supremacy challenged by other professors of anatomy, some of them brilliant men who attracted large classes of students. Among these free-lance professors was Dr Robert Knox.

Dr Knox lectured, and Dr Knox advertised his lectures. 'Two Demonstrations to be delivered daily,' so his handbills ran, 'To gentlemen attending the rooms for Practical Anatomy. These demonstrations so arranged so as to comprise complete courses of the descriptive anatomy of the human body, with its application to pathology and an operative surgery. The dissections and operations to be under the superintendence of Dr Knox. *Arrangements have been made to secure as usual an ample supply of anatomical subjects.*' Then follows a statement of fees charged, which were very moderate, and a footnote: 'An additional fee of 3 guineas includes subjects.' This means, I suppose, that for this extra payment the student was allotted a 'subject' which he might dissect for himself.

The italics in which Dr Knox's statement of the 'ample supply' has been printed, are mine and not his. But he might very well have used special type to call attention to this feature of his lectures. For an ample supply of subjects was a difficult thing to arrange in those days. The law was great on the sanctity of the human body, and took very little heed of the needs of lecturers on anatomy.

In 1505 the Edinburgh surgeons – who in those days were also barbers – were allowed the body of one executed criminal per annum; and that only on condition that they prayed for the man's soul – which perhaps they did. The Renaissance and the

Reformation increased the world's respect for science, while diminishing its faith in a perfectly literal resurrection of the body. At the end of the seventeenth century the Edinburgh surgeons were granted for the purposes of dissection the bodies of those who died in prison, of foundlings who died before apprenticeship and of suicides. Probably a good many people died in prison in those days and it would have been a rash society which ensured the life of a foundling up to the date of his apprenticeship. But even so the supply of 'subjects' – bodies for dissection – was lamentably short of the demand. The official professor, Alexander Monro the third, must have had first claim on the bodies legally disposed of, and even he wanted more than he got. The free-lance professors had to seek their subjects elsewhere and get them as best as they could without respect for the law.

When Dr Knox was at the height of his fame in 1828 or thereabouts, he had a class of three or four hundred students, and he advertised, as we have seen, 'an ample supply of subjects'. Unlike some other advertisers, he kept his faith with his clients. There was 'an ample supply' on the tables of his lecture-rooms, and Dr Knox, an enthusiast for his science, spent £700 or £800 a year to secure it.

Who had the money and how did they earn it? Mr Jeremiah Cruncher, the 'honest tradesman' in Dickens' novel, could have answered these questions.

There existed a regular traffic in bodies dug out of their graves after decent interment. There was, apparently, a fixed scale of prices, and these were so high that it was well worth while taking the risks which the 'resurrectionists' certainly took. And these risks were grave. In the first place the trade was illegal, and severe penalties were inflicted on such 'body-snatchers' as were caught. Smuggling was also illegal and the penalties severe. But the 'resurrectionists' ' trade, unlike the smugglers', had public opinion against it. Most right-minded people sympathized with the smugglers and the agents of the law were the only enemies they had to face. The 'resurrectionist' was in danger of being mobbed by the populace if the law failed to deal with him. A sexton in the neighbourhood of Edinburgh actually was mobbed, on suspicion, though he protested his innocence. It was felt, I suppose, that his business put irresistible temptation in his way. A gardener, suspected of digging in a graveyard deeper than the planting of flowers required, had his house burnt. But the trade went on. Edinburgh was the chief market, for Edinburgh's medical schools were large and active; but the supply came from places as far afield as London and the North of Ireland. The bodies from these places were shipped to Edinburgh or Glasgow. I remember seeing – and the thing may still exist – a very strongly built stone vault in a Co. Antrim churchyard. It was used for the safe keeping of bodies until, by the natural process of decay, they were no longer any use to the anatomists. Then they were taken out of their temporary vault and buried in ordinary graves. Other means were adopted elsewhere to defeat the 'resurrectionists', but the business flourished.

Nor was it always a sordid matter of earning money by a nauseous kind of crime. Sometimes the 'resurrectionists' were, so to speak, amateurs, who worked without pay. Students adopted this way of securing material for the dissecting tables of their professors. Perhaps the pure love of science actuated them, but there must often have been a love of adventure and risk for its own sake, and, no doubt, a delight in the gruesome. Wild Tales are told of the deeds of these student body-snatchers, and wild deeds were certainly done by them.

In 1827, when the 'resurrectionist' trade was enjoying its last and greatest boom, there were living in Edinburgh two Irishmen – William Burke and William Hare. They both belonged to the class of unskilled labourers. Both of them had left their native land, as Irishmen of this class did then and still do, in the hope of earning, or at all events gaining, a living in Scotland. Both of them worked for a time on a canal then being built between Edinburgh and Glasgow. But work, it seems, was unattractive to them. They preferred to live without it, if possible. Each had a woman as partner in iniquity. Burke's associate was one Helen Macdougal. She was Scottish and by religious profession a Presbyterian; but indeed the religious profession of the whole crew – Burke and the Hares were Roman Catholics – is not a thing which matters much. Hare, when he came to be sworn in court, preferred a Bible with a cross on it, which shows – What does that show? Perhaps that some memory of childish faith survives in the worst of us. Perhaps that even the most debauched and callous murderers like to wrap some rags of superstition around them. Both women, Helen Macdougal and Margaret Hare, were thoroughly immoral, in the special sense in which that word is used of women. Neither of them was married to the man with whom she lived, though Margaret Hare used her associate's name.

The Hares kept a lodging-house. It was the lowest possible house of the kind. The guests slept two or three in a bed and there were eight beds to let. The lodgers only paid twopence or threepence a night for this accommodation, so the Hares were not likely to grow rich or even to earn a comfortable livelihood and enough money for the whisky they craved. Burke, with his Helen Macdougal, lived in another miserable house near by. He earned what he did earn, but it must have been very little, by cobbling shoes, a trade which he had learned late in life, after he had given up the more arduous work of digging canals.

In the Hares' lodging-house there lived an old army pensioner called Donald. In November, 1827, this man died, and died owing the Hares £4. It seemed difficult, if not impossible, to recover the debt. But Hare was not content to write it off as 'bad'. He consulted his friend Burke. Together they hit on the idea of selling the old man's body to the doctors.

Like most people they had heard of this trade in bodies, and though they knew little or nothing about the details, they saw no reason why they should not make a little money that way if they could.

The early proceedings were simple enough. The old pensioner's body had been coffined for burial by the parish officer. Hare prized off the lid, took out the body, filled the coffin with rubbish and nailed down the lid again. He hid the body in a bed. The parish authorities, unsuspectingly, buried the coffin.

That night Burke and Hare went together to Surgeons' Square, where not less than six professors of anatomy lectured to their students. Here they sold their goods, afterwards delivered in a sack, to three young assistants of Dr Knox. Their original intention had been to deal with Professor Monro, whose name they had probably heard; but when Dr Knox's assistants met them they were easily persuaded to deal with him. It did not much matter to Burke and Hare to whom they sold their body, so long as the money was forthcoming.

It was forthcoming, a surprisingly large sum. Dr Knox, who inspected the corpse himself, was prepared to pay, and did pay, £7 10s. for the body of the dead army pensioner. This, as Burke and Hare learned from the assistants, was by no means a top price. As much as £10 was often paid for bodies delivered in good condition. Burke and Hare were warmly invited to return when they had another body to dispose of. There was no fear of the market being over-stocked.

With this £7 10s. safely in pocket, Burke and Hare returned home. No doubt they discussed their unexpected good fortune. No doubt they celebrated the occasion with copious whisky drinking. No doubt the two women joined in the festivities and the consultation which followed. For there was a consultation. Here was a chance of easy and abundant money, a glorious possibility of being able to live in comfort without doing any work.

If only a sufficient number of dying army pensioners could be induced to spend their last hours in Hare's lodging-house! Army pensioners or anybody else, man or woman, old or young, who was dying. No doubt Hare's customers were the sort of people who died easily. They were the poorest of the poor. They were for the most part vicious and drink-sodden. For such people the end comes swiftly. But not swiftly enough for Burke and Hare.

To whom did the idea of hastening the work of nature first occur? Was it Burke, debonair and civil-spoken, with a touch of the humorous Irishman about him, who suggested the idea to others? Was it Hare, a more ferocious man and more callous, to whom the great thought occurred? Or did Mrs Hare, vivacious, and vital in her wickedness, hint, half jokingly, that it was not absolutely necessary to wait for the victims to die? Or perhaps the morose dour Scotswoman, Helen Macdougal, Burke's partner and mistress, growled out the suggestion that corpses might be made as well as found. We shall never know. Only of this we are certain: the idea occurred to one of the four and was welcomed by the other three.

Then began the famous series of sixteen murders for which in the end Burke alone suffered on the scaffold. But no one – not even Burke and Hare – plumbs the utmost depths of iniquity all at once. The first two murders were such as might be justified or excused to each other by the four people concerned. They were the murders of men who were already ill, perhaps dying. Joseph, or Miller, fell ill of a fever, and, unfortunately for himself, fell ill in Hare's house. It was very easy to argue that the man would die in any case and that it was no heinous crime to hasten his end. It was easy to argue – and Hare actually did argue – that the presence of a lodger with fever in his house would keep other lodgers away and so hinder his legitimate business. So 'Joseph the miller' was murdered. Burke laid a small pillow on his mouth. 'Hare lay on the body and kept down the arms and legs.' These are the words of Burke's confession.

The body was disposed of to Dr Knox, who – Burke notes this particularly – 'did not ask any questions'. The next victim was also a sick man, an Englishman who was unfortunate enough to get jaundice in Hare's house. In his case there was a slight variation of method. A pillow was no longer used. The man was suffocated 'by holding his mouth'. Afterwards this method was invariably adopted, death in every case being by suffocation.

The murder of sick men, likely to die in any case, was one thing. The murder of perfectly healthy people was another, and no doubt, even to Burke and Hare, there was a considerable difference between the two. But the gulf could be bridged and was bridged by the ingenious device of making a healthy person sick and then assuming the probability of death. This was what happened in the case of the third victim. An old woman called Abigail Simpson came to Edinburgh from Gilmarton to receive a pension allowed to her. She spent the night in Hare's house as a casual lodger. Here is Burke's account of what happened to her, taken from the confession which he made in gaol while under sentence of death.

'She was a stranger and she and Hare became merry and drank together; and the next morning she was very ill in consequence of what she got and she sent for more drink and she and Hare drank together, and she became very sick and vomited; and at that time she had not risen from bed, and Hare said they would try and smother her in order to dispose of her body to the doctors. She was lying on her back on the bed and quite insensible from drink, and Hare clapped his hand on her mouth and nose and the declarant (Burke) laid himself across her body to prevent her making any disturbance, and she never stirred; and they took her out of bed and undressed her and put her into a chest; and they mentioned to Dr Knox's young men that they had another subject, and Mr Miller sent a porter to meet them in the evening at the back of the castle, and the declarant (Burke) and Hare carried the chest till they met a porter and they accompanied the porter with the chest to Dr Knox's class room and Dr Knox came in when they were there; the body was cold and stiff. Dr Knox approved of its being so fresh, but did not ask any questions.'

Dr Knox did not ask any questions. He was a doctor, very highly skilled in his profession. There was probably no reason why he should have asked any questions. He must have known or guessed how Abigail Simpson came to die. But if he asked no questions he surely thought some thoughts. What were they? Is the advancement of science – Dr Knox was an enthusiast for that – an all-justifying end? A man may be a despiser of all religions and all churches – Dr Knox apparently was – does this make him indifferent to all morality? In spite of his brilliance and his enthusiasm and his wit, Dr Knox is not an attractive personality. We scarcely wonder at the bitter contempt felt for him by a man like Sir Walter Scott.

The record of sixteen murders makes dreary reading once the first shock of horror is dulled by the repetition of the abominable details. There is a horrible monotony about the whole business. The sordid, filthy lodging-house, the drink and drink and drunkenness, the suffocations by hands held over mouth and nose, and the infernal iteration of the final sentences of each story 'was disposed of in the same manner' – Who wants to read such stuff over and over again?

Burke and Hare worked as business men, partners in a paying enterprise. They had a regular scale for the division of their profits. Of each ten pounds paid by Dr Knox Hare took £6 and

Burke £4. This departure from the natural fifty-fifty system of division was adopted because Mrs Hare claimed £1, a kind of royalty, on each transaction. She was, or claimed to be, the owner of the house in which the murders were done, and on that account deemed herself entitled to her ten per cent. This pound was deducted from Burke's share and added to Hare's. He, we presume, handed it over to the woman who called herself Mrs Hare. There was no formal deed of partnership. The firm kept no books, though in case of doubt reference could be made to Dr Knox's. But there never seems to have been any quarrelling about the money. Indeed, so 'honest' were these 'tradesmen' that Hare on at least one occasion paid his partner's share in the profits of a transaction though Burke was absent from Edinburgh when the sale was made.

Of the remaining murders only three were specially interesting, that of Mary Patterson, that of 'Daft' Jamie and that of the old woman Docherty. The last is interesting because it was the last and led to the arrest and trial of Burke. In the other two horror rises to a climax, and the details in each throw a sinister light on the character of Dr Knox.

Mary Patterson was a beautiful girl, strikingly beautiful, according to Dr Knox, who must have known something about the subject. He used her body as an example to his students of what a young woman's figure ought to be at its best. Mary Patterson was also a girl of spirit with a taste for adventure. That, perhaps, is why she became what the French call a *fille de joie*, a member of a profession which promises and sometimes begins by giving a specious kind of gaiety, which invariably ends in unutterable misery. But Mary Patterson never got as far as the final misery. Her career came to an abrupt end when she was only eighteen years old.

Mary Patterson had a friend called Janet Brown, another girl of eighteen, another member of that most unhappy profession. One evening the two girls incurred the suspicion or the resentment of the police and were shut up for the night. The experience must be common enough for such girls, and it was probably not the first night that Mary had spent in a cell. But she resented it. So, perhaps, did Janet. I dare say they were troublesome and behaved themselves badly. They certainly

Above: Raymond Fernandez (centre) and Martha Beck (right), the Lonely Hearts Killers who lured lonely women with promises of love. *(Associated Press)*
Below: Deadly Triangle: In a jealous rage, Freddie Bywaters (left), who was having a secret affair with Edith Thompson (centre), murdered her husband (right). *(Popperfoto)*

Above: Nathan Leopold (left) and Richard Loeb (right) thought they were teenage supermen, and kidnapped young Bobbie Franks to prove it – with deadly results. *(Hulton Deutsch)*

Below: 'Ricky' (real name Karl Hulten) tried to impress 'Georgina' (really Elizabeth Jones of Hammersmith) by posing as a big-time American gangster. Their spree ended in murder. *(Topham Picture Source)*

The real Bonnie and Clyde looked nothing like the Hollywood duo Fay Dunaway and Warren Beatty in the movie, but willingly posed tough for a friend's camera. *(Hulton Deutsch)*

AUTHENTIC CONFESSIONS OF WILLIAM BURK,

Who was Executed at Edinburgh, on 28th January 1829, for Murder, emitted before the Sheriff-Substitute of Edinburgh, the Rev. Mr Reid, Catholic Priest, and others, in the Jail, on 3d and 22d January.

EDINBURGH:
Printed and Sold by R. Menzies, Lawnmarket.
1829.
Price Tuppence.

TITLE-PAGE OF "AUTHENTIC CONFESSIONS OF WILLIAM BURK."
(Edinburgh, 1829.)

Above: Two Williams: Burke (left) and Hare (right), the original Bodysnatchers, supplied corpses to Dr Knox – but from where? *(Hulton Deutsch)*

Left: The execution of Burke drew large crowds. *(The Mansell Collection)*

Above, left: The Papin Sisters, Christine (left) and Léa (right), the religious housemaids who tore out their employers' eyeballs . . .
(Topham Picture Source)

Below: Alma Rattenbury with her son from her first marriage and her elderly second husband. Frustrated and discontent, she began a deadly affair with chauffeur/handyman Percy Stoner (above, right). *(Popperfoto)*

Nathalis Gaudry (far left) was cold-heartedly used by Jenny Amenaide Brécourt, alias Jeanne de la Cour and later the Widow Gras. She manipulated him to blind her lover thus ensuring his lifetime devotion. *(Bibliothèque Nationale)*

The Kray Twins, Ronnie (left) and Reggie (right): Britain's best-known gangsters as young contenders. *(Popperfoto)*

The Tiger Woman, Ruth Snyder, and the corset-salesman, Judd Gray. Together, they committed adultery and murder; in court, they hated each other. *(Topham Picture Source)*

New Zealand's strangest murderers: Pauline Parker (right) and Juliet Hulme (left) planned to 'moider' Pauline's mother, then run away and write crime novels. *(Hulton Deutsch)*

Charlie Starkweather thought he looked like James Dean. With fourteen-year-old Caril Ann Fugate he went on the bloody murder trip that inspired the movie *Badlands*. *(Associated Press)*

Lewis Staunton (left), found guilty of murdering his wife in the most heartless way. Alice Rhodes (right) seemed to be taking her place before she was dead . . . *(Hulton Deutsch)*

Above: Myra Hindley teamed up with Ian Brady to form Britain's most lethal couple, sadistically torturing and killing children. *(Hulton Deutsch)*
Below: Ian Brady was given three life sentences for the murders of three children. Hanging had been abolished in England just one month before he was arrested. *(Popperfoto)*

made themselves thirsty. When released the next morning they went together to the house of a Mrs Laurie, a friendly, kindly and sensible woman, though probably no puritan in her morality. From Mrs Laurie's house they went forth to search for a drink, being, as has been said, very thirsty after their experiences with the police. They found what they wanted in the house of one William Swanston. What they particularly wanted was whisky, and Mr Swanston supplied them with a gill each. He had another customer in his shop when the girls entered it. This was Burke, and he was drinking rum.

Burke's business led him to associate with the helpless and friendless, with those who led irregular lives, who would not be much missed if they disappeared, about whom inconvenient inquiries were not likely to be made. Such, obviously, were Mary and Janet. Burke spoke to them. He was a pleasant-spoken scoundrel when he chose. He gave them more drinks, for in the way of business he could be generous. He flattered them. Finally he invited them to go home with him to his lodgings. Mary was quite willing to go. Janet demurred. But in the end both girls went. Burke presented them each with a bottle of whisky before leaving Swanston's shop.

Burke took them to the house of a brother of his called Constantine. It was a miserable one-roomed tenement. Constantine Burke and his wife were in bed when the party arrived. William Burke played host. A fire was soon lit and a surprisingly good breakfast provided. Constantine and his wife, emerging from their bed, joined the party. After breakfast Constantine went off to work at his unsavoury job of city scavenging. The rest of the party sat on. The two bottles of whisky were opened and nearly finished. Mary Patterson fell sound asleep. She had spent the night in a police cell, very likely a sleepless and exhausting night. She had drunk her own gill of whisky and the three gills of rum provided by Burke in Swanston's shop. She had eaten a good breakfast. She had drunk her share of two bottles of whisky. She slept soundly, and Burke felt pretty sure of her.

Janet Brown was still awake and, if not strictly sober, at all events not helplessly drunk. Burke took her out to a neighbouring shop, where he fed her again and gave her more drink. They returned to Constantine's house and finished the two bottles of whisky. Helen Macdougal, Burke's horrible female associate, arrived and began to abuse the girl. Her tongue was rough. Her voice was loud. She frightened Janet, but she did not wake Mary, who by this time was lying helpless and unconscious on one of the beds with which the room was furnished. Janet, thoroughly terrified, left the house and went back to Mrs Laurie. Poor Mary remained asleep on the bed, in the company of Constantine's wife, Helen Macdougal and Burke. Was ever a girl in a worse plight?

Janet told the story of her morning's adventure to Mrs Laurie, and Mrs Laurie did not like the sound of it at all. She sent Janet back to fetch Mary, and sent with her a maidservant, surely an insufficient guardian.

When Janet and the maid reached the house Mary Patterson was lying dead, smothered as usual and concealed in the bed. The two Hares were there and invited Janet to come in. Her friend, they said, had gone out with Burke, but would soon come in. More whisky was produced. Mrs Laurie's servant was sent home. The unsuspecting Janet sat down to drink within a few feet of the body of her murdered friend.

Mrs Laurie's maid went back to her mistress and told her what Janet was doing. Mrs Laurie - what did she suspect or fear? - sent the girl off again with strict orders to fetch Janet. Janet, though she must have been very far from sober by that time, had sense enough to leave the house when the servant came for her. Mary - or rather her body - left the same house later in the day packed in a tea-chest, and her destination was Dr Knox's dissecting room.

Janet was a faithful friend. For a long time afterwards she made inquiries about Mary. She was told a story which scarcely satisfied her of Mary's departure to Glasgow in company with a packman. The landlady with whom Mary lodged also made inquiries. Nobody else did. Nobody else was particularly interested. Neither Janet nor the landlady reported the disappearance to the police. It was perhaps scarcely to be expected of such women that they should court the notice of the guardians of law and order.

Mary's body was received at Dr Knox's rooms by 'Mr

Ferguson' – I am again quoting from Burke's confession – 'and a tall lad who seemed to have known the dead woman by sight.' One or other of them asked where Burke got the body. Burke replied that he had purchased it from an old woman. This is the only time that a question was asked in Dr Knox's room about any body brought there. Mr Ferguson afterwards became a baronet, and 'Sergeant Surgeon to Queen Victoria'. Did that eminent lady ever ask him what he thought when Mary Patterson's body was brought to him? Probably not. The world is very merciful in forgetting 'the sins and offences of our youth', so perhaps Queen Victoria had never heard of Ferguson's reception of Mary Patterson in Dr Knox's room.

'The tall lad' was not, it seemed, the only one of Dr Knox's students who recognized or thought he recognized Mary. Her body excited general admiration, a thing which must be very rare in the dissecting room. Dr Knox brought an artist to sketch it, so Burke tells us. Many of the students sketched it, according to David Patterson, the door-keeper of Dr Knox's room, who knew a good deal about what went on there. Dr Knox used the body for some time as the best possible illustration of the female form in its muscular development. Then it was allowed to achieve dissolution on the dissecting table.

Burke and Hare only got £8 for Mary Patterson's body, surely an inadequate sum. But perhaps Dr Knox himself was in a position to drive a hard bargain. The story of the sale of the body by an old woman in Canongate can scarcely have been wholly satisfactory to the 'tall lad' who thought he knew her.

James Wilson, like Mary Patterson, was eighteen years old when he came into the clutches of Burke and Hare. He was a tall, strong, physically well-formed young man, but of weak intellect. The Edinburgh people called him 'Daft Jamie'. In our modern jargon we should describe his case as one of arrested development. In his young manhood he still had the mind of a child. Also, apparently, the amiability of a good-tempered child. He was accustomed to wandering about the streets of the city, picking up his food where he could get it, sleeping in any casual and convenient shelter. While a boy, he had quarrelled with his mother, and though she seemed to have some interest in him he refused to live in her house. His amiability and his fondness for feeble jokes endeared him to those who knew him, and they were many, for Daft Jamie was, in his way, a public character in Edinburgh.

His murder is noticeable among the sixteen committed by Burke and Hare for several reasons. He was the only one of their many victims who made any serious resistance. He was the only one of all the sixteen whom the murderers robbed after they had killed him. The production by Dr Knox of a body so easily recognized by so many people showed that long impunity had rendered him, as it had rendered the actual murderers, almost reckless.

It was Mrs Hare who found Jamie in the street and lured him into the murder den. Burke, who, after his usual custom, was having a drink in a public-house, saw her leading Jamie along. He says 'that he was led as a dumb lamb to the slaughter and as a sheep to the shearers'. The devil, as we know, can quote Scripture for his purpose, so there is nothing astonishing about the production of 'holy witness' by this 'evil soul'. What is a little surprising is that an Irish peasant should quote Scripture so glibly, even though he quoted it a little inaccurately. But it appears that Burke was no more faithful to the disciplinary regulations of his Church than he was to the moral precepts of the Decalogue. He had a fondness, surely an odd one, for attending revivalist meetings. It was no doubt at one of them that he became familiar with the words of the prophet Isaiah.

Mrs Hare led Jamie to her house and left him there in the company, perhaps we should say the custody, of Hare. She herself went to the public-house to seek for Burke, whose help was certain to be wanted. She found him and asked him for a dram, which he obligingly supplied. While drinking it she stamped on his foot. 'He immediately knew what he was wanted for,' so Burke's confession goes, and he then went after her. When in the house she said, 'You have come too late. The drink is all done! and Jamie had the cup in his hand.'

Daft Jamie, like many a saner man, liked a drink; but he was never known to take too much. Nor did he exceed that day in Hare's house; though 'another half mutchkin was sent for' after Burke's arrival, 'and they urged him to drink. She took a little with them.' Altogether, in spite of strong temptation, Jamie did not drink more than one glass of whisky, according to Burke's account. For some reason, or perhaps without reason, but with the instinct of an animal nearing the slaughter-house, Jamie was uneasy. 'He was always very anxious, making inquiries for his mother, and was told she would be there immediately.'

Jamie was not drunk, nor likely to be; but it was possible that he might be sleepy. He was 'invited in the little room, and advised to sit down on a bed'. At this stage of the proceedings Mrs Hare went out. She had no desire to witness the final scene of the drama for which she had set the stage. We can scarcely credit her with squeamishness or suspect her of nerves. She probably regarded the actual murder as the men's part of the job, and went out to have a drink while they did it. 'Jamie sat down on the bed.' This is Burke's account again. 'He then lay down on the bed, and Hare –' Hare attempted to smother him in the usual way, but Jamie fought for his life and fought desperately. Burke had to come to his partner's assistance. Between them they at last overpowered Jamie. 'They never quitted their gripe till he was dead. He never got up, nor cried any.' Then came the usual stripping of the body and the unusual robbery. The victims of Burke and Hare were all of them too poor to offer much temptation to murderers to turn robbers as well. Mary Patterson had $2^1/2d$. clasped tight in her hand, and Burke and Hare made no effort to take it from her. Perhaps one of Dr Knox's young men got it in the end. And there was one Mrs Hosler who had ninepence in her hand. But although the victims had little or no money they all of them had clothes, and the clothes even of the poorest are worth something, at all events worth as much as Daft Jamie's were. He was bare-footed and bare-headed when Mrs Hare met him in the street. But the clothes of all the victims were burnt after they were stripped from their bodies, perhaps as a precaution. For clothes may be recognized, though bodies, after an anatomist has done with them, cannot. Jamie's clothes, oddly enough, were not burnt. They were given to the children of Burke's brother, the same Constantine in whose house Mary Patterson was murdered, and these amiable brats quarrelled over the division of the spoil when the parcel was opened. From Jamie's pockets were taken a brass snuff-box and a copper snuff-spoon. Hare kept the box and Burke the spoon.

The body was, as usual, delivered to Dr Knox, who gave £10 for it. Why, one wonders, did he give two pounds more than he gave for Mary Patterson's, the perfect specimen of young womanhood?

As might have been expected, the body was recognized by some of the students, though Knox himself, when he was told of the recognition, persisted that it was not the body of Daft Jamie. Nevertheless the immediate dissection of the body was ordered. A judge, if there were such a person, appointed to consider questions of moral, not merely legal guilt, might well hesitate to decide which were the greatest villain, Burke, Hare, or the brilliant Dr Knox. 'Burke declares,' – our imaginary judge would here take into consideration this passage from Burke's confession – 'Burke declares that Dr Knox never encouraged him, neither taught him nor encouraged him to murder any person, neither any of his assistants.' But beside it he would have to set this sentence: 'That worthy gentleman Mr Ferguson was the only man that ever mentioned anything about the bodies. He inquired where we got the body of that young woman Patterson.' And this: 'They always met with a ready market; that when they delivered the body they were always told to get more.'

All things come to an end, even the careers of the most successful criminals. Burke was brought to the gallows for a murder which looked as easy and as safe as any of the many which he had committed.

One October morning Burke was 'taking his dram', as his custom was, in the shop of a man called Rymer. There came in a little old woman who begged from him. Now little old women who beg were as interesting to Burke as Chippendale chairs to one of our connoisseurs of furniture. Old women who beg very seldom have many friends. Often they are people of no fixed abode. Like Gilbert's undesirable people they are not likely to be missed if anything happens to them. Burke talked to this little old woman in a friendly manner and very soon discovered that she was Irish. Then Burke became even more civil, for Irish people in Edinburgh are likely to be very lonely souls. The old woman had come to Edinburgh to search for a son who had left her. So far, up to the time of her meeting with Burke, she had found no trace of him. Her name was Docherty. When Burke heard that he said that his name too was Docherty and that he was, without doubt, a relation of the old woman's. He invited her to make her home with him while she remained in Edinburgh and promised to help her in the search for her son.

The old woman was delighted. Who would not be delighted at the unexpected discovery of a hospitable relative in a strange city? She willingly went to Burke's house with him and was received with warm friendliness by Helen Macdougal. Burke went out to find Hare – these partners always worked together – and discovered him, where no doubt he looked first, in Rymer's shop drinking whisky. Hare was told that there was work on hand. He at once left his whisky and went home with Burke.

There was one obstacle to the fulfilment of Burke's hospitable intention. He already had lodgers in his house, a Mr and Mrs Gray with their child, and there was only one room in the house. It was plainly inconvenient to introduce another lodger, particularly as there was only one bed and a kind of pallet. But the claims of a relative plainly rank above those of strangers. The Grays were turned out. But Burke very civilly arranged that accommodation should be found for them in the Hares' house.

It was Hallow Eve, a day celebrated with certain festivities both in Ireland and Scotland. The party in Burke's house determined to make a night of it. Whisky was brought in, in considerable quantities. There were songs, the native songs of Old Ireland, and both Burke and Mrs Docherty joined in singing them. There was dancing, and one or two of the neighbours came in to enjoy the fun. Later on, after the neighbours had gone home to bed, there was fighting. Burke and Hare had a tussle and old Mrs Docherty was frightened. The other two women, Mrs Hare and Helen Macdougal, took the fighting as a matter of course. Perhaps they were thoroughly accustomed to it. Perhaps they knew that it was not thoroughly meant, but just part of a well-staged performance. In the course of the scrimmage between the two men the old woman Docherty was knocked down and was too drunk to get up again. The awaited opportunity had come. A quarter of an hour later her body was stripped and hidden in a heap of straw between the end of the bed and the door of the room.

Next morning the Grays came back to breakfast. They noticed at once that the old woman, for whose sake they had been turned out the night before, was no longer there. But Helen Macdougal had a story ready to account for her absence. She had been 'too familiar' with Burke the night before and she – out of natural jealousy or perhaps out of a regard for morality – had kicked the old woman out of the house. That was possible, or at all events it appeared to be possible, to the Grays. The party had breakfast together and then Mrs Gray lit a pipe.

Close beside her, as she sat smoking, was the heap of straw which covered the body of old Mrs Docherty. Mrs Gray, her eye roaming round the room, noticed the straw, and it occurred to her that her child's stockings might be hidden there. She had packed her belongings hurriedly the day before and had left the stockings behind her. The heap of straw seemed to her a likely place to find them. Perhaps she kept them and other spare clothes in that straw while she lodged at the Burkes'. She rose from her chair and went to look. Burke stopped her at once. The stockings might be there or might not. Mrs Docherty's body certainly was.

A little while afterwards Mrs Gray went over to the bed. Potatoes, she knew, were kept under the bed, and Mrs Gray thought it was time that some of them were put on to boil for dinner. Burke stopped her again. Old Mrs Docherty's clothes were under the bed.

Mrs Gray became a little curious; but she had sense enough not to argue with Burke. She waited her opportunity. It came during the latter part of the afternoon. Burke went out, on the necessary business of offering the body to Dr Knox. But he was not quite such a fool as to leave the Grays alone in the house with the corpse. Helen Macdougal was there, lying on the bed. And a boy called Broggan was there, a nephew of Helen Macdougal's. They might be trusted, so Burke felt, to see that Mrs Gray did not search the straw for her child's stockings. But as it turned out neither Helen Macdougal nor the boy was trustworthy. First one of them and then the other went out. Mrs Gray seized her chance and went over to the heap of straw.

Fatima's surprise and horror when she opened the door of Bluebeard's forbidden chamber can scarcely have been greater than Mrs Gray's when she turned over the straw. Under it was the nude body of a dead woman. Both she and her husband recognized it at once. It was the body of old Mrs Docherty. The Grays left the house at once. In the passage outside they met Helen Macdougal. Gray at once questioned her. Helen Macdougal's power of invention had been equal to a disappearance in the morning. They failed her when she had suddenly to account for a corpse in her house. She could think of nothing except an offer of money in return for a promise of silence from the Grays. The Grays refused to be bribed. The offer was increased, until at last £10 a month was promised if only they would say nothing about what they had seen. The Grays still refused. Then Mrs Hare appeared and she had a proposal to make. The party, she suggested, might go together to a neighbouring public-house and settle their little difference amicably there. Great was Mrs Hare's faith in the virtues of whisky. A corpse might look much less like a corpse through eyes dimmed with drink. A bribe would certainly appear more desirable when the heart was merry with wine. But the Grays remained incorruptible. Instead of going to the public-house they went to the police station and there told their story. At eight o'clock the police visited Burke's house. They found him and Helen Macdougal there, but they did not find the body of old Mrs Docherty though they did find her clothes. The body was already in the rooms of Dr Knox. Burke, ever prompt in matters of business, had taken it there, crushed into a box too small for it between the time of Mrs Gray's discovery and the visit of the police. Burke and Helen Macdougal were taken to the police station and kept there.

Early next morning the police visited the rooms of Dr Knox. What put it into their heads to go there? We do not know. In matters like this the police are often reticent and we have to be content with the usual formula 'information received'. But the police knew before they visited Burke's house that the body had been removed. Here is part of the examination in court of John Fisher, the policeman who visited the house.

'What house did you go to?'

'I went to the house of William Burke, the prisoner.'

'What did you go there for? . . . Was it to search for the body?'

'No. I understood that the body was removed before I went there. It was to see if I saw anything suspicious.'

It was also to 'see if I could see anything suspicious' that John Fisher went to Dr Knox's rooms the next morning. There he found what he wanted, what, it appears, he expected to find.

Patterson, the doorkeeper, was all civility, all innocence and all readiness to help in any way in his power. He conducted the police to a cellar. He pointed out a box, which, so he said, had arrived the night before. He had no idea where it came from, but the police could of course examine it for themselves if they liked. They did examine it, and found in it the body of a woman. Gray was sent for and identified it as the body of old Mrs Docherty. One of the guests at Burke's Hallow Eve party was sent for and she also identified the body. Burke and Helen Macdougal were shown the body, but they denied that they had ever seen it before. Mr and Mrs Hare, who were also shown it, said exactly the same thing. They were even more emphatic. Neither dead nor alive had they ever seen it.

But these blank denials did not carry the prisoners very far towards safety. The fact that the body had been in the house hidden under the straw could not be denied. The testimony of the Grays was strong and clear on that point. It remained to explain the awkward fact. Burke, after a suitable pause for thought, produced a story perhaps as good as could have been invented, but scarcely plausible.

He was a cobbler of shoes. What more innocent occupation? To him on Hallow Eve there came a man, a stranger, with a pair of shoes to be mended. Burke's mending, like the pressing of trousers in America, was done while the customer waited, and the customer was able to take a leisurely view of the room while Burke cobbled the shoes. It struck him as a 'quiet place' and he asked if he might leave a box there. Burke, ever willing to oblige, said yes. The stranger went out. Burke had lent him an old pair of shoes to wear while his own were being mended, a convenient custom, kept up until quite lately by watchmakers. The stranger soon came back with a box which he unroped. Burke heard, but did not see what was done. He was too busy cobbling the shoes to watch. Then he heard the stranger rustling the straw in the corner between the bed and the door. But that, though it must have been an unexpected noise, did not tempt the diligent Burke to look up from his work. The stranger paid sixpence for the mending of his shoes and went away. Only then did Burke display any curiosity. He looked at the box and found it empty. He looked at the straw and found a corpse. He was by no means so horrified as the Grays were when they made the same discovery, nor did he, like the Grays, go straight for the police. He waited.

His patience was soon rewarded. The stranger came back, and Burke protested, mildly and civilly, against having corpses dumped in his bedroom. The stranger, with equal courtesy, admitted that Burke had some cause for complaint and promised to have the thing removed the next day. He kept his word. On Saturday evening at 6 p.m. he came back, accompanied by a porter, packed his corpse into the box again and took it away.

That was Burke's story. Few men in his position could have invented a better one, but he could scarcely have expected anyone to believe it. Nobody did; but the thinness of the story did not make it any more certain that either Burke or any of his partners could be convicted of murder.

In fact, only Burke was convicted, and even his conviction was not by any means so easy a matter to obtain as might be supposed.

The first business of the Lord Advocate, who had charge of the prosecution, was to establish the fact that a murder had been committed. All Edinburgh was buzzing with stories of the sixteen victims; but that brought the Lord Advocate no nearer producing proof of a single deed of violence. The four prisoners were kept in separate cells, and from time to time they were examined, but with great wisdom and perfect unanimity they denied everything. The doctors who were called in to examine the body of old Mrs Docherty talked learnedly about 'forcible flexures', the 'contractibility of muscles', and 'extravasation', and other things near to doctors when they do not want to commit themselves. They declined to say definitely that the woman had been murdered. Only the police surgeon, Mr Alexander Black, ventured an opinion, and even he hedged a little. His 'private' opinion was that the woman died by violence and that (he says) 'I really and truly believe'. But 'medically' he could give no opinion. Mr Alexander Black held no medical degree. He was merely 'a surgeon to the police'. Dr Robert Christison, who was highly qualified, was not much more helpful. He thought it was 'probable' but 'nothing more', that the woman had been smothered. The Lord Advocate was scarcely in a position to come into court and assert that a murder had been committed.

He was no better off if he shied away from that point and went on to show who the murderer was. He had evidence of the drunken spree in Burke's house during the night. He had evidence that the old woman was there. He could prove that her dead body was found the next morning by Mrs Gray, but he had not a scrap of evidence to show who murdered her. It might have been Burke. It might have been Hare, or Helen Macdougal, or Mrs Hare, or the boy Broggan, or any of the guests at the Hallow Eve party. No public prosecutor, anxious to see justice done, dare present so shaky a case to a jury. The prisoner's lawyer would have knocked it to pieces in half an hour.

The only course open to the Lord Advocate was to induce one of the prisoners to act as King's evidence, that is to say to bear witness against the rest. This involved immunity for the fortunate informer. Nobody, certainly not the Lord Advocate, wanted any of the four to escape, but there was no other way out of the difficulty. After consideration Hare was chosen to give evidence. Burke, for some reason, was regarded as the worst of the four, and it was feared that neither of the women might know enough to make conviction certain.

Hare, as might have been expected, jumped at his opportunity. But Hare could not give evidence against his wife. And no one seemed sure that Mrs Hare was not his wife, according to Scottish law. So she had to be let off too. She joined Hare in giving evidence against Burke and Helen Macdougal. She was accused of being (in Scots Law phrase) 'art and part' of the murder, that is to say accessory to it.

The trial began with a long legal argument. The accusation against Burke was threefold: That he had murdered Mary Patterson, that he had murdered James Wilson (Daft Jamie), and that he had murdered old Mrs Docherty. The prisoner's counsel objected that the threefold accusation prejudiced the case of Helen Macdougal. She was only accused of participating in one murder. To receive evidence about the other two might raise a presumption of guilt against her in the third, her particular case. The objection was held to be sound and just. Only evidence bearing on the Docherty murder was given in court. We must, I think, regret the decision. It would have been interesting to hear what Janet Brown could have told about the day she spent going in and out of Constantine Burke's house. It would have been very interesting to hear what some of Dr Knox's pupils had to say about the body of Daft Jamie.

But, though two of the charges were dropped, the third was sufficient to secure the thoroughly well-merited punishment of Burke. Helen Macdougal got off with the Scottish verdict of Not Proven.

Burke was hanged. Helen Macdougal was at all events tried. The Hares had to relate in open court the story of their own infamy – not that they seemed to mind that very much or to feel any shame. Dr Knox escaped scot-free. The body of the woman Docherty was the only one of the whole series he had not seen. None of his assistants had seen it. It had reached his room in a box which remained unopened until the police officer came. And it was the only body with which the court was concerned at the trial. There was no excuse for putting Dr Knox or any of his associates into the witness-box. The law could not touch him. It could not even force him to speak.

Dr Knox was a remarkable man. He was a brilliant lecturer and an eminent scientist. He was almost worshipped by his pupils. He was heartily disliked by every one else. He had a bitter tongue which he used to belittle his professional brethren. He was inordinately vain. He was entirely contemptuous of public opinion. The press hinted dark things about him. The press spoke out pretty plainly. Public opinion ran strongly against him. A mob burned him in effigy. Men whose opinion mattered far more than the passion of the mob – men like Christopher North of the *Noctes Ambrosianae* – denounced him. Knox remained obstinately and contemptuously silent. He had matter for a hundred libel actions, but he refused to go into court to vindicate his character. For a long time he refused even to give a reason for not going into court. When at last he was goaded into making some kind of an apologia he wrote a letter to the press which scarcely bettered his position. His reason for not defending his honour was this: 'The disclosure of the most innocent proceedings of even the best conducted dissecting-rooms must always shock the public and be hurtful to science.' Could any disclosure shock the public more than the things which were freely said about Dr Knox and remained uncontradicted? Science, if it can be hurt at all by the sins of its votaries, would scarcely have suffered an additional pang by any dissecting-room story that could have been told.

But if Dr Knox dared not face a court he was not unwilling to seek such shelter as he could find behind the findings of a committee 'which was never meant to be anything but private'. Some members of the committee, he tells us, were his personal friends. Others were acquaintances. Others he did not know even by sight. Perhaps the Marquis of Queensberry, the original Chairman, belonged to this last group. He withdrew from the committee before its work was finished and 'no reason was assigned for his action'.

The committee did its best for Dr Knox; but its best was feeble and hesitating. Dr Knox professed to be in the main satisfied with the vindication of his honour. He must have been very easily satisfied indeed. But on one point he was not wholly satisfied. In the last paragraph of their report the committee ventured on a very mild criticism of Dr Knox's methods. Here it is: 'The extent to which (judging from the evidence they had been able to procure) the committee think that Dr Knox can be blamed on account of the transactions with Burke and Hare is, that by the laxity of the regulations under which bodies were received into his rooms, he unintentionally gave a degree of facility to the disposal of the bodies of the victims of their crimes which under better regulations would not have existed.'

This, the committee thought, was doubtless 'a matter of deep and lasting regret' to Dr Knox. The amiable committee must have been a little startled to discover that it was not. In the face even of a suggestion of pardonable carelessness, Dr Knox was defiant. 'I cannot,' he writes, 'be supposed to be a candid judge of my own case, and therefore it is extremely probable that any opinion of mine on the last view adopted by the committee is incorrect and theirs right.' But it remained his opinion all the same.

Burke died on the scaffold. His body, appropriately enough, was dissected. His patrons, the men of science, quarrelled over his skull. Hare died a blind beggar in the streets of London. Helen Macdougal, after being hunted about various parts of England and Scotland, disappeared. She is supposed to have died in Australia. Mrs Hare was also hunted and harried by mobs. In the end she was shipped back to Ireland where alone her peculiar talents were likely to be appreciated. Dr Knox, after applying, vainly, for various appointments, became a general practitioner in London. He died full of years if not of honour, in Hackney at the age of seventy-one.

Janet Flanner

MURDER IN LE MANS

When, in February, 1933, the Papin sisters, cook and housemaid, killed Mme. and Mlle. Lancelin in the respectable provincial town of Le Mans, a half-dozen hours from Paris, it was not a murder but a revolution. It was only a minor revolution – minor enough to be fought in a front hall by four females, two on a side. The rebels won with horrible handiness. The lamentable Lancelin forces were literally scattered over a distance of ten bloody feet, or from the upper landing halfway down the stairs. The physical were the most chilling details, the conquered the only dull elements in a fiery, fantastic struggle that should have remained inside Christine Papin's head and which, when it touched earth, unfortunately broke into paranoiac poetry and one of the most graceless murders in French annals.

On the day he was to be made a widower, M. Lancelin, retired lawyer, spent his afternoon at his respectable provincial club; at six forty-five he reported to his brother-in-law, M. Renard, practising lawyer, at whose table they were to dine at seven *en famille*, that, having gone by the Lancelin home in the Rue La Bruyère to pick up his wife and daughter Geneviève, he had found the doors bolted and the windows dark – except for the maid's room in the attic, where, until he started knocking, there was a feeble glow. It had appeared again only as he was leaving.

Two lawyers this time set off for the Lancelin dwelling, to observe again the mansard gleam fade, again creep back to life as the men retreated. Alarmed (for at the least a good dinner was drying up), the gentlemen produced a brace of policemen and a brigadier, who, by forcing Lancelin's window, invited Lancelin to walk into his parlour, where he discovered his electric lights did not work. Two of the police crept upstairs with one flashlight and the brother-in-law. Close to the second floor the trio humanely warned the husband not to follow.

On the third step from the landing, all alone, staring uniquely at the ceiling, lay an eye. On the landing itself the Lancelin ladies lay, at odd angles and with heads like blood puddings. Beneath their provincial petticoats their modest limbs had been knife-notched the way a fancy French baker notches his finer long loaves. Their finger-nails had been uprooted, one of Geneviève's teeth was pegged in her own scalp. A second single orb – the mother's, this time, for both generations seemed to have been treated with ferocious nonpartisanship – rested shortsightedly gazing at nothing in the corner of the hall. Blood had softened the carpet till it was like an elastic red moss.

The youngest and third policeman (his name was Mr Truth) was sent creeping toward the attic. Beneath the door a crack of light flickered. When he crashed the door, the light proved to be a candle, set on a plate so as not to drip, for the Papins were well-trained servants. The girls were in one bed in two blue kimonos. They had taken off their dresses which were stained. They had cleaned their hands and faces. They had, the police later discovered, also cleaned the carving knife, hammer and pewter pitcher which they had been using to put them neatly back where they belonged – though the pitcher was by now too battered to look tidy. Christine, the elder (Léa, the younger, was never after to speak intelligibly except once at the trial) did not confess; she merely made their mutual statement: they had done it. Truth took what was left of the candle – the short-circuiting electric iron had blown out the fuse again that afternoon and was at the bottom of everything, Christine kept saying, though the sensible Truth paid no attention – and lighted the girls downstairs, over the corpses, and out to the police station. They were still in their blue kimonos and in the February air their hair was wild, though ordinarily they were the tidiest pair of domestics in Le Mans.

Through a typographical error the early French press reports printed the girls' name not as Papin, which means nothing, but as Lapin, which means rabbit. It was no libel.

Waiting trial in the prison, Christine, who was twenty-eight years of age and the cathartic of the two, had extraordinary holy visions and unholy reactions. Léa, who was twenty-two and looked enough like her sister to be a too-long-delayed twin,

151

had nothing, since the girls were kept separate and Léa thus had no dosage for her feeble brain.

Their trial at the local courthouse six months later was a national event, regulated by guards with bayonets, ladies with lorgnettes and envoys from the Parisian press. As commentators *Paris-Soir* sent a pair of novelists, the Tharaud brothers, Jean and Jérôme, who, when they stoop to journalism, write themselves as 'I' and nearly even won the Goncourt Prize under this singular consolidation. Special scribes were posthasted by *Détective*, hebdomadal penny dreadful prosperously owned by the *Nouvelle Revue Française*, or France's *Atlantic Monthly*. *L'Œuvre*, as daily house organ for the Radical-Socialist Party (supposedly friendly to the working classes till they unfortunately shot a few of them in the Concorde riot), sent Bérard, or their best brain.

The diametric pleas of prosecution and defence facing these historians were clear: either (*a*) the Papins were normal girls who had murdered without a reason, murdering without reason apparently being a proof of normalcy in Le Mans, or else (*b*) the Rabbit sisters were as mad as March Hares, and so didn't have to have a reason. Though they claimed to have one just like anybody else, if the jury would only listen: their reason was that unreliable electric iron, or a mediocre cause for a revolution. . . . The iron had blown out on Wednesday, been repaired Thursday, blown again Friday, taking the houselights with it at five. By six the Lancelin ladies, in from their walk, had been done to death in the dark – for the dead do not scold.

While alive, Madame had once forced Léa to her housemaid knees to retrieve a morsel of paper overlooked on the parlor rug. Or, as the Tharauds ponderously wrote in their recapitulation of the crime, 'God knows the Madame Lancelins exist on earth.' This one, however, had been rare in that she corroborated Léa's dusting by donning a pair of white gloves, she commented on Christine's omelettes by formal notes delivered to the kitchen by Geneviève – both habits adding to the Papins' persecution complex, or their least interesting facet. Madame also gave the girls enough to eat and 'even allowed them to have heat in their attic bedroom,' though Christine did not know if Madame was kind, since in six years' service she had never spoken to them, and if people don't talk, how can you tell? As for the motive of their crime, it was again the Tharauds who, all on the girls' side, thus loyally made it clear as mud: 'As good servants the girls had been highly contraried' when the iron blew once. Twice 'it was still as jewels of servants who don't like to lose their time that they became irritated. Perhaps if the sisters had been less scrupulous as domestics the horror which followed would never have taken place. And I wish to say,' added Jean and Jérôme, without logic and in unison, 'that many people still belong to early periods of society.'

Among others, the jury did. They were twelve good men and true, or quite incompetent to appreciate the Papin sisters. Also, the trial lasted only twenty-six hours, or not long enough to go into the girls' mental rating though the next forty or fifty years of their lives depended on it. The prosecution summoned three local insane-asylum experts who had seen the girls twice for a half hour, and swore on the stand that the *prisonnières* were 'of unstained heredity' – i.e., their father having been a dipsomaniac who violated their elder sister, since become a nun; their mother having been an hysteric 'crazy for money'; a cousin having died in a madhouse and an uncle having hanged himself 'because his life was without joy.' In other words, heredity O.K., legal responsibility 100 percent.

Owing to the girls' weak, if distinguished defence – high-priced French lawyers work cheaply for criminals if bloody enough, the publicity being a fortune in itself – their equally distinguished psychiatrist's refutation carried no weight. Their lawyer was Pierre Chautemps, cousin to that Camille Chautemps who, as Prime Minister, so weakly defended the French republic in the 1933 Boulevard Saint-Germain riots; their expert was the brilliant Parisian professor, Logre, whose 'colossal doubt on their sanity' failed to count since under cross-examination he had to admit he had never seen the girls before even for five minutes; just knew all about them by sitting back in his Paris study, ruminating. He did, too, but the jury sniffed at the stuck-up city man.

Thus, they also missed Logre's illuminating and delicate allusion to the girls as a 'psychological couple,' though they'd understood the insane-asylum chief's broader reference to

Sappho. Of paramount interest to twelve good men and true, the girls' incest was really one of the slighter details of their dubious domesticity. On the jury's ears Christine's prison visions also fell flat. Indeed it was not until six months after she was sentenced to be beheaded that these hallucinations were appreciated for their literary value in a scholarly essay entitled '*Motifs du Crime Paranoïaque: ou Le Crime des Soeurs Papins*,' by Docteur Jaques Lacan, in a notable surrealist number of the intelligentsia quarterly *Minotaure*.

In court, however, Christine's poetic visions were passed over as a willful concoction of taradiddles that took in no one - except the defence, of course. Yet they had, in the limited data of lyrical paranoia and modern psychiatry, constituted an exceptional performance. Certain of the insane enjoy strange compensations; having lost sight of reality they see singular substitutes devoid of banal sequence, and before the rare spectacle of effect without cause are pushed to profound questions the rest of us are too sensible to bother with. 'Where was I before I was in the belly of my mother?' Christine first inquired, and the fit was on. She next wished to know where the Lancelin ladies might now be, for, though dead, could they not have come back in other bodies? For a cook she showed, as the Tharauds said, 'a bizarre interest in metempsychoses,' further illuminated by her melancholy reflection, 'Sometimes I think in former lives that I was my sister's husband.' Then while the prison dormitory shuddered, Christine claimed to see that unholy bride hanging hanged to an apple tree, with her limbs and the tree's limbs broken. At the sad sight crazed Christine leapt in the air to the top of a ten-foot barred window where she maintained herself with muscular ease. It was then that Léa, whom she had not seen since their incarceration six months before, was called in as a sedative. And to her Christine cried with strange exultation, 'Say yes, say yes,' which nobody understands to this day. By what chance did this Sarthe peasant fall like the Irish Joyce in the last line of *Ulysses* on the two richest words in any tongue - those of human affirmation, Yes, yes. . . .

Thus ended the lyrical phase of Christine's seizure, which then became, maybe, political. At any rate she hunger-struck for three days, like someone with a cause, went into silence, wept and prayed like a leader betrayed, traced holy signs with her tongue on the prison walls, tried to take Léa's guilt on her shoulders, and, when this failed, at least succeeded in freeing her own of her strait jacket.

'Wasn't all of that just make-believe?' the prison officials later asked her. (All except escaping from the strait jacket, of course, a reality that had never occurred in French penal history before.) 'If Monsieur wishes,' said Christine politely. Both the girls were very polite in prison and addressed their keepers in the formal third person, as if the guards were company who had just stepped into the Lancelins' parlour for tea.

During the entire court proceeding, report on visions, vices and all, from one thirty after lunch of one day to three thirty before breakfast of the next, Christine sat on the accused bench with eyes closed. She looked like someone asleep or a medium in a trance, except that she rose when addressed and blindly said nearly nothing. The judge, a kind man with ferocious moustaches was, in his interrogation, finally forced to examine his own conscience, since he couldn't get Christine to talk about hers.

'When you were reprimanded in your kitchen, you never answered back but you rattled your stove lids fiercely; I ask myself if this was not sinful pride. . . . Yet you rightly think work is no disgrace. No, you also have no class hatred,' he said with relief to find that he and she were neither Bolsheviks. 'Nor were you influenced by literature, apparently, since only books of piety were found in your room.'

(Not that printed piety had taught the girls any Christian mercy once they started to kill. The demi-blinding of the Lancelins is the only criminal case on record where eyeballs were removed from the living head without practice of any instrument except the human finger. The duplicating of the tortures were also curiously cruel; Christine took Madame in charge, the dull Léa followed suit by tending to Mademoiselle; whatever the older sister did to the older woman, the younger sister repeated on fresher flesh in an orgy of obedience.)

As the trial proceeded, the spectators could have thought the court was judging one Papin cadaver seen double, so much the

155

sisters looked alike and dead. Their sanity expert had called them Siamese souls. The Papins' was the pain of being two where some mysterious unity had been originally intended; between them was a schism which the dominant, devilish Christine had tried to resolve into one self-reflection without ever having heard of Narcissus or thinking that the pallid Léa might thus be lost to view. For, if Christine's eyes were closed to the judge, Léa's were as empty in gaze as if she were invisible and incapable of sight. Her one comment on the trial for her life was that, with the paring knife, she had 'made little carvings' in poor spinster Geneviève's thighs. For there, as her Christine had said, lay the secret of life. . . .

When the jury came in with their verdict Christine was waiting for them, still somnambulant, her hands clasped not as in prayer but as if pointing down into the earth. In the chill predawn both sisters' coat collars were turned up as if they had just come in from some domestic errand run in the rain. With their first effort at concentration on Léa, whom all day the jury had tried to ignore, the foreman gave her ten years' confinement and twenty of municipal exile. Christine was sentenced to have her head cut off in the public square of Le Mans which, since females are no longer guillotined, meant life – a courtesy she, at the moment, was ignorant of.

When Christine heard her sentence of decapitation, in true belief she fell to her knees. At last she had heard the voice of God.

Charles Franklin

ALMA RATTENBURY

Until recently women guilty of sexual immorality were at some disadvantage when up against English justice. Edith Thompson (1923), Charlotte Bryant (1936) and Ruth Ellis (1955) were all immoral women. Certainly the last two were murderesses. But all three were hanged.

The execution of Edith Thompson is generally considered a blot on English justice. Found guilty, with her lover, Frederick Bywaters, of the murder of her husband, she was hanged for adultery rather than murder. The first Lord Birkenhead - who, as F. E. Smith, had successfully defended Ethel Le Neve of being an accessory after the fact in the murder of Cora Crippen - defended Edith Thompson's execution by saying, 'Anyhow, she had the will to destroy her husband for the sake of her lover,' even though he confessed to a lingering doubt as to whether she was present at the crime for which she was hanged.

Few shared his view. Public opinion was, in fact, so shocked at the monstrous thing done to Edith Thompson that when twelve years later Alma Rattenbury was accused, with her lover, of a similar murder of passion, the Bywaters-Thompson case hung over the trial like an awful warning. Not many people believed that Mrs Rattenbury would be hanged, but her acquittal was by no means a foregone conclusion.

Alma Rattenbury was not really an attractive character. At first the evidence against her seemed overwhelming. She appeared to be a loose, immoral, drunken, callous woman who seduced a youth young enough to be her son, and after sleeping with him constantly, in the same room as her own child, she finally took part in the brutal murder of her wealthy husband.

This picture of Alma Rattenbury emerged when the case was first brought in sensational style before the public in the spring of 1935. But at usual the public image was distorted. The story was only half told. Mrs Rattenbury's sexual immorality dominated the public mind, and if she had been less fortunate in the judge who presided over her trial, it would probably have lessened her chances of justice; for one of the least admirable of Anglo-Saxon attitudes is that people found guilty of gross immorality are considered capable of almost any crime.

Alma Victoria Clark was born at Victoria, British Columbia in 1897, the daughter of a printer. She grew up a talented musician and wrote many popular songs under the name 'Lozanne'. She became a quite well-known musician in Western Canada. Men found her extremely attractive. On the outbreak of war, when she was eighteen, she married a young Englishman named Caledon Dolly who joined the Canadian forces. She followed him to England where she got a job in Whitehall. When her husband was killed in action, she became a transport driver. After the war she married a man whose wife had divorced him citing her as co-respondent. A son named Christopher was born in 1922. The marriage failed. She returned to Canada and stayed with an aunt at Victoria.

Here she met Francis Mawson Rattenbury, a wealthy and successful architect of about sixty. Though married himself, he fell in love with Alma, then about thirty, and had an affair with her. His wife divorced him, citing her. Alma and Rattenbury got married in 1928, but owing to the scandal of the divorce had to leave Victoria. They came to England and rented a house, Villa Madeira, Manor Park Road, Bournemouth. In 1929 a child was born to them named John. After that they ceased marital relations.

Alma Rattenbury who a few years later was to be pilloried as the most evil woman of her day was devoted to her two sons, John and Christopher. The latter spent his holidays at Villa Madeira, and when John went to school, he came home every week-end. Alma had the domestic assistance of a companion-help, Miss Irene Riggs, who was extremely loyal to her and remembered her as the kindest and most generous person she had ever met. They were friends rather than mistress and servant and addressed each other as 'darling'. They went out together to the theatre, or to London.

Life at Villa Madeira, between the years 1928 and 1934, was

very much like that in many other respectable Bournemouth homes. Rattenbury was a dull sort of man who took no great interest in his wife. He looked older than his years and had grown deaf. He grew worried about his finances which had been affected by the slump, and even talked of suicide on that account. Though he drank the better part of a bottle of whisky each day, he was not a drunkard but rather a quiet, pleasant, intelligent man who was as disappointed in his marriage as he was about his financial affairs.

Occasionally he lost his temper. Once when he was talking about suicide, Alma exclaimed impatiently to him: 'It's a pity you don't do it, instead of always talking about it.' This infuriated him and he hit her across the face, giving her a black eye. But she was not one to bear malice and they soon made it up.

He was generous and allowed her £1,000 a year, out of which she had to run the whole household, pay the food and drink bills, the servants' wages and the boys' school fees. But she was not a wise spender. She was often overdrawn and there were frequent quarrels about money.

Rattenbury ran a car, but by 1934 found driving difficult. Alma advertised in the *Bournemouth Daily Echo*: 'Daily willing lad, 14-18, for housework. Scout-trained preferred.' This was answered by an eighteen-year-old youth named George Percy Stoner who had worked in a garage and could drive a car. He was considered eminently suitable, particularly in view of his driving ability and was given the job of chauffeur-handyman. This was in September. Two months later he had become Alma's lover and was living in the house.

Stoner was a raw youth, barely literate, not very bright, though a decent enough lad. Alma Rattenbury was a sophisticated, gay, sentimental woman, talented in her way.

She was thirty-seven. He was eighteen. It is easy to see what was the attraction so far as he was concerned. She was still good to look at, and he was full of youthful lust beneath his quiet exterior. She seduced him and completely turned his head. But why was she so attracted to this immature, rather loutish youth?

The whole tragedy turned upon Alma's physical make-up.

Nature had endowed her with extremely strong sexual desires. Since the birth of John, she had developed pulmonary tuberculosis and the illness inflamed her sexual appetite. For six years she had been deprived of sexual satisfaction. By the time Stoner appeared on the scene she was on the verge of nymphomania and could endure the torment no longer. She grasped at the lad almost in despair and when the young man's virility gave her what she had so long wanted, she fell in love with him, or imagined that she had.

His virility was in fact the main attraction so far as she was concerned. 'Love' to her was the physical enjoyment of sex. But it was not as simple as that. Like many women of loose morals, she was generous-hearted and loyal. Her affair with Stoner in no way turned her against her husband, for whom she maintained a constant affection. Nor did it make her less of a devoted mother to her two sons.

No one can pretend that Alma Rattenbury was a woman of taste. That she entertained her young lover in her bedroom at Villa Madeira when her six-year-old son was asleep in the same room, was a profoundly shocking thing for which there could be little excuse. At first she admitted it and tried to excuse it in the witness-box. She said in court that she did not consider it a dreadful thing, for little John was always sound asleep. Indeed, as the family doctor confirmed, he knew of no child with a sounder sleep and John noticed nothing of what was going on around him. But the revelation did irreparable damage to her character and she later tried to deny it.

But the love affair did not make her a murderer, as Mr Justice Humphreys, one of England's great judges, was at pains to point out to the jury.

According to Stoner, Alma Rattenbury seduced him shortly after he entered her employment during a trip to Oxford which, she told her husband, was a visit to relatives in Sunderland. She said the seduction took place somewhat later, on 22 November, 1934 – in fact, just before Stoner took up residence in the house. It is of scant importance. The fact remains that throughout the winter of 1934 and the spring of 1935 the two of them regularly slept together. The adultery took place both in his bedroom and in hers.

During this time Francis Rattenbury was constantly in the house and slept downstairs. It was generally believed that he knew what was going on and did not care. Alma said at her trial: 'He must have known about it, because he told me to live my own life quite a few years ago.' The Judge called him 'not a nice character – what the French call *un mari complaisant*, a man who knew his wife was committing adultery and had no objection to it.'

No one can say for certain that Rattenbury knew what was going on. Apart from being very deaf, incurious and tired of life, he drank so much every night that not only would his marital relations have been impossible, even if he desired them any longer, but in his alcohol haze the noises of the incautious lovers on the floor above never came to his ears. There was certainly something pathetic about him, but those who knew him – Irene Riggs and his doctor – were of the opinion that he was not the contemptible character who would consciously permit his wife to go to bed regularly with his chauffeur-handyman.

The person who was perhaps most distressed by the affair between Alma and Stoner was Irene Riggs. For her it meant the end of a pleasant and delightful intimacy with the mistress she loved with exemplary loyalty. Alma told her about the affair with Stoner. Irene considered Stoner a quite unsuitable person to enjoy the favours and love of Alma Rattenbury who at least should have chosen someone more of her own age and class. She found the liaison shocking at first, though she was forced to accept it. It meant the end of many pleasant little outings with her mistress which had given her so much pleasure. Now Mrs Rattenbury was obsessed by her teenage lover. Naturally enough, Irene Riggs resented Stoner and he didn't like her very much, though there was no open enmity between them.

In March, 1935 Alma's bank account was considerably overdrawn. She cajoled £250 out of her husband on the pretence that she had to go to London for a minor operation. She had had several such operations in the past. Rattenbury had always paid generously for them.

On 19 March Alma went to London, taking Stoner with her. They stayed at the Royal Palace Hotel, Kensington, as brother and sister, occupying rooms opposite each other. In return for the enjoyment Stoner gave her in bed, she took him to Harrods and bought him two new suits, shirts, handkerchiefs, ties, gloves, three pairs of crêpe-de-chine pyjamas, two sets of underwear and a mackintosh. He was not above taking £15 10s. from her to buy a ring which she solemnly accepted as a present.

They stayed in London four days. The experience thoroughly turned Stoner's head and was directly responsible for the tragedy which followed. Here he was no longer the servant, but the equal. He was addressed as 'sir', was waited on, ate at the same table as his mistress and was intoxicated by the presents she showered upon him. A simple labourer's son, he had never experienced anything like this before and the taste of 'high life' in London increased his vanity and his determination to make the most of the situation in which he found himself.

They returned to Villa Madeira on 22 March. It is possible that Stoner would have resigned himself once more to the easy-going life there, had not Mr and Mrs Rattenbury decided to go away together.

Rattenbury asked no questions. He did not even inquire about the operation his wife was supposed to have gone to London for. He was utterly depressed, reading a book in which a man married to a young wife had committed suicide, and he expressed his admiration for anyone who had the courage to take his own life. In an attempt to cheer him up, Alma suggested that they should go to Bridport and see a friend of theirs, a Mr Jenks. She had no desire, it would seem, for her husband to commit suicide.

Rattenbury agreed to go. Jenks was a wealthy businessman who was associated with a block of flats for which Rattenbury was to have been the architect and which was delayed owing to the economic depression. Alma suggested that Jenks could help Rattenbury with regard to his financial worries. She telephoned Bridport, found they would be welcome at Mr Jenks's home and made arrangements to go there the following day.

The telephone was in Rattenbury's bedroom which opened off the drawing-room, and while his wife was phoning he remained in his drawing-room. During the telephone conversation Stoner, who had overheard the arrangements Alma was making, came into the bedroom in a state of fury. He held an air pistol in his hand which she took to be a revolver. He told her bluntly that if she went to Bridport with her husband he would kill her. Afraid of her husband overhearing and apparently not taking his threat seriously, Alma took Stoner into the dining-room where he accused her of having had sexual intercourse with her husband that afternoon behind closed doors in the bedroom.

Stoner was beside himself with jealousy. He knew he would have to drive Mr and Mrs Rattenbury to Bridport, and in the Jenks's big house his place would be among the servants. To be reminded of his menial status so soon after the dazzling luxury of the Royal Palace Hotel where he had stayed with Alma as her equal was intolerable. He believed that at the Jenks's house Mr and Mrs Rattenbury would have to share a bedroom, and he told Alma that if they went to Bridport he would refuse to drive them there.

Alma Rattenbury was a persuasive as well as a sympathetic woman, and she was not unaware of the way her lover felt. She assured him most convincingly, in the first place, that there had been no intercourse between herself and her husband that afternoon – indeed there hadn't been for years; and in the second place, that she and her husband would not share a room at the Jenks's. They had stayed with the Jenks before and had always had separate rooms. Her assurances only partly mollified Stoner who left brooding darkly. That evening he went to his grandparents' house and borrowed a carpenter's mallet.

It was generally assumed that Stoner was completely dominated by Alma Rattenbury. That great student of crime, the late Miss R. Tennyson Jesse, was of the opposite opinion. 'There is no woman so much under the dominance of her lover as the elderly mistress of a much younger man,' she observed and quoted Benjamin Franklin's words: 'As in the dark all cats are grey, the pleasure of corporal enjoyment with an old woman is at least equal and frequently superior; every knack being by practice capable of improvement. . . . Lastly, they are so grateful.'

Alma Rattenbury was neither elderly nor old. She was a desirable woman in her late thirties with a potent sexuality that would have appealed strongly to any man. Miss Jesse who attended her trial described her as being very attractive to men. 'In the witness box she still showed us a very elegant woman. She had a pale face, with a beautiful egg-like line of the jaw, dark grey eyes and a mouth with a very full lower lip. She was undoubtedly, and always must have been, a *femme aux hommes*, that is to say . . . first and foremost a woman to attract men and be attracted by them.'

There is nothing unusual in a youth being obsessed by such a woman. The magic of first love and the first experience of sex have a powerful effect upon the young. Every man treasures his first experience of physical passion and remembers how he confused it with love. To be initiated into the mysteries of sex by an older, experienced woman is no small advantage to a young man, though he may well suffer agonies at the time, as Stoner obviously did. Alma unfortunately did not understand how he felt about going to Bridport with her and her husband as their servant, though there is no doubt at all that she loved him dearly and was even prepared to give her life for him.

And so the inexorable events of 24 March, 1935 led them all to tragedy, death and ruin.

It was Irene Riggs's night out. Alma sat at home and played cards with her husband, kissed him good night, then went upstairs between nine-thirty and ten to pack for the trip to Bridport. Irene returned about ten-fifteen, going straight to her room. About ten minutes later she went downstairs intending to get something to eat in the kitchen, but her purpose was distracted by the sound of heavy breathing. She looked into Rattenbury's bedroom, switched on the light and saw that he was not in bed. The sound of heavy breathing seemed to come from the drawing-room. She concluded that Rattenbury had fallen asleep in his chair, as he often did after drinking nearly a bottle of whisky as a night-cap. Irene returned to her room and came out again later to go to the lavatory.

She found Stoner hanging over the banisters at the top of the stairs.

'What's the matter?' she asked.

'Nothing,' he replied. 'I was just looking to see if the lights were out.'

Irene noticed that the lights were out. She returned to her room. A little later Alma Rattenbury came in and told her about the proposed trip to Bridport. They were going by car, but she did not know whether Stoner or her husband would be driving.

Alma then returned to her own room and got into bed. About ten minutes later Stoner came into the room. She was expecting him as usual and he got into bed with her. She anticipated, and indeed wanted, the usual sexual intercourse, for she would be deprived of it while she and her husband were away at Bridport. But there was no thought of sex in Stoner's mind on that night. She immediately noticed that he was greatly agitated.

'What's the matter, darling?' she asked. He replied that he was in great trouble, but could not tell her what it was. 'But you must tell me,' she said. He told her it was so awful that she could not bear it. Alma replied she was strong enough to bear anything.

Finally he told her, 'You won't be going to Bridport tomorrow, as I have hurt Ratz.'

She did not realize quite what he meant by this remark until she heard her husband groaning downstairs. Stoner told her that he had hit Rattenbury on the head with a mallet. Alarmed, Alma jumped out of bed, saying she must go to him.

She fled down the stairs in her bare feet, into the drawing-room where she found her husband leaning back in his chair, one of his eyes swollen and discoloured. He was unconscious and there was a large pool of blood on the floor. She stumbled around the table and trod on his false teeth with her bare feet. She screamed, a wave of hysterical nausea coming over her. Yelling for Irene, she grabbed the whisky bottle thinking the neat spirit would calm her stomach which was rising in her throat. Swallowing the whisky, she picked up a towel and put it around her husband's head, then was violently sick.

After that, Alma Rattenbury swore, she remembered no more of what had happened that night. The story was taken up by Irene Riggs who came rushing down to find her mistress in a state of hysteria, begging her to phone the doctor and crying, 'Oh, poor Ratz! Poor Ratz! Can't someone do something?'

To Irene Riggs Mr Rattenbury seemed to be just sitting asleep in the chair, but then she observed his black eyes and the blood on the floor near him. She phoned Dr William O'Donnell who had been both physician and friend to the Rattenburys for a number of years.

Meanwhile Alma was 'raving about the house,' drinking whisky, being violently sick, and telling Irene to wipe up the blood in case her little boy should see it. Irene fetched a bowl and a cloth and bathed Rattenbury's eye, not suspecting the gravity of his injuries. She called Stoner who helped them carry the injured man to his bed.

Dr O'Donnell arrived at Villa Madeira at a quarter to midnight. He found Mrs Rattenbury drunk and hysterical, and her husband lying in bed, a bloodstained towel around his head which was itself now covered in blood.

As the doctor tried to make an examination, Alma kept getting in the way, crying, 'Look at him! Look at him! Somebody has finished him,' and trying to take his clothes off.

It was obvious to Dr O'Donnell that the insensible man was in need of urgent surgical attention. He phoned Mr Alfred Rooke, a Bournemouth surgeon, who arrived at Villa Madeira shortly after midnight.

Alma Rattenbury's behaviour again made proper examination impossible. Owing to her condition the doctors decided to remove the injured man to the Strathallan Nursing Home where they detected three deep skull wounds which looked as though caused by a blunt instrument. The skull was seriously fractured and the smashed bone driven into the brain. It was obvious that he could not live for long. Dr O'Donnell had no option but to phone the police who arrived at Villa Madeira about two o'clock.

Inspector Mills took charge of the case. They found Mrs Rattenbury very much the worse for the drink – but, in their estimation, not drunk.

She already had intimated to Constable Bagwell, the first on the scene: 'At nine o'clock I was playing cards with my husband in the drawing-room and I went to bed about ten-thirty. I heard a yell. I came downstairs and saw him sitting in a chair. I sent for Dr O'Donnell and he was taken away.'

When Inspector Mills informed her that her husband was in a critical condition she exclaimed: 'Will this be against me?' He cautioned her. She confessed: 'I did it. He has lived too long. I will tell you in the morning where the mallet is. Have you told the Coroner yet? I shall make a better job of it next time. Irene does not know. I have made a proper muddle of it. I thought I was strong enough.'

It was obvious that the woman was rambling in a semi-alcoholic condition, but the Inspector could hardly ignore what she said.

Dr O'Donnell left the nursing home about 3.30 a.m. When he came out Stoner, who had driven him there in the Rattenbury's car, was peacefully asleep at the wheel, which on the surface appeared to be an indication of a clear conscience.

When the doctor arrived back at Villa Madeira he found all the lights on, the door open, and the radiogram playing. There were four police officers in the house, endeavouring to conduct an investigation amid the uproar.

Alma's hysterical conduct had caused them considerable embarrassment. When the Inspector had left the house to go to the nursing home to inquire about Rattenbury's condition P.C. Bagwell stayed alone with Alma and Irene. According to his statement Alma approached the constable with the words: 'I did it with a mallet. Ratz had lived too long. It is hidden. No, my lover did it. I would like to give you £10. No, I won't bribe you.' She then became maudlin and amorous and tried to kiss the constable. She so pestered him with her attentions that he went outside the house. She tried to follow him, but Irene prevented her, locked the door and finally had to push her into a chair and sit on her to keep her in the house.

In Dr O'Donnell's opinion, Mrs Rattenbury was in no fit condition to make a statement, for she obviously did not know what she was saying. She was in a state of uncontrollable excitement, running about saying wild things to the police officers.

When Inspector Mills asked her who she thought had done it, she named Rattenbury's son of his first marriage. Dr O'Donnell knew that the son, who was a man of thirty-two, was not in England, and he told the Inspector that Mrs Rattenbury could have no idea what she was saying, and was in no condition to be asked any questions. She was then taken to bed and the doctor gave her a large shot of morphia.

But she did not sleep for long. The police were in the house all night. Even drug-induced sleep was impossible in the state Alma was in. At six the police had her up again, and called in a police matron. They realized that she was a sick woman who had been drinking half the night and was still under the influence of the morphia. All the same, they took a statement from her at eight in the morning, an action for which they were subsequently severely criticized.

In the statement she alleged: 'About 9 p.m. on 24 March I was playing cards with my husband when he dared me to kill him, as he wanted to die. I picked up a mallet and he then said, "You have not the guts to do it." I then hit him with the mallet. I hid the mallet outside. I would have shot him if I had had a gun.' Detective-Inspector William G. Carter, to whom this statement was made, later recalled that she read it over aloud and then signed it.

Carter then arrested her. Before she left the house she had a moment alone with Irene Riggs and requested of her: 'You must get Stoner to give me the mallet.'

No one really knew what went on in Alma's mind during the hours after the discovery of her fatally injured husband. Afterwards she swore that everything was a total blank, and no amount of pressure would make her say otherwise. If her story of what Stoner said to her in bed was true, then she knew he had administered those terrible injuries to her husband. Judging by her actions, it seems that her very first thoughts were for her husband, her second for her young son, and her third for her lover whom she wished to save from the consequences of his deed.

She was taken to Bournemouth police station and at 8.45 a.m. was charged with causing grievous bodily harm to her husband with intent to murder.

In answer to the charge, she said: 'That is right. I did it deliberately and would do it again.'

Medical opinion considered that she was not normal when she made these statements, and many people thought that a charge should not have been made against her in view of this. When Dr O'Donnell saw her at Bournemouth police station later during the same day, she could not stand up without support. She looked dazed and her pupils were still contracted as the result of the morphia he had given her. Three days later Dr Morton, of Holloway Prison, stated his opinion that she was still suffering from confusion of mind as the result of the alcohol and the morphia. 'She kept repeating the same sentences over and over again.'

The police were in a difficult position. The victim of the assault was dying and they knew the ultimate charge would be murder. Alma Rattenbury had confessed to the crime and had in fact admitted it over and over again. They may well have underestimated the confused state of her mind, but they had no alternative but to charge her with the crime.

Later, when it seemed that after all she had not struck the fatal blow the Director of Public Prosecutions was exposed to criticism for putting her on trial; but legal authorities held that in view of her confession the D.P.P. was bound to proceed against her in the circumstances.

While Alma Rattenbury was in Holloway Prison, London, Irene Riggs and Stoner were left alone at Villa Madeira. Irene hated being in the house alone with Stoner. She was convinced of her mistress's innocence. She knew that Alma was quite incapable of hurting anyone, let alone her husband of whom she was very fond.

Dr O'Donnell had been asked by Mr Rattenbury's relatives to keep an eye on Villa Madeira. When he called there he was, however, unable to have a word alone with Irene Riggs. Stoner would not leave them and was all the time hovering suspiciously in the background.

O'Donnell called again on 28 March when Stoner had gone to Holloway to see Mrs Rattenbury. Irene told him that her mother had seen Stoner drunk the previous night. He had been going up and down the road shouting, 'Mrs Rattenbury is in jail and I have put her there.'

Irene informed him also that Mrs Rattenbury had not committed the crime. Stoner had confessed to her that he had done it. He had told her there would be no fingerprints on the mallet because he had worn gloves. Dr O'Donnell took her to Bournemouth police station where she made a statement.

The following day Francis Rattenbury died and Stoner was

arrested for murder on his return to Bournemouth. He asked: 'Do you know Mrs Rattenbury had nothing to do with this affair?'

After being cautioned, he told the police: 'When I did the job I believe he was asleep. I hit him and then went upstairs and told Mrs Rattenbury. She rushed down then. You see, I watched through the french window and saw her kiss him goodnight and then leave the room. I waited and crept in through the french window which was unlocked. Still, it ain't much use saying anything.' He then added, a little touchingly: 'I suppose they won't let her out yet?'

The Director of Public Prosecutions had a clear case against George Stoner, though not against Alma Rattenbury. She now denied all knowledge of what had passed at Villa Madeira during that dreadful night, and claimed to know nothing of confessions she had made. In fact she now denied all knowledge of the crime.

All the same her confessions could not be ignored; and if the view was taken that she had made them in an attempt to protect her lover, then the assumption was irresistible that there may have been a conspiracy between them to get rid of Rattenbury. This, in the circumstances, would have been extremely difficult to prove.

On the other hand, to have released Alma Rattenbury unconditionally would have aroused a storm of criticism in view of her behaviour – the sympathy with Stoner, as the teenage victim of her lust and wanton immorality, would have been overwhelming both among the public and in the jury box.

The D.P.P. took the only course available to him. He placed them both on trial charged with the murder and left it to the jury to decide.

Mr R. P. Croom-Johnson, K.C., put it like this in court: 'It is the contention of the prosecution that one or other of the accused delivered a blow or blows to the head of Mr Rattenbury. And if that is right the prosecution suggests for your consideration that these two people, with one common object and one common design, set out to get rid of Mr Rattenbury, who, as I suggested earlier, stood in their way.'

The defence of both prisoners presented great difficulties.

Alma refused to accuse Stoner, though she was prepared to go into the box and tell the truth of what had happened, but only after much pressure from her legal advisers. Her counsel, Mr Terence O'Connor, K.C., had the almost impossible task of presenting her as a sympathetic character. The prejudice against her was overwhelming, so much so that the case could not be tried at the county assizes and was transferred to the Old Bailey.

Stoner presented his counsel, Mr J. D. Casswell, with perhaps even greater difficulties. He pleaded not guilty and insisted that he was a cocaine addict. There was no evidence at all to support this, and the theory that he had attacked the murdered man in a fit of uncontrollable jealousy while the balance of his mind was upset by the drug, was quite ridiculous and made not the slightest impression on the court. Stoner didn't even know what cocaine looked like. When asked, he said it was brown with black specks in it.

When Mr Casswell went to see Stoner in Brixton Prison before the trial, he was well aware that all the young man was concerned about was ensuring that Alma was not convicted, which was considerably to his credit.

It seemed to Casswell that Stoner did not care whether he himself was convicted or not, and at the interview he was almost completely uncooperative. Though all this might be said to be very much in Stoner's favour, it put Casswell in a most difficult position. He had little hope of saving his client, except by his own art of persuasion. To put him in the box would be fatal. The only way of saving Stoner, Casswell knew, was to get the jury to believe that Mrs Rattenbury struck the fatal blows, and if he then were to put Stoner in the box he would passionately deny it and confess it was his doing.

It told heavily against Stoner that he failed to go into the witness-box while Alma did. Was he really prepared to die for her? And she for him? If so, it was certainly a great romance, whatever else might be said about the characters of this strangely-assorted Romeo and Juliet who appeared at the Old Bailey before Mr Justice Humphreys on 27 May, 1935.

Stoner's counsel has said that he did not know that Alma was going to give evidence until the morning when the trial opened and her counsel informed him that she would be giving evidence against Stoner. It was a shock to Casswell, and he took it to mean that Alma was going to give sworn evidence against her ex-lover in order to try and save her own neck.

Actually, it was not until almost the last minute that Alma had been persuaded by her counsel to give evidence. Though she was faithful to Stoner in her fashion, the first thought in her life was her children, and the terrible thing they would inherit if she was found guilty. It was this, more than anything else, that induced her to go into the box and tell the truth, and the consensus of opinion about this strange and complicated case is that Alma Rattenbury did tell the truth in the witness-box.

The prosecution's main witness was Irene Riggs, though she could only be persuaded to say very little which told against the female defendant. But what she did mention about Stoner was very damaging, and it came out dramatically in court.

Mr O'Connor, Alma's counsel, cross-examined Irene. On the Monday morning, she recollected, Stoner had said to her: 'I suppose you know who did it?' She asked back: 'Well?' But he gave no reply.

O'Connor then sat down, supposing that his cross-examination was completed, when Irene added: 'There was something else on the Tuesday that I remember. I asked Stoner why he had done it.'

There was an astonished pause in court, a sudden rising of tension.

Casswell was about to rise and cross-examine her on behalf of Stoner, and naturally he would not be expected to pursue a point so damaging to his client.

Mr Justice Humphreys immediately intervened.

'Wait a minute. Do you want to put any further questions, Mr O'Connor?'

O'Connor was on his feet again in an instant. He was not going to let an opportunity like this go by.

'My lord, I think I will follow this up, if I may.'

From the witness-box Irene Riggs said: 'I should have said it when he asked me another question.'

'What was it?' asked O'Connor.

'On the Tuesday I asked Stoner why he had done it,' replied Irene.

'What did he say?'

'He said because he had seen Mr Rattenbury "living with" Mrs Rattenbury in the afternoon.'

The damage was done. It was irreparable. There was little Casswell could do to retrieve the situation as far as his client was concerned. If young Stoner had struck the blows, then he was guilty of a despicable murder.

But so far as Alma Rattenbury was concerned, it was different. The terrible Bywaters–Thompson case cast its awful shadow over the Rattenbury–Stoner trial. The consciousness of the savage fate which Edith Thompson had met at the hands of English justice in its harshest mood doubtless held back the hands of Judge, counsel and jury alike. The unease caused by the hanging of Edith Thompson not only went a long way to saving Alma Rattenbury from the hangman; it also marked the beginning of the end of capital punishment in England.

Alma's performance in the witness-box caused a deep impression. She told the story of what happened on the day of her husband's death in a way which seemed both earnest and truthful. She made no attempt to evade or excuse her immoralities. Her story could not be shaken even after the most searching cross-examination.

The trial lasted four days. Observers remarked that it aged Alma by twenty years. Day by day her physical aspect changed. She seemed to grow old in the court as though time itself had in some strange way been speeded up. Stoner, on the other hand, appeared unmoved by the whole drama.

Alma Rattenbury was fortunate in her judge. Travers Humphreys's summing up was a masterly exposition of the law. But he did not spare her character. He called her 'a woman so lost to all sense of decency, so entirely without any morals that she would stop at nothing to gain her ends, particularly her sexual gratification, and if that be true, then, say the prosecution, do you think that woman would stop at the killing of her husband, particularly if she had not to do it herself?'

Speaking of the 'degradation to which this wretched woman has sunk', he went on: 'You will remember that she gave evidence herself that she was committing adultery – she is an adulteress of course – regularly in bed with her husband's servant in her bedroom and that in that bedroom in a little bed there was her own child of six, and counsel asked her: 'Do you really mean that you chose that room when if you wanted to gratify your passions you could have gone into the man's room which was just along the passage and done it there? Did you really choose the room where your child was asleep? And you will remember that the woman who was in the witness-box seemed surprised that anyone should put such a question to her, and her answer was apparently given in perfectly good faith: 'Why not? The little boy was asleep. He was a sound sleeper.'

After conceding that no one could have sympathy with this woman whose morals and depravity he had so soundly berated, the Judge gave the jury a stern warning that they must not convict her of the crime of murder 'because she is an adulteress, and an adulteress, you may think, of the most unpleasant type.' The case against her, the Judge pointed out, depended neither on her character, nor on the theories of the prosecution, but solely on her statements, and these she had made only after she had drunk considerable quantities of alcohol.

The jury took forty-seven minutes to reach their verdict. They found Mrs Rattenbury not guilty and Stoner guilty, adding a recommendation to mercy with their verdict. Mr Justice Humphreys had no alternative but to sentence Stoner to death, but he added a strong recommendation of his own to the jury's plea for mercy.

Alma left the court with barely any feeling of relief. She was overwhelmed with remorse and shame, haunted with grief over the fate of Stoner, desperately miserable about her children. Hounded by the Press, execrated by society, ill physically and mentally, she did not – could not – vanish from the scene like the mysterious Adelaide Bartlett, and leave not a trace behind.

Her husband's relatives who treated her with great charity took her away with them. But wherever they went they were pursued by the Press. Even when she was finally removed to a nursing home in London, newspapermen followed her; one of them called out to the doctor who was with her: 'It doesn't matter where you take her, we will follow you.'

She was admitted to the nursing home on 3 June for 'rest and treatment'. The following afternoon, she borrowed two pounds from one of the officials at the home, saying she was going out and would be back at nine o'clock. She appeared normal and the doctor allowed her to go out.

The following day her body was found by the side of a stream near Christchurch. She had stabbed herself six times in the chest with a knife which three times she had driven into her heart. The agony, despair, self-hatred and remorse which had caused her to do this was reflected in letters which were found in her handbag. Some of these were read at the inquest.

> I want to make it perfectly clear that no one is responsible for what action I may take regarding my life. I quite made up my mind at Holloway to finish things should Stoner (*sic*) and it would only be a matter of time and opportunity. Every night and minute is only prolonging the appalling agony of my mind.

A letter addressed to the Governor of Pentonville Prison said:

> If I only thought it would help Stoner, I would stay on, but it had been pointed out to me all too vividly that I cannot help him. That is my death sentence.

Another letter read:

> Eight o'clock. After so much walking I have got here. Oh, to see the swans and the spring flowers and just smell them. And how singular I should have chosen the spot Stoner said he nearly jumped out of the train once at. It was not intentional my coming here. I tossed a coin, like Stoner always did, and it came down Christchurch. It is beautiful here. What a lovely world we are in! It must be easier to be hanged than to have to do the job oneself, especially in these circumstances of being watched all the while. Pray God nothing stops me tonight. Am within five minutes of Christchurch now. God bless my children and look after them.

Yet another:

I tried this morning to throw myself under a train at Oxford Circus. Too many people about. Then a bus. Still too many people about. One must be bold to do a thing like this. It is beautiful here and I am alone. Thank God for peace at last.

Stoner lost his appeal, but he was reprieved. His mistress died in the belief that he would be hanged.

Although he had admitted in his statement to the police that he had killed Rattenbury with the mallet, Stoner later maintained that he was totally innocent of the crime.

His new story of the fatal night was that he had fetched the mallet for an innocent reason, put it in the coal shed and then went to bed. Later he went on to the landing and was looking downstairs to see if the old man had gone to bed so that he could go to Alma's bedroom as usual. This was when Irene Riggs saw him. Afterwards he went to Alma's bedroom and found her in bed terrified. He heard a sound of groaning, and Alma said, 'Hear him!' Then she got out of bed and ran downstairs. Later he found the mallet on the floor of the drawing-room and he hid it in the garden where it was subsequently found by the police.

What was the truth of the affair? Many have chosen to believe Alma Rattenbury, that sad, unbalanced, passionate creature whom society convicted and sentenced to death when judge and jury acquitted her.

H. B. Irving

THE WIDOW GRAS

I

Jenny Amenaide Brécourt was born in Paris in the year 1837. Her father was a printer, her mother sold vegetables. The parents neglected the child, but a lady of title took pity on her, and when she was five years old adopted her. Even as a little girl she was haughty and imperious. At the age of eight she refused to play with another child on the ground of her companion's social inferiority. 'The daughter of a Baroness,' she said, 'cannot play with the daughter of a wine-merchant.' When she was eleven years old, her parents took her away from her protectress and sent her into the streets to sell gingerbread – a dangerous experience for a child of tender years. After six years of street life, Amenaide sought out her benefactress and begged her to take her back. The Baroness consented, and found her employment in a silk manufactory. One day the girl, now eighteen years old, attended the wedding of one of her companions in the factory. She returned home after the ceremony thoughtful. She said that she wanted to get married. The Baroness did not take her statement seriously, and on the grocer calling one day, said in jest to Amenaide, 'You want a husband, there's one.' But Amenaide was in earnest. She accepted the suggestion and, to the Baroness' surprise, insisted on taking the grocer as her husband. Reluctantly the good lady gave her consent, and in 1855 Amenaide Brécourt became the wife of the grocer Gras.

A union, so hasty and ill-considered, was not likely to be of long duration. With the help of the worthy Baroness the newly married couple started a grocery business. But Amenaide was too economical for her husband and mother-in-law. Quarrels ensued, recriminations. In a spirit of unamiable prophecy husband and wife foretold each other's future. 'You will die in a hospital,' said the wife. 'You will land your carcase in prison,' retorted the husband. In both instances they were correct in their anticipations. One day the husband disappeared. For a short time Amenaide returned to her long-suffering protectress, and then she too disappeared.

When she is heard of again, Amenaide Brécourt has become Jeanne de la Cour. Jeanne de la Cour is a courtesan. She has tried commerce, acting, literature, journalism, and failed at them all. Henceforth men are to make her fortune for her. Such charms as she may possess, such allurements as she can offer, she is ready to employ without heart or feeling to accomplish her end. Without real passion, she has an almost abnormal, erotic sensibility, which serves in its stead. She cares only for one person, her sister. To her Jeanne de la Cour unfolded her philosophy of life. While pretending to love men, she is going to make them suffer. They are to be her playthings, she knows how to snare them: 'All is dust and lies. So much the worse for the men who get in my way. Men are mere stepping-stones to me. As soon as they begin to fail or are played out, I put them scornfully aside. Society is a vast chess-board, men the pawns, some white, some black; I move them as I please, and break them when they bore me.'

The early years of Jeanne de la Cour's career as a Phryne were hardly more successful than her attempts at literature, acting and journalism. True to her philosophy, she had driven one lover, a German, to suicide, and brought another to his death by overdoses of cantharides. On learning of the death of the first, she reflected patriotically, 'One German the less in Paris!' That of the second elicited the matter-of-fact comment, 'It was bound to happen; he had no moderation.' A third admirer, who died in a hospital, was dismissed as 'a fool who, in spite of all, still respects women.' But, in ruining her lovers, she had ruined her own health. In 1865 she was compelled to enter a private asylum. There she is described as 'dark in complexion, with dark expressive eyes, very pale, and of a nervous temperament, agreeable, and pretty.' She was suffering at the time of her admission from hysterical seizures, accompanied by insane exaltation, convulsions and loss of speech. In speaking of her humble parents she said, 'I don't know such people'; her manner was bombastic, and she was fond of posing as a fine lady.

After a few months Jeanne de la Cour was discharged from the asylum as cured, and on the advice of her doctors went to Vittel. There she assumed the rank of Baroness and recommenced her career, but this time in a more reasonable and businesslike manner. Her comments, written to her sister, on her fellow guests at the hotel are caustic. She mocks at some respectable married women who are trying to convert her to Catholicism. To others who refuse her recognition, she makes herself so mischievous and objectionable that in self-defence they are frightened into acknowledging her. Admirers among men she has many, ex-ministers, prefects. It was at Vittel that occurred the incident of the wounded pigeon. There had been some pigeon-shooting. One of the wounded birds flew into the room of the Baroness de la Cour. She took pity on it, tended it, taught it not to be afraid of her and to stay in her room. So touching was her conduct considered by some of those who heard it, that she was nicknamed 'the Charmer'. But she is well aware, she writes to her sister, that with the true ingratitude of the male, the pigeon will leave her as soon as it needs her help no longer. However, for the moment, 'disfigured as it is, beautiful or ugly,' she loves it. 'Don't forget,' she writes, 'that a woman who is practical and foreseeing, she too enjoys her pigeon-shooting, but the birds are her lovers.'

Shortly after she left Vittel an event occurred which afforded Jeanne de la Cour the prospect of acquiring that settled position in life which, 'practical and foreseeing,' she now regarded as indispensable to her future welfare. Her husband, Gras, died, as she had foretold, in the Charity Hospital. The widow was free. If she could bring down her bird, it was now in her power to make it hers for life. Henceforth all her efforts were directed to that end. She was reaching her fortieth year, her hair was turning grey, her charms were waning. Poverty, degradation, a miserable old age, a return to the wretched surroundings of her childhood, such she knew to be the fate of many of her kind. There was nothing to be hoped for from the generosity of men. Her lovers were leaving her. Blackmail, speculation on the Bourse, even the desperate expedient of a suppositious child, all these she tried as means of acquiring a competence. But fortune was shy of the widow. There was need for dispatch. The time was drawing near when it might be man's unkind privilege to put her scornfully aside as a thing spent and done with. She must bring down her bird, and that quickly. It was at this critical point in the widow's career, in the year 1873, that she met at a public ball for the first time Georges de Saint Pierre.*

Georges de Saint Pierre was twenty years of age when he made the acquaintance of the Widow Gras. He had lost his mother at an early age, and since then lived with relatives in the country. He was a young man of independent means, idle, of a simple, confiding and affectionate disposition. Four months after his first meeting with the widow they met again. The end of the year 1873 saw the commencement of an intimacy, which to all appearances was characterised by a more lasting and sincere affection than is usually associated with unions of this kind. There can be no doubt that during the three years the Widow Gras was the mistress of Georges de Saint Pierre, she had succeeded in subjugating entirely the senses and the affection of her young lover. In spite of the twenty years between them, Georges de Saint Pierre idolised his middle-aged mistress. She was astute enough to play not only the lover, but the mother to this motherless youth. After three years of intimacy he writes to her: 'It is enough for me that you love me, because I don't weary you, and I, I love you with all my heart. I cannot bear to leave you. We will live happily together. You will always love me truly, and as for me, my loving care will ever protect you. I don't know what would become of me if I did not feel that your love watched over me.' The confidence of Georges in the widow was absolute. When, in 1876, he spent six months in Egypt, he made her free of his rooms in Paris, she was at liberty to go there when she liked; he trusted her entirely, idolised her. Whatever her faults, he was blind to them. 'Your form,' he writes, 'is ever before my eyes; I wish I could enshrine your pure heart in gold and crystal.'

The widow's conquest, to all appearances, was complete. But

---

*For obvious reasons I have suppressed the real name of the widow's lover.

Georges was very young. He had a family anxious for his future; they knew of his *liaison*; they would be hopeful, no doubt, of one day breaking it off and of marrying him to some desirable young person. From the widow's point of view the situation lacked finality. How was that to be secured?

One day, towards the end of the year 1876, after the return of Georges from Egypt, the widow happened to be at the house of a friend, a ballet dancer. She saw her friend lead into the room a young man; he was sightless, and her friend with tender care guided him to a seat on the sofa. The widow was touched by the spectacle. When they were alone, she inquired of her friend the reason of her solicitude for the young man. 'I love this victim of nature,' she replied, 'and look after him with every care. He is young, rich, without family, and is going to marry me. Like you, I am just on forty; my hair is turning grey, my youth vanishing. I shall soon be cast adrift on the sea, a wreck. This boy is the providential spar to which I am going to cling that I may reach land in safety.' 'You mean, then,' said the widow, 'that you will soon be beyond the reach of want?' 'Yes,' answered the friend, 'I needn't worry any more about the future.' 'I congratulate you,' said the widow, 'and what is more, your lover will never see you grow old.'

To be cast adrift on the sea and to have found a providential spar! The widow was greatly impressed by her friend's rare good fortune. Indeed, her experience gave the widow furiously to think, as she revolved in her brain various expedients by which Georges de Saint Pierre might become the 'providential spar' in her own impending wreck. The picture of the blind young man tenderly cared for, dependent utterly on the ministrations of his devoted wife, fixed itself in the widow's mind; there was something inexpressibly pathetic in the picture, whilst its practical significance had its sinister appeal to one in her situation.

At this point in the story there appears on the scene a character as remarkable in his way as the widow herself, remarkable at least for his share in the drama that is to follow. Nathalis Gaudry, of humble parentage, rude and uncultivated, had been a playmate of the widow when she was a child in her parents' house. They had grown up together, but after Gaudry entered the army, had lost sight of each other. Gaudry served through the Italian war of 1859, gaining a medal for valour. In 1864 he had married. Eleven years later his wife died, leaving him with two children. He came to Paris and obtained employment in an oil refinery at Saint Denis. His character was excellent; he was a good workman, honest, hard-working, his record unblemished. When he returned to Paris, Gaudry renewed his friendship with the companion of his youth. But Jeanne Brécourt was now Jeanne de la Cour, living in refinement and some luxury, moving in a sphere altogether remote from and unapproachable by the humble workman in an oil refinery. He could do no more than worship from afar this strange being, to him wonderfully seductive in her charm and distinction.

On her side the widow was quite friendly towards her homely admirer. She refused to marry him, as he would have wished, but she did her best without success to marry him to others of her acquaintance. Neither a sempstress nor an inferior actress could she persuade, for all her zeal, to unite themselves with a hand in an oil mill, a widower with two children. It is typical of the widow's nervous energy that she should have undertaken so hopeless a task. In the meantime she made use of her admirer. On Sundays he helped her in her apartment, carried coals, bottled wine, scrubbed the floors, and made himself generally useful. He was supposed by those about the house to be her brother. Occasionally, in the absence of a maid, the widow allowed him to attend on her personally, even to assist her in her toilette and perform for her such offices as one woman would perform for another. The man soon came to be madly in love with the woman; his passion, excited but not gratified, enslaved and consumed him. To some of his fellow-workmen who saw him moody and preoccupied, he confessed that he ardently desired to marry a friend of his childhood, not a working woman but a lady.

Such was the situation and state of mind of Nathalis Gaudry when, in November, 1876, he received a letter from the widow, in which she wrote, 'Come at once. I want you on a matter of business. Tell your employer it is a family affair; I will make up your wages.' In obedience to this message Gaudry was absent from the distillery from the 17th to the 23rd of November.

The 'matter of business' about which the widow wished to consult with Gaudry turned out to be a scheme of revenge. She told him that she had been basely defrauded by a man to whom she had entrusted money. She desired to be revenged on him, and could think of no better way than to strike at his dearest affections by seriously injuring his son. This she proposed to do with the help of a knuckle-duster, which she produced and gave to Gaudry. Armed with this formidable weapon, Gaudry was to strike her enemy's son so forcibly in the pit of the stomach as to disable him for life. The widow offered to point out to Gaudry the young man whom he was to attack. She took him outside the young man's club and showed him his victim. He was Georges de Saint Pierre.

The good fortune of her friend, the ballet-dancer, had proved a veritable toxin in the intellectual system of the Widow Gras. The poison of envy, disappointment, suspicion, apprehension had entered into her soul. Of what use to her was a lover, however generous and faithful, who was free to take her up and lay her aside at will? But such was her situation relative to Georges de Saint Pierre. She remembered that the wounded pigeon, as long as it was dependent on her kind offices, had been compelled to stay by her side; recovered, it had flown away. Only a pigeon, maimed beyond hope of recovery, could she be sure of compelling to be hers for all time, tied to her by its helpless infirmity, too suffering and disfigured to be lured from its captivity. And so, in accordance with her philosophy of life, the widow, by a blow in the pit of the stomach with a knuckle-duster, was to bring down her bird which henceforth would be tended and cared for by 'the Charmer' to her own satisfaction and the admiration of all beholders.

For some reason, the natural reluctance of Gaudry, or perhaps a feeling of compunction in the heart of the widow, this plan was not put into immediate execution. Possibly she hesitated before adopting a plan more cruel, more efficacious. Her hesitation did not last long.

With the dawn of the year 1877 the vigilant apprehension of the widow was roused by the tone of M. de Saint Pierre's letters. He wrote from his home in the country, 'I cannot bear leaving you, and I don't mean to. We will live together.' But he adds that he is depressed by difficulties with his family, 'not about money or business but of a kind he can only communicate to her verbally.' To the widow it was clear that these difficulties must relate to the subject of marriage. The character of Georges was not a strong one; sooner or later he might yield to the importunities of his family; her reign would be ended, a modest and insufficient pension the utmost she could hope for. She had passed the meridian of her life as a charmer of men, her health was giving way, she was greedy, ambitious, acquisitive. In January she asked her nephew, who worked as a gilder, to get her some vitriol for cleaning her copper. He complied with her request.

During Jeanne de la Cour's brief and unsuccessful appearance as an actress she had taken part in a play with the rather cumbrous title, *Who Puts Out the Eyes Must Pay for Them*. The widow may have forgotten this event; its occurrence so many years before may have been merely a sinister coincidence. But the incident of the ballet-dancer and her sightless lover was fresh in her mind.

Early in January the widow wrote to Georges, who was in the country, and asked him to take her to the masked ball at the Opera on the 13th. Her lover was rather surprised at her request, nor did he wish to appear with her at so public a gathering. 'I don't understand,' he writes, 'why you are so anxious to go to the Opera. I can't see any real reason for your wanting to tire yourself out at such a disreputable gathering. However, if you are happy and well, and promise to be careful, I will take you. I would be the last person, my dear little wife, to deny you anything that would give you pleasure.' But for some reason Georges was unhappy, depressed. Some undefined presentiment of evil seems to have oppressed him. His brother noticed his preoccupation.

He himself alludes to it in writing to his mistress: 'I am depressed this evening. For a very little I could break down altogether and give way to tears. You can't imagine what horrid thoughts possess me. If I felt your love close to me, I should be less sad.' Against his better inclination Georges promised to take the widow to the ball on the 13th. He was to come to Paris on the night of the 12th.

II

On the afternoon of January 11, Gaudry called to see the widow. There had been an accident at the distillery that morning, and work was suspended for three days. The widow showed Gaudry the bottle containing the vitriol which her nephew had procured for her use. She was ill, suffering, she said; the only thing that could make her well again would be the execution of her revenge on the son of the man who had defrauded her so wickedly: 'Make him suffer, here are the means, and I swear I will be yours.' She dropped a little of the vitriol on to the floor to show its virulent effect. At first Gaudry was shocked, horrified. He protested that he was a soldier, that he could not do such a deed; he suggested that he should provoke the young man to a duel and kill him. 'That is no use,' said the widow, always sensitive to social distinctions; 'he is not of your class, he would refuse to fight with you.' Mad with desire for the woman, his senses irritated and excited, the ultimate gratification of his passion held alluringly before him, the honest soldier consented to play the cowardly ruffian. The trick was done. The widow explained to her accomplice his method of proceeding. The building in the Rue de Boulogne, in which the widow had her apartment, stood at the end of a drive some twenty-seven and a half yards long and five and a half yards wide. About half-way up the drive, on either side, there were two small houses, or pavilions, standing by themselves and occupied by single gentlemen. The whole was shut off from the street by a large gate, generally kept closed, in which a smaller gate served to admit persons going in or out. According to the widow's plan, the young man, her enemy's son, was to take her to the ball at the Opera on the night of January 13. Gaudry was to wait in her apartment until their return. When he heard the bell ring, which communicated with the outer gate, he was to come down, take his place in the shadow of one of the pavilions on either side of the drive, and from the cover of this position fling in the face of the young man the vitriol which she had given him. The widow herself, under the pretence of closing the smaller gate, would be well behind the victim, and take care to leave the gate open so that Gaudry could make his escape.

In spite of his reluctance, his sense of foreboding, Georges de Saint Pierre came to Paris on the night of the 12th, which he spent at the widow's apartment. He went to his own rooms on the morning of the 13th.

This eventful day, which, to quote Iago, was either to 'make or fordo quite' the widow, found her as calm, cool and deliberate in the execution of her purpose as the Ancient himself. Gaudry came to her apartment about five o'clock in the afternoon. The widow showed him the vitriol and gave him final directions. She would, she said, return from the ball about three o'clock in the morning. Gaudry was then sent away till ten o'clock, as Georges was dining with her. He returned at half-past ten and found the widow dressing, arraying herself in a pink domino and a blonde wig. She was in excellent spirits. When Georges came to fetch her, she put Gaudry into an alcove in the drawing-room which was curtained off from the rest of the room. Always thoughtful, she had placed a stool there that he might rest himself. Gaudry could hear her laughing and joking with her lover. She reproached him playfully with hindering her in her dressing. To keep him quiet, she gave him a book to read, Montaigne's 'Essays'. Georges opened it and read the thirty-fifth chapter of the second book, the essay on 'Three Good Women', which tells how three brave women of antiquity endured death or suffering in order to share their husband's fate. Curiously enough, the essay concludes with these words, almost prophetic for the unhappy reader: 'I am enforced to live, and sometimes to live is magnanimity.' Whilst Georges went to fetch a cab, the widow released Gaudry from his place of concealment, exhorted him to have courage, and promised him, if he succeeded, the accomplishment of his desire. And so the gay couple departed for the ball. There the widow's high spirits, her complete enjoyment, were remarked by more than one of her acquaintances; she danced one dance with her lover, and with another young man made an engagement for the following week.

Meanwhile, at the Rue de Boulogne, Gaudry sat and waited in the widow's bedroom. From the window he could see the gate and the lights of the cab that was to bring the revellers home. The hours passed slowly. He tried to read the volume of

Montaigne where Georges had left it open, but the words conveyed little to him, and he fell asleep. Between two and three o'clock in the morning he was waked by the noise of wheels. They had returned. He hurried downstairs and took up his position in the shadow of one of the pavilions. As Georges de Saint Pierre walked up the drive alone, for the widow had stayed behind to fasten the gate, he thought he saw the figure of a man in the darkness. The next moment he was blinded by the burning liquid flung in his face. The widow had brought down her pigeon.

At first she would seem to have succeeded perfectly in her attempt. Georges was injured for life, the sight of one eye gone, that of the other threatened, his face sadly disfigured. Neither he nor anyone else suspected the real author of the crime. It was believed that the unfortunate man had been mistaken for some other person, and made by accident the victim of an act of vengeance directed against another. Georges was indeed all the widow's now, lodged in her own house to nurse and care for. She undertook the duty with every appearance of affectionate devotion. The unhappy patient was consumed with gratitude for her untiring solicitude; thirty nights she spent by his bedside. His belief in her was absolute. It was his own wish that she alone should nurse him. His family were kept away, any attempts his relatives or friends made to see or communicate with him frustrated by the zealous widow.

It was this uncompromising attitude on her part towards the friends of Georges, and a rumour which reached the ears of one of them that she intended as soon as possible to take her patient away to Italy, that sounded the first note of danger to her peace of mind. This friend happened to be acquainted with the son of one of the Deputy Public Prosecutors in Paris. To that official he confided his belief that there were suspicious circumstances in the case of Georges de Saint Pierre. The judicial authorities were informed and the case placed in the hands of an examining magistrate. On February 2, nearly a month after the crime, the magistrate, accompanied by Macé, then a commissary of police, afterwards head of the Detective Department, paid a visit to the Rue de Boulogne. Their reception was not cordial. It was only after they had made known their official character that they got audience of the widow. She entered the room, carrying in her hand a surgical spray, with which she played nervously while the men of the law asked to see her charge. She replied that it was impossible. Macé placed himself in front of the door by which she had entered, and told her that her attitude was not seemly. 'Leave that spray alone,' he said; 'it might shoot over us, and then perhaps we should be sprinkled as M. de Saint Pierre was.' From that moment, writes Macé, issue was joined between the widow and himself.

The magistrate insisted on seeing the patient. He sat by his bedside. M. de Saint Pierre told him that, having no enemies, he was sure he had been the victim of some mistake, and that, as he claimed no damages for his injuries, he did not wish his misfortune to be made public. He wanted to be left alone with his brave and devoted nurse, and to be spared the nervous excitement of a meeting with his family. He intended, he added, to leave Paris shortly for change of scene and air. The widow cut short the interview on the ground that her patient was tired. It was inhuman, she said, to make him suffer so. The magistrate, before leaving, asked her whither she intended taking her patient. She replied, 'To Italy.' That, said the magistrate, would be impossible until his inquiry was closed. In the meantime, she might take him to any place within the Department of the Seine; but she must be prepared to be under the surveillance of M. Macé, who would have the right to enter her house whenever he should think it expedient. With this disconcerting intelligence the men of the law took leave of the widow.

She was no longer to be left in undisturbed possession of her prize. Her movements were watched by two detectives. She was seen to go to the bachelor lodgings of Georges and take away a portable desk, which contained money and correspondence. More mysterious, however, was a visit she paid to the Charonne Cemetery, where she had an interview with an unknown, who was dressed in the clothes of a workman. She left the cemetery alone, and the detectives lost track of her companion. This meeting took place on February 11. Shortly after the widow left Paris with Georges de Saint Pierre for the suburb of Courbevoie.

Macé had elicited certain facts from the porter at the Rue de

Boulogne and other witnesses, which confirmed his suspicion that the widow had played a sinister part in her lover's misfortune. Her insistence that he should take her to the ball on January 13; the fact that, contrary to the ordinary politeness of a gentleman, he was walking in front of her at the time of the attack; and that someone must have been holding the gate open to enable the assailant to escape – it was a heavy gate, which, if left to itself after being opened, would swing too quickly on its hinges and shut of its own accord – these facts were sufficient to excite suspicion. The disappearance, too, of the man calling himself her brother, who had been seen at her apartment on the afternoon of the 13th, coupled with the mysterious interview in the cemetery, suggested the possibility of a crime in which the widow had had the help of an accomplice. To facilitate investigation it was necessary to separate the widow from her lover. The examining magistrate, having ascertained from a medical report that such a separation would not be hurtful to the patient, ordered the widow to be sent back to Paris, and the family of M. de Saint Pierre to take her place. The change was made on March 6. On leaving Courbevoie the widow was taken to the office of Macé. There the commissary informed her that she must consider herself under provisional arrest. 'But who,' she asked indignantly, 'is to look after my Georges?' 'His family,' was the curt reply. The widow, walking up and down the room like a panther, stormed and threatened. When she had in some degree recovered herself, Macé asked her certain questions. Why had she insisted on her lover going to the ball? She had done nothing of the kind. How was it his assailant had got away so quickly by the open gate? She did not know. What was the name and address of her reputed brother? She was not going to deliver an honest father of a family into the clutches of the police. What was the meaning of her visit to the Charonne Cemetery? She went there to pray, not to keep assignations. 'And if you want to know,' she exclaimed, 'I have had typhoid fever, which makes me often forget things. So I shall say nothing more – nothing – nothing.'

Taken before the examining magistrate, her attitude continued to be defiant and arrogant. 'Your cleverest policemen,' she told the magistrate, 'will never find any evidence against me. Think well before you send me to prison. I am not the woman to live long among thieves and prostitutes.' Before deciding finally whether the widow should be thrown into such uncongenial society, the magistrate ordered Macé to search her apartment in the Rue de Boulogne.

On entering the apartment the widow asked that all the windows should be opened. 'Let in the air,' she said; 'the police are coming in; they make a nasty smell.' She was invited to sit down while the officers made their search. Her letters and papers were carefully examined; they represented a strange mixture of order and disorder. Carefully kept account books of her personal expenses were mixed up with *billets doux*, paints and pomades, moneylenders' circulars, bella-donna and cantharides. But most astounding of all were the contents of the widows' *prie-Dieu*. In this devotional article of furniture were stored all the inmost secrets of her profligate career. Affectionate letters from the elderly gentlemen on whom she had imposed a supposititious child lay side by side with a black-edged card, on which was written the last message of a young lover who had killed himself on her account. 'Jeanne, in the flush of my youth I die because of you, but I forgive you. – M.' With these genuine outpourings of misplaced affection were mingled the indecent verses of a more vulgar admirer, and little jars of hashish. The widow, unmoved by this rude exposure of her way of life, only broke her silence to ask Macé the current prices on the Stock Exchange.

One discovery, however, disturbed her equanimity. In the drawer of a cupboard, hidden under some linen, Macé found a leather case containing a sheaf of partially-burnt letters. As he was about to open it the widow protested that it was the property of M. de Saint Pierre. Regardless of her protest, Macé opened the case, and, looking through the letters, saw that they were addressed to M. de Saint Pierre and were plainly of an intimate character. 'I found them on the floor near the stove in the dining-room,' said the widow, 'and I kept them. I admit it was a wrong thing to do, but Georges will forgive me when he knows why I did it.' From his better acquaintance with her character Macé surmised that an action admitted by the widow to be 'wrong' was in all probability something worse. Without delay he took the prisoner back to his office, and himself left for Courbevoie, there to enlighten, if possible, her unhappy victim as to the real character of his enchantress.

The interview was a painful one. The lover refused to hear a word against his mistress. 'Jeanne is my Antigone,' he said. 'She has lavished on me all her care, her tenderness, her love, and she believes in God.' Macé told him of her past, of the revelations contained in the *prie-Dieu* of this true believer, but he could make no impression. 'I forgive her past, I accept her present, and please understand me, no one has the power to separate me from her.' It was only when Macé placed in his hands the bundle of burnt letters, that he might feel what he could not see, and read him some passages from them, that the unhappy man realised the full extent of his mistress' treachery. Feeling himself dangerously ill, dying perhaps, M. de Saint Pierre had told the widow to bring from his rooms to the Rue de Boulogne the contents of his private desk. It contained some letters compromising to a woman's honour. These he was anxious to destroy before it was too late. As he went through the papers, his eyes bandaged, he gave them to the widow to throw into the stove. He could hear the fire burning and feel its warmth. He heard the widow take up the tongs. He asked her why she did so. She answered that it was to keep the burning papers inside the stove. Now from Macé he learnt the real truth. She had used the tongs to take out some of the letters half burnt, letters which in her possession might be one day useful instruments for levying blackmail on her lover. 'To blind me,' exclaimed M. de Saint Piere, 'to torture me, and then profit by my condition to lie to me, to betray me – it's infamous – infamous!' His dream was shattered. Macé had succeeded in his task; the disenchantment of M. de Saint Pierre was complete. That night the fastidious widow joined the thieves and prostitutes in the St Lazare Prison.

It was all very well to imprison the widow, but her participation in the outrage on M. de Saint Pierre was by no means established. The reputed brother, who had been in the habit of attending on her at the Rue de Boulogne, still eluded the searches of the police. In silence lay the widow's only hope of baffling her enemies. Unfortunately for the widow, confinement told on her nerves. She became anxious, excited. Her very ignorance of what was going on around her, her lover's silence made her apprehensive; she began to fear the worst. At length – the widow always had an itch for writing – she determined to communicate at all costs with Gaudry and invoke his aid. She wrote appealing to him to come forward and admit that he was the man the police were seeking, for sheltering whom she had been thrown into prison. She drew a harrowing picture of her sufferings in jail. She had refused food and been forcibly fed; she would like to dash her head against the walls. If any misfortune overtake Gaudry, she promises to adopt his son and leave him a third of her property. She persuaded a fellow-prisoner, an Italian dancer undergoing six months' imprisonment for theft, who was on the point of being released, to take the letter and promise to deliver it to Gaudry at Saint Denis. On her release the dancer told her lover of her promise. He refused to allow her to mix herself up in such a case, and destroyed the letter. Then the dancer blabbed to others, until her story reached the ears of the police. Macé sent for her. At first she could remember only that the name Nathalis occurred in the letter, but after visiting accidentally the Cathedral at Saint Denis, she recollected that this Nathalis lived there, and worked in an oil factory. It was easy after this for the police to trace Gaudry. He was arrested. At his house, letters from the widow were found, warning him not to come to her apartment, and appointing to meet him in Charonne Cemetery. Gaudry made a full confession. It was his passion for the widow, and a promise on her part to marry him, which, he said, had induced him to perpetrate so abominable a crime. He was sent to the Mazas Prison.

In the meantime the Widow Gras was getting more and more desperate. Her complete ignorance tormented her. At last she gave up all hope, and twice attempted suicide with powdered glass and verdigris. On May 12 the examining magistrate confronted her with Gaudry. The man told his story, the widow feigned surprise that the 'friend of her childhood' should malign her so cruelly. But to her desperate appeals Gaudry would only reply, 'It is too late!' They were sent for trial.

The trial of the widow and her accomplice opened before the Paris Assize Court on July 23, 1877, and lasted three days. The widow was defended by Lachaud, one of the greatest criminal advocates of France, the defender of Madame Lafarge, La Pommerais, Troppmann, the Marshal Bazaine. M. Demange (famous later for his defence of Dreyfus) appeared for Gaudry. The case had aroused considerable interest. Among those present at the trial were Halévy, the dramatist and Mounet-Sully and Coquelin, from the Comédie Française. Fernand Rodays thus described the widow in the *Figaro*: 'She looks more than her age, of moderate height, well made, neither blatant nor ill at ease, with nothing of the air of a woman of the town. Her hands are small. Her bust is flat, and her back round, her hair quite white. Beneath her brows glitter two jet-back eyes – the eyes of a tigress, that seem to breathe hatred and revenge.'

Gaudry was interrogated first. Asked by the President the motive of his crime, he answered, 'I was mad for Madame Gras; I would have done anything she told me. I had known her as a child, I had been brought up with her. Then I saw her again. I loved her, I was mad for her, I couldn't resist it. Her wish was law to me.'

Asked if Gaudry had spoken the truth, the widow said that he lied. The President asked what could be his motive for accusing her unjustly. The widow was silent. Lachaud begged her to answer. 'I cannot,' she faltered. The President invited her to sit down. After a pause the widow seemed to recover her nerve.

President: Was Gaudry at your house while you were at the ball?

Widow: No, no! He daren't look me in the face and say so.

President: But he is looking at you now.

Widow: No, he daren't! (She fixes her eyes on Gaudry, who lowers his head.)

President: I, whose duty it is to interrogate you, look you in the face and repeat my question. Was Gaudry at your house at half-past ten that night?

Widow: No.

Prlesident: You hear her, Gaudry?

Gaudry: Yes, Monsieur, but I was there.

Widow: It is absolutely impossible! Can anyone believe me guilty of such a thing?

President: Woman Gras, you prefer to feign indignation and deny everything. You have the right. I will read your examination before the examining magistrate. I see M. Lachaud makes a gesture, but I must beg the counsel for the defence not to impart unnecessary passion into these proceedings.

Lachaud: My gesture was merely meant to express that the woman Gras is on her trial, and that under the circumstances her indignation is natural.

President: Very good.

The appearance in the witness box of the widow's unhappy victim evoked sympathy. He gave his evidence quietly, without resentment or indignation. As he told his story the widow, whose eyes were fixed on him all the time, murmured: 'Georges! Georges! Defend me! Defend me!' 'I state the facts,' he replied.

The prisoners could only defend themselves by trying to throw on each other the guilt of the crime. M. Demange represented Gaudry as acting under the influence of his passion for the Widow Gras. Lachaud, on the other hand, attributed the crime solely to Gaudry's jealousy of the widow's lover, and contended that he was the sole author of the outrage.

The jury by their verdict assigned to the widow the greater share of responsibility. She was found guilty in the full degree, but to Gaudry were accorded extenuating circumstances. The widow was condemned to fifteen years' penal servitude, her accomplice to ten years' imprisonment.

It is dreadful to think how very near the Widow Gras came to accomplishing successfully her diabolical crime. A little less percipitancy on her part, and she might have secured the fruits of her cruelty. Her undoubted powers of fascination, in spite of the fiendishness of her real character, are doubly proved by the devotion of her lover and the guilt of her accomplice. At the same time, with that strange contradiction inherent in human nature, the Jekyll and Hyde elements which, in varying degree, are present in all men and women, the Widow Gras had a genuine love for her young sister. Her hatred of men was reasoned, deliberate, merciless and implacable. There is something almost sadic in the combination in her character of erotic sensibility with extreme cruelty.

Edgar Lustgarten

THE KRAY TWINS

Any attempt to generalize about the brothers Kray is bedevilled by the fact that they were twins. Assumptions may follow that in this case are unfounded. Without recourse to science or statistics, simply and solely from personal experience, many believe that twins – especially of the same sex – possess an almost supernatural affinity; that their mental processes and emotional reactions make them into carbon copies of each other. Life does provide examples. I could name some. But, as it happens, they do not include the Krays.

Of course Ronnie and Reggie had certain things in common. Physical appearance: until their mid-twenties, when Ronnie's face grew puffy, people really 'couldn't tell the two of them apart' (a fact which they sometimes turned to some advantage in effecting escapes and arranging alibis). Early upbringing: their nursery, their playground, their fount of education, had been the asphalt jungle depths of Bethnal Green, where even infants neither asked nor granted quarter. Adolescent hell raising: they were precocious tearaways, provoking and relishing and revelling in brawls, toting guns at the ripe age of sixteen. At seventeen, they both became professional boxers, the only honest work that either ever did. Called up for National Service, they spent their military careers in the glasshouse or AWOL. As fugitives, as captives, they sought similar associates, consorting with criminals, inveterate or incipient. They re-entered the civilian world with a fixed resolve to attain, in concert, the commanding heights of crime.

Far more important, though, than these or other likenesses was one fundamental difference between the twins.

Ronnie was a madman. By strictest definition. Once he was certified and held in an asylum; more than once he was put in a strait-jacket. His madness took the form of paranoid schizophrenia – delusions of grandeur in which the deranged person often identifies with some famous figure. There is a tale told of Bonaparte, anxious to inspect conditions in a Paris madhouse, arriving late one night, unescorted, unannounced, imperiously demanding immediate admission. 'And who do you think *you* are?' said the janitor. 'I am Napoleon,' the visitor replied. 'Oh,' said the janitor, opening the gates. 'Come in. We've got ten of you inside already.' Substitute Capone for Napoleon, and Ronnie Kray might well have been one of the ten. He had devoured Capone until Capone had devoured him. No thrill could equal that of being his idol's avatar. While not unmindful of material rewards, Ronnie was in the Gangster game primarily for kicks.

Reggie presented the reverse of the Kray coin. Amoral as his twin, he was absolutely sane. Like Ronnie, he asked himself: What's in it for me? But he gave himself a very different answer. He was a master of, not a slave to, violence, regarding it as a useful means to a desired end. He may sometimes have employed the means with positive enjoyment. A Capone streak ran through his Costello character. He would not, however, risk the end simply for the means. And Reggie was in the Gangster game primarily for profit.

Thus the Krays were engaged in two concurrent conflicts. One visible – as allies. One concealed – as opponents. Furious quarrels erupted privately; Reggie would charge Ronnie with idiotic recklessness, Ronnie would charge Reggie with inglorious timidity. These exchanges never endangered their alliance; they always stood together against the outside world. It cannot be denied, though, that there was a clash of wills, and not infrequently the madman's will prevailed. This is evident from their history.

No such clashes were anticipated, even by themselves, when they embarked upon their first joint venture: the Regal, a seedy billiard hall in Mile End. (By a typical stratagem – organizing shindies that gradually drove ordinary habitués away – they had leased it from the owner at a knockdown rent.) Billiards continued, but now as a screen; they transformed the hall into an *entrepôt* for crooks – and a catchment area for mugs. Ronnie was the magnet, Reggie was the manager. The design evolved has been depicted by John Pearson in *The Profession of Violence*. 'Ronnie would bring the crowds in, Reggie would fleece them. Ronnie would make their "name" for violence, Reggie would market it. When there was a serious fight, they could both still join in.' To that extent, until that time, Mr Pearson's summing up is wholly justified: 'the ideally complementary couple'. They held out the promise (or the threat) of the ideal Gangster partnership.

The 'Firm' (local euphemism for their Gang) was born in the billiard hall, grew up, and spread out. They started operating in the small change of 'protection', and were naturally caught up in territorial disputes. These had formerly been resolved by inconspicuous pressures. The Firm introduced more spectacular solutions. Ronnie soon found an excuse to use his Luger; the wound was not serious but the repercussions were. While Reggie stormed ('One day you'll get us hanged') and – by immense exertions – suppressed the evidence, other mobsters pondered and, both angry and alarmed, felt that guns could only be met with guns. Gang warfare, Chicago style, was coming to the boil when Ronnie – after another incident where he had put the boot in – received a three year sentence on a charge of GBH (underworld shorthand for 'causing grievous bodily harm').

As a brother, Reggie must have heard that sentence with regret. As a colleague, he may have heard it with relief. He would miss the companion to whom he was devoted. He would find it easier to run the Firm alone. Without the constant fear of Ronnie's crazy impulses, he could pursue a calculated policy, win much larger prizes, take much smaller risks. While Ronnie was inside, Reggie (supported by elder brother Charles) gave the Firm a new look, a new orientation. He turned his back upon their gutter monarchy, and set his sights on high society and showbiz. The medium was gaming, the bait was ritzy clubs – at first in outré, and hence titillating, settings. He opened 'The Double R', first of its kind in the East End; catching West End fancy too, it was a big success. He opened 'The Wellington Way' nearby; it was an even bigger one. These were precursors of, and pacemakers for, 'Esmeralda's Barn' in fashionable Wilton Place; most celebrated and most chic of the Kray casinos. Smooth professional gamblers mixed with stage and film celebrities, peers of the realm with felons in tuxedos. The recipe spelt riches. 'Esmeralda's Barn' yielded each twin £40,000 a year. All seemed headed for prosperity – and peace. Until Ronnie, freed, reappeared on the changed scene.

Reggie was now content. Ronnie was not. Reggie did not hanker after the old life. Ronnie did. Chatting up posh birds, hob-nobbing with swells – all very well, if you liked that sort of thing. As relaxation. But relaxing from what? Where was the excitement, the violence, the *action*? Without it, you cut no ice; you were a nobody, a nothing. Soon Ronnie was cutting ice again; a somebody, a something. It took only two or three relapses into pointless rough stuff to undermine all that had been steadily built up. Reggie's restraining influence progressively diminished, vanishing altogether when – as much by misfortune as misfeasance – he himself was put away for eighteen months. During his absence, Ronnie had himself a ball. He killed the goose that laid the golden eggs in 'Esmeralda's Barn'; his entourage of nubile boys and blatant hoodlums stripped off the veneer and dispersed the clientele. He revived the sordid rackets that had been virtually laid off. He replenished the Firm with new strongarm men and cut-throats. He reloaded, and resumed carrying, his Luger. Reggie returned too late to stop the rot. He gave up the struggle – and the leadership. His loyalty to Ronnie, however, was unswerving. That meant the twins were finally set on a disaster course.

The nature of their march along that course is well exemplified by the two murders for which they are best known.

The first was that of George Cornell, an old antagonist who had lately joined a Gang led by the brothers Richardson. Smaller, less powerful, their Gang did not cover the same area as the Krays. A feud existed, though, that did not terminate – at least for Ronnie – with the Richardsons' arrest. That followed a Gang fight, unconnected with the Krays, but in which an old friend of Ronnie's had been killed. It was enough. The Richardsons were out of reach, but subordinates were at large. One of them must be made to pay – and must be seen to pay. On an evening in March 1966, Ronnie walked into 'The Blind Beggar' pub in Whitechapel. George Cornell was drinking at the bar. 'Just look who's here,' he said. Ronnie shot him through the head and walked out into the night. Several saw it happen. Nobody talked – then.

The second murderee was Jack McVitie ('Jack the Hat' – his Gang monicker might have come straight out of Damon Runyon). A Gangster's casual handyman, breaking up through drink, he bungled a killing with which Ronnie had entrusted him. Furthermore, he retained some money paid to him in advance. Furthermore, in public he reviled the twins, loudly proclaiming that he was going to shoot them both. Had he been sober, Jack the Hat would not have said it. Being drunk he sowed the wind and reaped the whirlwind. On an evening in October 1967 he was decoyed to a 'party' at a woman's flat; when he arrived, there was no woman and no party – only the Kray twins and some of their plug-uglies. Ronnie had devised and engineered the plot, but stopped short of casting himself as the executioner. Not from squeamishness. For a less creditable reason. He taunted Reggie, 'I've done my one, and made a job of it.' Seconds later, Reggie had done his.

Justice – although by then crippled as well as blind – prevailed in the end to the fullest extent which the hamstrung law allowed.

Leonard Gribble

CORSETS AND CHLOROFORM

She was a bobbed-haired blonde who liked sprung-maple floors and the music of Irving Berlin and Cole Porter. She liked male companionship in much the same way she liked French pastries and ice-cream. She was thirty-two and had to start thinking about her figure. Possibly that is why corsets became important to her. And as one thing led to another in a most incredible and utterly human pattern, so corsets led to Judd Gray, and Judd Gray led to murder and the electric chair. Yet none of her friends or neighbourhood acquaintances would have termed Ruth Snyder an adventuress.

Albert Snyder was an art editor on the staff of a magazine for owners of motor-boats. In 1915 he had married Ruth Brown, his typist, and eight years later moved to Queen's Village, on Long Island. There the Snyders, with their daughter Lorraine, lived a normal middle-class American life until Ruth Snyder met Judd Gray in a restaurant, and began to think seriously about her figure. Why a woman of Ruth Snyder's vivacious temperament looked twice at Judd Gray is one of those fundamental mysteries of the sexes that can never be solved. Gray was short and wore glasses. There was nothing romantic about him. He hadn't an ounce of masculine glamour. And he gained his livelihood in a fashion popular only in the broadest of Hollywood comedies. He was a corset salesman.

Undoubtedly Ruth Snyder was bored with the everyday smoothness of her Long Island life. She was like someone doomed to watch the placid waters of a smiling lake when she longed for the excitement of a shelving beach with surf-singing breakers beating towards her. Perhaps Judd Gray entered her life at a moment when she was near to despair. Perhaps he really did capture her interest when he talked of corsets. Whatever the reason, she found herself meeting him unbeknown to her husband. Judd Gray had received some training as a salesman. He called at the Snyder home with samples of his wares. He was introduced to a husband whose mind was given to the presentation of glossy photographs of sleek rivercraft. If Albert Snyder thought anything of Judd Gray he kept it to himself. Corset salesmen did not belong in his tony magazine. Indeed, they had no real place in Queen's Village. It is quite possible that Albert Snyder did not consider Judd Gray as a real person.

But Gray was real enough, and was receiving real letters from Ruth Snyder. She was no longer asking about the latest lines in corsets. She was being introspective and unwisely amorous in her literary style.

One day she wrote:

> My own sweetheart boy. All I keep thinking of is U – you damn lovable little cuss. I could eatch aall up. Could I get lit and put out this blaze that is so much bother to me? Hurry home, darling. I'll be waiting for you. Could I meet you at the train? I can't sit still enough to write what I am thinking about you.
>
> Good-bye, sweetie old darling. All my love.
>
> Love and kisses,
>
> Your Momie.

From which one can deduce fairly accurately the passionate and utterly irrational nature that had been disturbed by the chance meeting in a restaurant. Certainly the illicit intrigue that was kept up by the unfaithful wife and the insignificant-looking lingerie hawker provides a striking demonstration of how complex and perverse can become normal human desires and frailties. The wife, in whose home the days passed in a pleasant atmosphere of intelligence, culture, and decency, lost all restraint in the company of this tenth-rate Casanova. Her taste deteriorated. Her mind, when she wrote to him, was untidy and lost any fastidiousness it had acquired. With Judd Gray she threw off restraint. Perhaps she had endured tortures for years in trying to conceal her innate common quality from her husband. With Gray she did not pretend. She was as common as he. Which means she was in truth a vastly different person from the woman her husband thought he had married.

The marriage ended abruptly on the night of March 19th, 1927.

The next day was a Sunday. Little Lorraine awoke about half-past seven. She sat up in bed, listening to a curious sound outside her bedroom. It was as though someone were tapping at bare floor-boards.

'Mummie!' she called. 'Mummie!'

Her mother did not answer, but the strange tapping sound continued. Not rhythmically or even regularly. It was a kind of fumbling sound. The child overcame her first fears, and climbed out of bed. She padded across the room and opened the door. A strange sight met her curious child gaze. Her mother lay on the floor of the corridor outside her room. Her hands and ankles were lashed with strands of wire. The tapping sound was made by the heels of Ruth Snyder's shoes. The woman was panting.

As Lorraine bent over, trembling and fearful, she cried: 'Phone Mr Mulhausen, Lorraine dear. Please don't stay asking questions. I was hit over the head, and I'm scared of what's happened to Daddy.'

Lorraine moved obediently to the telephone and called their neighbour. A few minutes later he arrived after dressing hurriedly and helped Ruth Snyder from her metal bonds. A strange story came brokenly from her. She mentioned three strangers who had gained entry to the house. They had attacked her, bound her limbs, and carried her into the corridor where she must have fainted. She seemed to remember lying there calling for her husband, and hearing no sound. She had been able to do nothing to help herself. Her limbs had become cramped.

Mr Mulhausen went into the front bedroom. He found Albert Snyder sprawled across the bed. The art editor was dressed in pyjamas. Blood spattered them. The blood had obviously come from two large wounds in his head.

Behind him rose a high-pitched scream. Mr Mulhausen turned in time to catch Ruth Snyder as she stumbled forward. As he gripped her she found her voice again.

'Oh, God, my jewels – they've been and taken my jewels!'

She tore away from the neighbour's grasp, and, ignoring the pathetic sight of her husband, began hunting for her pieces of jewellery. She stood up.

'They're gone!' she exclaimed.

Mr Mulhausen frowned. 'I'll call the police,' he said, and escaped from the room.

The police arrived promptly that Sunday morning, and heard how Ruth Snyder had been awakened by a man who looked like an Italian. It must have been in the middle of the night, she claimed. She had been hit over the head, and while she was confused they had dragged her from the bed and out of the room.

Plain-clothes men examined the body of Albert Snyder. One thing was obvious at first glance. His death had not been accidental. The wounds on Snyder's head had been caused by a blunt weapon. One wound was on the back of his head, one at the side. Several strands of picture-wire had been drawn tightly around his neck. Caught in the hairs of his moustache was a small piece of cotton waste. The killers had seemingly made assurance doubly sure by chloroforming their victim.

The first glaring clue to this mysterious attack could not be overlooked. Burglars had come for jewellery and taken up a great deal of time killing a man who might recognize them. Or so it appeared at first glance. In any case, it appeared cock-eyed, as a policeman told the reporters.

Equally cock-eyed was the disarray of the furniture in the Snyder home.

Burglars who had seemingly entered to steal jewellery had bothered to throw cushions from chairs and settee, pull up carpets and tear down curtains. Even more fantastic and inexplicable was a revolver found in the rumpled bedcovers. It had been broken open, the chambers were empty, and the cartridges lay under one of the covers. Shown the gun by the police, Mrs Snyder readily admitted it was her husband's. But the open revolver was not all. That bed was too freely strewn with clues. There was also a blue cotton hankerchief that had been screwed into a ball. Also a torn piece of a newspaper printed in Italian.

Cock-eyed indeed.

Inspector Arthur Carey tried to discover what this crazy quilt of obvious clues concealed. He started by asking fresh questions of the tearful widow. While she was explaining the loss of her rings and bracelets the men Carey had put to search the house found the missing articles. In, of all places, Ruth Snyder's bed, tucked under the mattress. The case was getting no less cock-eyed as it progressed. Ruth Snyder must have thought as much, for she suddenly decided that she had put the jewellery where it was found. For safety. Only, she was so worried, she had forgotten all about it. Except its disappearance.

Carey strove not to have a sense of humour that memorable Sunday. It would have been too embarrassing to find himself laughing in the widow's face.

The bereaved wife told of the previous evening. She and her husband had gone to a party. She had taken only a drink or two. Her husband had felt festive. He wasn't walking too straight when they came home. She continued with the entry of the raiders, and her story varied in several details from the one she had blurted out to Mr Mulhausen.

She told Carey that she was wakened by a noise in her daughter's room. She rose to find out what was happening, and found a dark-skinned man with a heavy moustache reaching for her. She had been tied up and dragged from her room.

'How old would you say this man was?' Carey asked.

'Around thirty-five, Inspector.' She had no hesitation.

'And the time?'

'I can't be sure. Around half after two, I guess.'

She knew no more until her daughter found her at half-past seven.

'You mean, Mrs Snyder,' Carey said, 'you remained for five hours in a dead faint?'

'I guess I must have, Inspector.'

Carey turned to the domestic matters, and found that the late Albert Snyder's widow talked very readily about her husband's work and their life together. Carey came to insurance. She told him her husband had been insured for only a thousand dollars until about a year before. Then she had taken out an accident and death policy.

'How much for?' Carey inquired.

'Twenty-five thousand dollars.'

Carey took particulars of the insurance and later checked with the company. He found that Mrs Snyder's memory in the matter of insurance benefits after her husband's death was every whit as shaky as when she had concealed her jewellery under the mattress of her bed. For instance, the amount she had insured her husband's life for was forty-five thousand dollars, and she had forgotten a quite important proviso. In the event of death by violence the company paid a double indemnity. In short, her husband's dying the way he had should mean a net gain to her in cash of ninety thousand dollars. The widow could consider herself comfortably placed for a few years.

Meantime a systematic search at the house had discovered in the basement a stained sash-weight. Medical evidence attested that this could have been the blunt weapon used to beat Snyder's head. The skull had not been fractured, which meant that the blows had not been delivered with sufficient force. In turn, this could mean that the assailant had been either a small man or a woman.

After the post-mortem examination Carey knew that the blows struck had been lighter than would normally be expected in the case of such a brutal attack. Snyder had been chloroformed and strangled while unconscious.

Carey posted men to make inquiries in the neighbourhood, while he continued to fill in pieces of the domestic scene. The child Lorraine could not help him. He went through Snyder's bankbook and papers, and drew a blank. He started on Mrs Snyder's, and became interested when he found a cancelled cheque signed by her to the order of H. Judd Gray. The sum was two hundred dollars.

'Who is Mr Gray?' he asked her.

'Oh, he's a corset salesman.'

'And this cheque is for goods he has supplied, Mrs Snyder?'

'Why, sure,' she smiled.

Carey looked at her figure, and decided she hadn't needed corsets as urgently as all that. He held out a letter.

'Did Mr Gray write this, Mrs Snyder?'

The letter had been posted in Syracuse, in New York State, on the Saturday evening. It had arrived at the Snyder home on

Long Island on the Monday morning after the crime. The uneven writing ran:

> Hello Momma! How the dickens are you this bright beautiful day, anyway? Gee, it makes you feel like living again after all that rain yesterday. If we only have a nice day tomorrow we will be all set. We have had so many miserable Sundays. Had just came over for a few minutes. He wanted me to go home with him. Have quite some work to do yet on the line, writing besides, then I am going up tomorrow for supper.
>
> I don't want to rub it in. If I get there in time, after supper may run over to a movie or vaudeville. This warm weather does not give one a lot of pep. I feel tired when the day is up. Tonight you go to R's party. Hope you have a lovely time, and have one for me.
>
> But see that you behave yourself. I want to call up Eve tomorrow and see her before I leave, as I haven't seen her since Christmas.
>
> I haven't much news, so will get this off. Take good care of yourself.
>
> As ever,
Sincerely
Jud.

'A rather familiar letter, Mrs Snyder,' Carey pointed out.

'Judd's a good friend of the family. My husband liked him. They got along fine.'

'Who is the Had he mentions?'

'Haddon Gray, a relation of Judd's.'

'And Eve?'

'Just a friend, Inspector.'

Ruth Snyder was completely calm when she answered the detective's searching questions. She maintained her composure even when Carey informed her that he had reason to suppose she and Gray had been more than friends. He went on to question her about a glass found on the dining-room table that Sunday morning. There had been whisky in the bottom. Also on the table had been a bottle of whisky. It looked to have been a new bottle, but about five glasses had been poured from it.

She told him she knew nothing about the bottle. But her fingerprints were on it. Only hers.

While she decked herself in deep mourning for her husband Carey had a consultation with the District Attorney. The result was the arrest of Ruth Snyder and Judd Gray. Under severe questioning each grew scared of what the other would say, and agreed to make a statement. Both admitted collusion to kill Albert Snyder and make the crime appear the work of unknown burglars. Both put full blame on the other. Both hinted that they had planned murder before.

But from the statements a fairly accurate and utterly revolting picture of the crime's commission was obtainable. Ruth Snyder, in her nightdress, had stolen away from her slumbering husband to admit the night-prowling lover. Judd Gray believed he had taken care of a useful alibi by asking a friend in Syracuse to post a letter. The same friend had been asked to rumple the bed in Gray's hotel bedroom. In the Snyder living-room Gray had held the scantily garbed woman in his gloved hands and kissed her while she explained that during the afternoon she had brought the sash-weight from the basement. Gray took it from her, went into the bedroom where Snyder slept, and smashed it across the head twice. Then the plotters tied the unconscious man's limbs, pushed rags soaked in chloroform up his nostrils and in his mouth. Next the pair set to work on the furniture. When, as they thought, it looked as though the room had been searched, they returned to the living-room. Gray fidgeted, jumped up suddenly and produced the picture-wire he had brought. He went back into the bedroom.

Afterwards they sat talking about the future! Quite accidentally Gray noticed blood on his shirt. He went into the bathroom and took it off.

'I can't leave without a shirt,' he called to her.

She went back into the bedroom where her husband lay and took a freshly laundered shirt from a drawer. Gray donned it, and knotted his tie. The two then went to the basement, where the woman took off her nightdress, which was bloodstained. She burned the shirt and the nightdress. By six o'clock there was a hint of daylight in the sky. Ruth Snyder lay down, Gray pushed some cheesecloth into her mouth, tied her up, and then let himself out of the house.

In a prison cell, awaiting trial, he maintained he did this while in a hypnotic trance. But although in a trance-like state, he recalled that Ruth Snyder was with him in the bedroom when the actual murder was committed. She produced the chloroform. She had the picture-wire handy.

For a hypnotist, she did a remarkably poor job on Judd Gray.

The accused pair entered the court-room in Long Island City on a warm day in May 1927. A seething throng of sensation hunters pushed and strove to gain admission, to sit in the close atmosphere for hours while snarling lawyers fought over the prisoners like dogs over two meaty bones. Counsel for each prisoner tried to lever the responsibility, moral and physical, on to the other. Love-letters were read aloud. Signed statements and depositions were haggled over, contested, admitted, re-examined. Slowly, hour by hour, the halting machinery of the law ground towards a conclusion, while court-room reporters ran to and fro to telephone each news-break to their papers.

The public interest in the case shown throughout the United States was precisely similar to the interest created in Britain by the case of Edith Thompson and Frederick Bywaters five years previously.

But whereas Edith Thompson had crumpled with fear, Ruth Snyder sat throughout the hearing in an attitude of detached calm. Whereas Bywaters faced the inevitable result pleading his mistress's innocence and trying to save her life, Judd Gray endeavoured to unload all responsibility for the treacherous murder on to his paramour and to save his life at the expense of hers.

The trial might have been sensational from a newspaper reporter's view-point. Viewed impartially, it was a shoddy spectacle of human nature betraying itself. The love the killers had known for each other had been a tawdry, fleshly business mantled in sad shame. In the shadow of death their stature shrank. They hated themselves and each other.

The District Attorney became scathing in his denunciations. He poured contumely on their threadbare pretence and transparent artifice. He bared their lies and mocked their uncloaked deceit.

Gray, in evidence, made point of having wrapped some paper around the sash-weight with which he battered Snyder's head. He felt that then it would not give the victim quite so much pain.

'It reminds me of the old woman,' cried District Attorney Newcombe, 'who, out of the same feeling of kindness, warmed the water in which she drowned the kittens.'

The grim-faced judge could not prevent laughter rippling across the court. But it was the kind of laughter that sounds like teeth chattering.

The prisoners were found guilty and sentenced to death. Shock unnerved Ruth Snyder. She fell in tears as hands reached out to support her.

Judd Gray, the bawdy-minded corset salesman, produced a prayer-book from his pocket and opened it. Whatever impression his reading from it was calculated to produce was spoiled as he was hustled away. The State of New York would provide ample time later for his prayers.

Lawyers fought an appeal, and lost. Months went by, and Christmas passed. On January 22nd, 1928, Ruth Snyder sat in the electric chair. At the same hour Judd Gray was to die.

Reporters watched. At a signal from the warden a switch was thrown. A blue flame seemed to dance across her head. There was a faint hissing sound.

One reporter turned away quickly, his stomach unable to take the sight without rebelling. Another released the shutter of a camera concealed in his clothing. The day she died the woman who had a passion for bright lights and dance music made the front page and shocked a nation for the last time.

Tom Gurr and H. H. Cox

DEATH IN A CATHEDRAL CITY

Christchurch is as English as a muffin. English cars are parked neatly in the square, across which falls the pointed shadow of the soaring spire of the cathedral. From the cars step red-faced hearty men wearing tweed trout-fishermen's hats and expensive but sagging suits of hairy-looking tweed. They hand out their ladies, who wear cashmere jumpers and tweed skirts and sensible shoes, and they walk into the hotels, the United Services and Warners, talking together in accents so entirely English that no county in all England can rival them for English purity.

These are the landed proprietors of the Canterbury Plains and their ladies, all financially comfortable after years and years of raising fat lambs for export in the best possible climate and on the best possible pastures. Transport them to the England whence their great-grandfathers came a century ago and more, and set them down upon landed estates, and they would become squires in a minute, and as naturally as breathing. Today they come into New Zealand's third city from their rich farms and they are happy in the Englishness of the atmosphere of the cathedral city.

In the spring, crowds of daffodils dance on the green banks of a winding little river, called, inevitably, the Avon, a river so English that you suspect it of being an art director's creation. The water, running crystal clear, is so shallow that the ridiculously fat trout have a hard time dodging the wheels of the bicycles which university undergraduates, their black gowns flapping, have a habit of riding along the river bed. Under the oaks, the willows, the planes and the beeches the roses riot.

You will see houses and shops similar to those of New Zealand's Christchurch in many an English provincial city, and when you are walking along the flat, tree-lined streets in the twilight, with the starlings twittering sleepily in the branches, you will experience the peace and the gentleness which you have felt in cities like Salisbury and Cambridge and Exeter.

The 'Canterbury Pilgrims', the 791 settlers who arrived here in 1848, found that Christchurch had been laid out for them with mathematical care by the founder, an Anglo-Irish Protestant named John Robert Godley, who, having selected the incredibly flat plain on the western side of the Port Hills, tidily staked out the home sites. From that day, everything about Christchurch had been tidy, from the street gutters to the thinking of the citizens.

Therefore the crime of the Murdering Girls struck Christchurch with cataclysmic force.

One was sixteen years of age. The other was fifteen. They wore the white blouses and blue tunics that were the uniform at Christchurch Girls' High School. Different as they were in family background, in appearance, and in manner, they were close friends, bound together, it seemed, in one of those intimacies which are so common among adolescents, which seem so tremendously important at the time, and which invariably end with schooldays. But this was no ordinary friendship. It was deep and dark, and it was to become terrible.

Pauline Yvonne Parker was the sixteen-year-old one, a dark and dumpy girl, five feet three inches tall, with cold brown eyes gleaming watchfully from her olive-skinned face. She walked with the suspicion of a limp. When she was five years old, she contracted osteomyelitis, as a result of which she spent several months in hospital, and for which, over a period of three years, she had a series of operations. While other little girls of her age were laughing and playing in the sunshine, little Pauline Parker had to lie in bed, weary month after weary month, and watch them through the window.

Because of her slight lameness, Pauline Parker at sixteen was unable to participate in the tennis and the running and the other sports at the girls' high school. Her friend and classmate, Juliet Hulme, owned a pony and often rode it when she came to visit her, and so Pauline had developed an interest in horses. Lameness did not matter, she said, when you are in the saddle.

For some time, she had been pestering her parents for permission to keep a pony, so that, like her friend Juliet, she could become a member of the Horse and Pony Club.

Pauline's father and mother said 'No'. Their daughter was becoming a constant worry to them. In the house she often pointedly ignored them. ('Pauline kept me out of her life,' the father said sadly.) She was constantly writing novels. One night, sitting before the fire, she volunteered that she was writing an opera. This was a rare kind of admission for her to make, but on this occasion, burning with the creative urge, she could not repress the information.

Then there was Pauline's friendship with Juliet Hulme. Pauline was crazy about Juliet, could not stop talking about her, seemed perpetually to be in her company. Pauline's mother and father could see all the factors which were responsible for their daughter's lack of progress at school. Possession of a pony, concentration on yet another craze, would result in marks even lower.

But Pauline had a pony! She kept it secretly in a paddock, had been keeping it there for weeks, ever since, with the advice of her good friend Juliet, she had bought it with money she obtained nobody knew where. That was typical of the slyness of the lame Pauline, who among other forbidden things had for a time been sneaking into a boy's bedroom at night.

When the news about the pony was broken to them by the dark and determined Pauline, her parents shrugged their shoulders in a resigned manner and agreed to let her keep it, seeing she had had it so long, and seeing, of course, that if they did not agree Pauline would metaphorically tear the house down.

And all Pauline's parents wanted was a happy home. They had been through so much trouble together during their twenty-three years as man and wife, had had so many difficulties to overcome.

In the first place, they were not married. The obstacle to the performance of a formal ceremony of marriage was not stated during the progress of the Christchurch case. Whatever the reason, the parents of Pauline Parker, in an extraordinary gesture of honesty, proclaimed the irregularity of their union for all the world to see. On the front door of the near-white painted house in a Christchurch suburb, the ground floor of which was their home, there was a carefully lettered notice: 'Mr Rieper ... Mrs Parker.'

Herbert Rieper, a gentle, pipe-smoking, carpet-slippered little man, owned a reasonably successful wholesale fish business in Christchurch city. Honora Mary Parker had been a good and loving wife to him. They had had four children. The eldest was eighteen-year-old Wendy, who had been no trouble at all to them, and who was an affectionate daughter. Then there was Pauline, over whom they had had all the worry and expense when she had the bad time with osteomyelitis as a little girl, and who, now that she was sixteen and had her head full of strange ideas, was still a worry.

There had been two others, and they didn't like to think about them. One had been a mongoloid, a flat-faced, drooling imbecile, who had been placed in an institution. And the fourth child had been born a 'blue baby', with a congenital heart defect. Mercifully it had died.

Pauline's schoolmate, Juliet Hulme, was the biggest worry of all for Herbert Rieper and Honora Mary Parker. The two girls were crazy about each other. They used to sprawl on the lawn of the Hulme home and write 'books' together. They had all kinds of secrets. It seemed they could not bear to be away from each other. Their mutual affection was so intense that it seemed to be abnormal. Mrs Parker had taken Pauline to Dr Bennett, and while their daughter waited in the consulting room had told him all about the friendship. The doctor had had Pauline into the surgery, and had examined her and talked to her.

When the mother suggested that Pauline should leave the high school, and go to another school where her progress might be better, Pauline surprisingly agreed.

And then, one day, Juliet's father called at the house, and said he was leaving New Zealand and was taking Juliet with him. This was the happiest news that Herbert and Honora Mary had heard for many a day. To Pauline, it meant disaster.

Juliet Hulme. Fifteen years of age. Tall for her age, five feet seven inches, and slim. Shoulder-length light brown hair. The clear pink-and-white complexion of an English hedge rose – Juliet was an English girl, bomb-shocked in the blitz at the age of two. Slanting grey eyes, the clear eyes of youth; high forehead; a slim and graceful body, and a confident air. Now she was intelligent and attractive. Soon she would be intelligent and beautiful.

Juliet Hulme (pronounced, in the English manner, Hume) was an intellectual, born and bred. The tall and stooping figure of her father, bespectacled, forty-six-year-old Dr Henry Rainsford Hulme, had been a familiar one during World War II in the corridors of the War Office. One of England's leading mathematical scientists, he was one of two 'boffins' who worked out the degaussing method which countered the German magnetic mine.

After the war, young Dr Hulme was being regarded as one of England's bright minds in the atomic era when he dismayed his colleagues by announcing that he was going to New Zealand to the £2,200 a year post of Rector of Canterbury University College at Christchurch, and to membership of the Senate of New Zealand University. Hulme was not running away from his work in atomic research because of ideological or any other reservations. He was leaving for the single and simple reason that his elder child, Juliet (there was a son, Jonathan, five years younger) was threatened with active tuberculosis. Doctors felt that the clear air of 'the colonies', away from industrial smog would benefit the girl tremendously. With his coolly aristocratic wife, Hilda Marion, and the children, Hulme arrived in New Zealand in 1948.

Early in 1953 they put Juliet in hospital. After four months' treatment she was discharged, but not as cured.

If there is any overseas city in which an expatriate Englishman can feel at home it is surely the cathedral city of Christchurch. Dr Hulme lived in a sixteen-roomed stone mansion with extensive grounds, called 'Ilam'. His salary, by New Zealand standards, was a good one. His wife, Hilda, was prominent in welfare work and in cultural movements. And his position as Rector of the university college established him in the front rank of the honoured citizens of Christchurch. The Anglican Bishop was one of his best friends.

Then Walter Andrew Bowman Perry, another Englishman, arrived in Christchurch, and the relationship between Henry and Hilda Hulme was never the same again.

Big, moustached Perry was an engineer, and a man of considerable charm. He was in Christchurch on a prolonged business visit, and, like the Hulmes, was interested in sociology. He promised to assist them in the conduct of a marriage guidance bureau. When the Hulmes suggested he might be more comfortable in a self-contained flat which was part of 'Ilam', he was glad to move in. At the beginning, they were all friends together, the donnish Rector, the calm and queenly Mrs Hulme, the lively young Jonathan, and Juliet. The latter could quote pages of the classical poets, knew something about good music, could model in clay like a born artist, could embroider like a maiden aunt or a ship's captain, and also wrote. A brilliant girl, Juliet. All of a sudden, like other brilliant people, this fifteen-year-old girl lost one of her enthusiasms: she had decided that riding no longer interested her, and wanted to sell her horse. The obliging Perry was glad to buy it for £50 from his little friend, who now had a secret reason for getting all the money she could.

Then, one afternoon, Juliet found her mother and Walter Andrew Bowman Perry in bed together. And, shortly afterwards, Dr Hulme resigned the rectorship of the university college to return to England, where his outstanding scientific talent was required in the British atomic research team led by Sir William Penney. He would, he told friends, take Jonathan with him. Mrs Hulme, however, would remain with Juliet: 'The girl's lungs aren't too strong, you know, and the English winter . . .'

Then the Hulmes, who had been aware of, and disturbed by, their daughter's obsession with her friend, the daughter of the fish-shop proprietor, made an alarming discovery. Juliet and the dumpy Parker girl, who often came to stay with Juliet at weekends, had written what they called 'novels'. Well, adolescents did things like that. But the alarming fact was, the girls had decided to go to America to sell their novels there. And, as everybody knew, they were two very determined young ladies. Their friendship could be quite unhealthy. Twice, Dr Hulme had called on that quiet fish-man, Rieper, and talked to him about it. In the circumstances, it would be an excellent plan to separate the girls before something embarrassing happened.

And so, Dr Hulme told Juliet he intended to take her with him and Jonathan as far as South Africa. She could return alone to her mother in Christchurch. (Looming over this father-daughter discussion was the affair between Perry and Mrs Hulme, which the father guessed at, and the daughter, on the evidence of her own eyes, knew about. But neither admitted it to the other. The relationship between a forty-six-year-old father and a bright fifteen-year-old daughter is not always an easy one.)

Juliet's reaction was a flat demand. Her friend Pauline must go to South Africa with her. Impossible, replied Dr Hulme tetchily. Impossible, said Honora Mary Parker, firmly, when the two girls put it to her.

For Honora Mary Parker, impossible was a fatal word. Her daughter and her daughter's intimate friend were already planning her murder, with all the enthusiasm and excitement which two high-school girls might display in arranging the details of a school dance.

At 3 p.m. on June 22nd, 1954, a grey winter's day, Honora Mary Parker, Pauline Parker and Juliet Hulme left a refreshment kiosk in Victoria Park, on the Cashmere Hills on the outskirts of Christchurch. Topcoated against the cold, they walked down the track.

Juliet Hulme hurried along in front. Her hand in her pocket clutched part of the plot - a collection of brightly coloured pebbles, picked up by the roadside during the preceding few days. When she had rounded a bend in the track and was out of sight of the Parkers, she scattered the pebbles.

Pauline Parker, walking by her mother's side with that suggestion of a limp, also had her hand in her coat pocket, and also clutched part of the plot - half a brick, which Juliet had brought from her home to the Parkers' at noon that day. Pauline had slipped the piece of brick into the foot of an old stocking, thus making an effective sling-shot.

Juliet was sixty yards in front, and still out of sight down the track, when Honora Parker caught sight of a pink pebble, and

Pauline remarked how pretty it was. Honora bent down to pick it up. Behind her, Pauline pulled the sling-shot from her pocket, braced her legs and swung. The brick crashed on her mother's head, and she collapsed.

And that was the moment when Pauline wished it hadn't happened. But some force possessed her, drove her on, some inner voice which commanded: It is too late to stop! She struck again, and again, and now Juliet, panting from a sprint along the track, was kneeling beside her, and swinging the sling shot. Blood was spurting from twenty-four wounds in Honora Parker's face and head. Sobbing hysterically, the girls looked at each other and at their victim. The blood was only trickling now. They had beaten Honora Mary Parker to death.

The plan had to be completed.

Blood was dripping from their hands when they ran the four hundred yards back to the kiosk. 'It's Mummy!' gasped Pauline to the proprietress, Mrs Agness Ritchie. 'She's terrible! I think she's dead. We tried to carry her. She was too heavy.'

'Yes, it's her mother!' Juliet burst out. Her voice was breaking with hysteria. 'She's covered with blood!'

Pauline pointed down the path, in the direction in which the body lay, and as she made the gesture Mrs Ritchie saw that blood was spattered upon her face. 'Don't make us go down there again!' Pauline breathed.

And then: 'We were coming back along the track. Mummy tripped on a plank and hit her head when she landed. She kept falling, and her head kept banging and bumping as she fell.'

'I'll always remember her head banging,' cried Juliet dramatically.

While Mrs Ritchie called her husband, the girls went to a sink to wash the blood off themselves, and Mrs Ritchie heard them laughing hysterically as they did so.

Kenneth Nelson Ritchie ran down the track. Under a tall pine tree by the track, and lying on a bed of pine needles, was the battered body of Honora Mary Parker. Ritchie hurried back to the kiosk and telephoned the police and the ambulance. The police took the girls away, and the ambulance took the body away. Doctors counted forty-five separate wounds upon it.

* * *

Three weeks later, a magistrate committed Pauline Yvonne Parker and Juliet Marion Hulme for trial on a charge of having murdered Honora Mary Parker.

The trial was the most tremendous event in the history of Christchurch. In a city where Rugby Union Football seems to challenge Anglicanism as the popular religion, it drew to the court-room, on one day of the hearing, a crowd of beribboned supporters of the opposing teams in an inter-provincial match, Canterbury *v.* Waikato, who remained in court until within a few minutes of the game.

To the reporters who had flown in from Australia, to the Crown Prosecutor and the defence, to the jury, and to the people of New Zealand, stirred as they never had been before by human tragedy, one single exhibit was the core of the case. It was Pauline Parker's diary, and its contents, together with medical evidence and legal argument, which were to decide the vital questions: Were Pauline Parker and Juliet Hulme sane?

Most decidedly they were, Crown Prosecutor Alan W. Brown told the jury. Furthermore, they were dirty-minded little girls. The motive for the murder, the Crown Prosecutor said in measured tones, arose from the opposition of Mrs Parker to the girls' plan to go overseas together. Their friendship was one of intense devotion. They spent a good deal of time in each other's beds (but the Crown Prosecutor did not add there was no real evidence of any immoral physical relationship between them). They scribbled, said Mr Brown scornfully, what they called novels (so, the Crown Prosecutor did not see fit to remark, have thousands of adolescents, some of whom eventually have become novelists, some of whom have become lawyers).

'You may feel pity for these girls, but pity and sentiment have no part in British justice,' declaimed the Crown Prosecutor to the twelve in the jury box.

And so, clearly and dispassionately, Crown Prosecutor Brown described the crime, and the confessions of Pauline Parker and Juliet Hulme, made shortly after its commission, to Senior Detective Macdonald Brown. Revealing passages of these statements to the police were:

From Juliet Hulme's: 'I gave the brick to Pauline. . . . I know it was put in the stocking. . . . I wasn't quite sure what was going to happen when we went to Victoria Park. I thought we might have been able to frighten Mrs Rieper [Parker] with the brick, and she would have given her consent for me and Pauline to stay together. I saw Pauline hit her mother with the brick in the stocking. I took it and hit her, too. After the first blow was struck, I knew it would be necessary for us to kill her. I was terrified, hysterical.'

From Pauline Parker's: 'I killed my mother. Had made up my mind to do it some days before. I don't know how many times I hit her; a great many, I imagine.'

The Crown Prosecutor produced the diary which had been found in Pauline's bedroom. It was a bound book, with a space for every day in the year, of the kind so many business men used to jot down in outline the record of their activities. The entries were written in ink, in clear, adult calligraphy. The story they told was one of the strangest ever read in a court of law; it became a phantasmagoria; the twisted shapes of a disordered imagination seemed to swirl visibly in the heavy air of the court-room. And the two adolescents sat in the dock and listened to its recital with calm detachment. Pauline with a brown felt hat shielding her cunning brown eyes, Juliet, a pale green Paisley scarf tied round her fair hair, staring coolly from her slanted eyes at one person in court after another. From time to time, Juliet leaned across the wardress who sat between them, and spoke to dumpy Pauline, who did little more than nod in reply.

The diary was not put in as evidence in its entirety. But, as the prosecution and the defence introduced passages from it, the diary was revealed as one of the strangest and most terrible exhibits in criminal history.

The diary referred to Juliet by the pet name of Deborah, and revealed that Pauline was affectionately known to her friend as Gina. Mr Brown read these extracts:

'February 13th, 1954: Why could not Mother die? Dozens, thousands of people are dying. Why not Mother, and Father too? Life is very hard.'

'April 28th: Anger against Mother boiling inside me as she is the main obstacle in my path. Suddenly, means of ridding myself of the obstacle occur to me. If she were to die . . .'

'June 20th: Deborah and I talked for some time. Afterwards,

we discussed our plans for moidering Mother and made them clear. But peculiarly enough, I have no qualms of conscience. Or is it peculiar? We are so made.'

(The term 'moider' had apparently been acquired by the pair in reading crime fiction. It is the Brooklyn pronunciation of the word 'murder'.)

'June 21st: Deborah rang and we decided to use a brick in a stocking rather than a sandbag. Mother has fallen in with plans beautifully. Feel quite keyed up.'

'June 22nd: I felt very excited last night and sort of night-before-Christmas, but I did not have pleasant dreams. I am about to rise.'

And the top of the page for June 22nd was headed in printed letters: 'The Day of the Happy Event.'

While his daughter was in custody awaiting trial, Dr Hulme left for England and his new career, taking the boy, Jonathan, with him. Mrs Parker lay in her grave in a Christchurch cemetery. And so the parents who were left to stand the ordeal of the gaping crowds in court, and the verbal probing of the barristers, were self-effacing Herbert Rieper and cool, composed Hilda Marion Hulme. She, however, had a bulwark to lean upon: the sturdy Walter Andrew Bowman Perry.

Rieper had two significant pieces of evidence to give: at lunch on the day of the murder, Pauline and Juliet were in high good humour, laughing and joking; and in 1953 Pauline had been interested in a boy (later identified by the name Nicholas) who had been staying with them. Rieper had had to send the boy away.

At this time, the mention of Nicholas did not appear to have any particular impact upon Juliet Hulme, who was engaged in a habit she developed through the police court hearing and the trial, of trying to outstare the occupants of the Press box, one after the other. . . . But soon there was to be a violent reaction.

A sensitive and demanding girl was her Juliet, Mrs Hulme told the court in her serene English accents. Because of the active threat of tuberculosis, she explained, Juliet had had to spend quite a lot of time resting in bed. Her friend Pauline would keep her company, sitting at the bedside. Oh yes, she had read one of the books Juliet had written, and considered it quite ordinary, certainly not over-exciting.

When Dr Reginald Warren Medlicott, of the southern and Scottish city of Dunedin, was called to give evidence of his psychiatric examination of the accused, there began the real battle to decide the fate of Pauline Parker and Juliet Hulme. He had talked to the girls, but the diary was the basis on which the prim and precise doctor had formed his views.

Juliet, he said, had told him that Pan was the favourite god of Pauline and herself. The girls believed they lived in 'a fourth world', and their god was a more powerful version of the humans' God, having greatly magnified powers.

The girls, said Dr Medlicott, had extraordinary conceit. A poem written by Pauline Parker was an example. It was called 'The Ones I Worship'. The second verse:

> I worship the power of these lovely two,
> With that adoring love known to so few,
> 'Tis indeed a miracle, one must feel,
> That two such heavenly creatures are real,
> Both sets of eyes though different far,
> Hold many mysteries strange,
> Impassively, they watch the race of man decay and change,
> Hatred burning bright in the brown eyes for fuel,
> Ivy scorn glitters in the grey eyes, contemptuous and cruel,
> Why are men such fools they will not realise,
> The wisdom that is hidden behind those strange eyes,
> And these wonderful people are you and I.

How did the girls feel after the murder? Pauline, said the doctor, showed signs of remorse only when she told him that she now tried always to sleep on her left side. When she slept on the right, her mother 'seemed to come back'. However, the girls believed that by their own standards what they had done was morally right. Pauline had told him that she and Juliet were sane. Everybody else was off the mark. The views of Juliet herself were much more logical and sensible.

Early in January, said Dr Medlicott, Pauline wrote in the diary about Juliet having tuberculosis of one lung, and added: 'I spent a wretched night. We agreed it would be wonderful if I could get TB, too.'

On January 29th, Pauline wrote excitedly about the latest scheme. 'We have worked out how much prostitutes should earn, and how much we should make in this profession,' wrote the enthusiastic Miss Parker. 'We have spent a really wonderful day, messing around and talking about how much fun we will have in our profession.'

An illuminating episode occurred at this stage of Dr Medlicott's evidence. The doctor was being questioned by the Crown Prosecutor about the diary's relations of Pauline making repeated nocturnal visits to the bed of the boy Nicholas. According to Pauline, said the doctor, the boy had had sexual relations with the girl only once.

Sexual relations.... Juliet Hulme, sitting calmly in the dock, her grey eyes gazing calmly at the official court reporter, suddenly became aware of what Dr Medlicott was saying. She looked as if she had been struck across the face! Hands clenched, eyes flashing, face suffused, teeth bared, she leaned across the wardress and hissed, rather than whispered, to the dark and impassive Pauline. It was the reaction of a mother who has found her young daughter in bed with the butcher boy.

The motivation of the murder, as the psychiatrist in the witness-box saw it, was the girls' decision to go to America together to have their novels published. The first reference to the planned death of Honora Parker appeared in the diary on February 12th. In March Pauline was visiting shipping companies. On April 30th (and this was one of the most important entries, in retrospect, in the entire case) she told Juliet that she intended to kill her mother. Early in May, the girls began a campaign of shoplifting to get money towards their projected American trip. On May 27th, Pauline set out alone, in the early hours of the morning, to rob the till in her father's fish shop, but the sight of a policeman on the beat caused her to go home to bed.

The diary rose to a febrile crescendo. On June 19th Pauline

wrote: 'Our main idea for the day is moider.' (Always the Brooklyn rendition of the terrible word which Pauline could never bring herself to write.) 'We have worked it out quite clearly.'

Now the Crown Prosecutor, who was most ably following his brief, which was to prove that the girls were sane murderers, referred Dr Medlicott to an entry in the diary of April 17th. Mrs Hulme had been 'perfectly beastly to Deborah'. It seemed that Juliet had gone to Perry's rooms and taken a gramophone record. Juliet had had to apologise, and this made the friends feel very cross, so they went to a field, sat on a log, and watched members of a riding club. 'We shouted nasty jeering remarks to every rider that passed. About fifty did. This cheered us up greatly, and we came back and wrote out all the Commandments so that we can break them.'

Now back to the deadly month of June. Passages from the diary: 'We are both stark, staring mad.' And 'Dr Hulme is mad – mad as a March hare.'

Then there were the Saints, to which the diary referred several times. They were creatures of the imagination, based on film stars, of whom Mario Lanza was one, and the girls had spent a delirious night in bed, imagining encounters with seven of them.

Did the girls know the legal penalty for the killing of Honora Parker, Dr Medlicott was asked?

In the dock Juliet Hulme answered him. She drew her finger across her slim throat, and Pauline Parker looked at her from under the brim of her brown felt hat and smiled.

The girls, said Dr Medlicott, were mad. They suffered from a form of insanity in which two persons were joined in their instability – *folie à deux*. They were a couple of paranoiacs, as all the evidence had gone to show.

And in support of Medlicott, the calm and cogent Dr Francis O. Bennett went into the witness-box. Of all the expert witnesses, he knew best the characters concerned. He was the Rieper-Parker family doctor, and he agreed that Pauline and Juliet were paranoiacs who were cases of *folie à deux*. Seven months before the murder, both Dr Hulme and Mrs Parker had consulted him about the close attachment of the two girls. He had thought that there was a homosexual relationship between them, and naturally had suggested that they be separated. The next time he saw them was in prison.

'They suffer from paranoia,' said Dr Bennett, 'and follow delusion wherever it is. They become antisocial and dangerous. They think they are superior to the general race of man. Intellectually they are a little higher than girls of their own age, but they are not intellectual giants. They had delusions of grandeur, formed a society of their own, and lived in it. In this society they were no longer under the censure and nagging of mothers.'

Again the diary; for April 3rd, 1953. Dr Bennett quoted Pauline: 'Today Juliet and I found the key to the fourth world. We saw a gateway through the clouds. We sat on the edge of a path and looked down a hill out over a bay. The island looked beautiful, the sea was blue, and everything was full of peace and bliss. We then realised we had the key. We know now that we are not genii, as we thought. We have an extra part of the brain, which can appreciate the fourth world.'

The girls, Dr Bennett related in his steady professional voice, had bathed together, gone to bed together, had dressed up and acted together on the lawn in the moonlight. They had made a little cemetery, and in it they had buried a dead mouse under a cross. When the Queen visited Christchurch, they made no attempt to see Her Majesty.

The Crown Prosecutor: 'Is their relationship homosexual physically?' . . . 'I don't know. I'm inclined to think not.'

The girls believed in survival after death. Heaven was for happiness, paradise was for bliss. There was no hell, Juliet had told him in the remand prison. The idea was 'so primitive'. 'The day we killed Mrs Parker,' Juliet had added, 'I think she knew beforehand what was going to happen. And she did not bear any grudge.'

The Crown now called its own medical witnesses, first the senior medical adviser of Avondale Mental Hospital, Auckland, Dr K. R. Stallworthy, who had examined each girl four times in remand prison, who had read the diary, and who was quite sure that neither girl had a disease of the mind, and that each had known the nature and quality of her act. They had written down what was going to happen. They had given clear accounts of what they had done. They knew it was wrong to murder, they knew they were murdering somebody, they knew it was against the law. A primary request for paranoia was the presence of delusions, which he did not admit with these girls. Juliet's mental calibre was that of a highly intelligent person of much greater age. Pauline's intelligence was considerably above average.

Dr Stallworthy had no doubt there had been a physical homosexual relationship.

Dr James Edwin Saville, medical officer at Sunnyside Mental Hospital, had interviewed each girl five times. They were sane now, and they were sane when they killed Mrs Parker, he said.

Dr James Dewar Hunter, superintendent of Sunnyside, echoed Saville: Five interviews, same conclusion. Both were sane, then and now.

In his final address, Crown Prosecutor Brown pithily summed up his submission: 'These girls are not incurably insane. They are incurably bad.'

For Pauline Parker, Dr A. L. Haslam, a brilliant pleader, traversed the evidence of 'this rottenness, this disease' which had made killers of two paranoiac girls. And for Juliet Hulme, Mr T. A. Gresson followed the same line. He told the jury that in 'this appalling case' the girls were incapable of forming a moral judgment of what they had done.

The jury was out for two hours and thirteen minutes. The girls returned to the court-room simultaneously with the jurymen, and they smiled and laughed with the gallant disdain of the daughters of French aristocrats arraigned before Fouquier-Tinville. They took the verdict of 'Guilty' calmly. With an air of indifference, they heard themselves sentenced to imprisonment during Her Majesty's pleasure.

The crowd streamed out of the grey stone court-house.

At his home, Herbert Rieper sat by the fire and smoked his pipe and sighed. Dr Hulme, having taken his son Jonathan off the liner *Himalaya* at Marseilles, had reached England by a circuitous route. And in Christchurch, Mrs Hulme was changing her name by deed poll to Mrs Perry.

They sent Pauline Parker to Arohata Borstal, near Wellington,

New Zealand's capital city, and Juliet Hulme to Mount Eden, the grim prison at Auckland where all New Zealand's hanging is done, and where, in her first year of sewing uniforms, there were four evening executions on New Zealand's portable steel scaffold.

At Arohata, Pauline Parker studied for a year under the Government's correspondence school scheme. In her cell, she sat for the school certificate, marking graduation from high school, and passed.

On her first day in Mount Eden in her prison dress of blue denim, Juliet Hulme was introduced to the sewing machine, and to enable her to operate it more efficiently a prostitute prisoner was kind enough to clip her long, well-cared-for-fingernails. Alone in her cell, Juliet knits, writes, according to competent judges, brilliantly, and studies languages. When she refers to the murder, which seems to be fading from her mind, she explains that she participated in it out of loyalty to 'Gina' – her dark friend, Pauline.

And, though 'Her Majesty's pleasure' is generally accepted as a sentence of twenty-five years, it would not be surprising if that of the two Christchurch girls, Juliet Hulme will be the one who will serve a short sentence; and it is possible that, under another name, the world in time will recognise a writer of talent.

This assumes that Juliet Hulme's tuberculosis (a disease found often in cases of sexual divergence) has been subdued, if not conquered; that the New Zealand prison system provides psychiatric treatment of a kind which, extended in 1953 to both Pauline Parker and Juliet Hulme, could have taken them out of the nightmare world they were making for themselves.

When Mr Justice Adams passed sentence, a man in the public gallery called 'I protest!' An Australian editorial writer heard in the minds of thousands of others an echo of this cry against the sentence, but for a different reason: 'It is that two young human beings should ever be in such a way the victims of a dark conspiracy of circumstance so evil in its purpose and so appalling in its outcome.

'The psychiatrists will explain it all, however, and contradict each other in the explanation. Less knowing people will ponder upon the fact that it was the same world of the normal child's imagination which Pauline Parker and Juliet Hulme extended into a universe of sinister fantasy and gross design. They had vicious and depraved tendencies, and without each other they might have remained problem children; but their coming together, as if by the magnetism of some strange force in the hinterland of their minds, was a fatal conjunction of abnormality.

'Sane, legally, the girls may have been when, threatened with separation, they committed the murder, but it was surely the kind of sanity that mocks at all reality. The normal mind shrinks from the implications of this tragic story. In many other crimes, lessons of some sort or other are to be found. Here there is little but horror, sadness, and bafflement.'

Jay Robert Nash

A LITTLE WORLD ALL OUR OWN

There was always something a little odd about Charlie Starkweather. Not his all-American love of comic books, hot rods, and hunting; he did strange things.

Once when he was driving a garbage truck in Lincoln, Neb., Charlie sat behind the wheel and shouted obscenities at passersby.

(From this confession: 'The more I looked at people the more I hated them because I knowed they wasn't any place for me with the kind of people I knowed. I used to wonder why they was here anyhow? A bunch of goddamned sons of bitches looking for somebody to make fun of . . . some poor fellow who ain't done nothin' but feed chickens.')

Still no one suspected little Charlie would become one of the bloodiest mass murderers of all time.

Starkweather, nineteen, was infatuated with the James Dean image and wore his red hair long (by 1950s standards). Small, stocky, and pigeon-toed, he wore a cheap pair of cowboy boots several sizes too large, the toes of which he stuffed with crumpled newspapers.

His small stature kept him from dating girls his own age. So he selected diminutive Caril Ann Fugate for his sweetheart.

Caril Ann was only fourteen but well developed. She had a sexy, hip-swinging way about her. And she was a rebel, like Charlie. She delighted in telling her stepfather, Marion Bartlett, to go to hell.

Little Red, as Starkweather was called by his friends, and Caril Ann made a mumbling, awkward pair of lovebirds. Charlie was on the shy side.

Yet it was this withdrawn boy who would blithely slaughter eleven people and terrify the Plains States area in the late, wintry days of January, 1958.

A lone victim of Starkweather's wrath was gas station attendant Robert Colvert. Little Red drove into Colvert's station on December 1, 1957 and robbed him at gunpoint. He then drove the 21-year-old Colvert to the open plains beyond Lincoln and killed him, shooting him several times in the head.

The mass slaughter began in Caril Ann's living room two months later. Charlie was waiting for her to come home from school. He had brought along his slide-action .22-calibre hunting rifle, the one possession he was seldom without.

Mrs Bartlett was annoyed. She didn't like Charlie, and his fondling of the rifle made her uneasy. Suddenly she started shouting angrily at him.

As Little Red remembered later: 'They said they were tired of me hanging around. I told Mrs Bartlett off and she got so mad that she slapped me. When I hit her back, her husband started to come at me, so I had to let both of them have it with my rifle.'

Caril Ann arrived just as the argument began. She watched the berserk bantam saunter into her little sister's room and choke two-year-old Betty Jean to death by pushing his rifle down her throat.

Then she switched on one of her favourite TV programs while Charlie made sandwiches in the kitchen.

Charlie hid Bartlett's body under rags and newspapers in the chicken coop behind the house. He dragged Mrs Bartlett's corpse to an abandoned outhouse a few yards away and covered it with newspapers.

Next he dumped the baby's body into a cardboard box and joined Caril Ann to watch television.

(From his confession: 'Don't know why it was but being alone with her [Caril] was like owning a little world all our own . . . lying there with our arms around each other and not talking much, just kind of tightening up and listening to the wind blow or looking at the same star and moving our hands over each other's face . . . I forgot about my bow-legs when we was havin' excitement. When I'd hold her in my arms and do the things we done together, I didn't think about bein' a red-headed peckerwood then . . . We knowed that the world had give us to each other. We was goin' to make it leave us alone . . . if we'd a been let a lone we wouldn't hurt nobody . . .')

Caril Ann worried that relatives might show up. So Charlie wrote on a piece of paper: 'Stay a Way. Every Body is Sick With the Flu.' They tacked the note to the front door.

It wasn't long before Mrs Bartlett's older daughter stopped to visit. She thought the note fishy and pounded on the door. Caril Ann refused to let her in.

Puzzled and angry, the sister told her husband the fourteen-year-old was acting strangely. He called the police.

When officers arrived, Caril Ann again refused to open up.

'Everybody in this house is sick with the flu,' she said. 'The doctor told me not to let anybody inside.'

'He didn't mean your relatives, did he?'

'I certainly wouldn't let my sister come in here with her baby.'

Caril Ann played her role faultlessly. Perhaps, as her lawyers argued later, she was protecting visitors from the killer who lurked behind the door.

The officers were persistent. 'Why would your brother-in-law call us over something like this?' one asked.

'Ask him. I don't know what goes on in his head. He doesn't like me, for one thing. And he always has to be worrying about something.'

Two days later, Caril Ann turned her grandmother away. The woman angrily went to Lincoln's assistant police chief, Eugene Masters.

'There's something fishy going on,' she asserted. 'Caril's voice just didn't sound right, like she was covering something up.'

Two officers accompanied the woman back to the Bartlett house. Ignoring the 'Flu' sign, they entered. The house was empty.

At first they thought the entire family may have gone to the doctor. Then the Bartlett son-in-law, followed by Starkweather's brother, found the bodies.

Police quickly learned that Caril Ann and Charlie had packed bags into Little Red's hot rod and roared off. They ordered their arrest on 'suspicion.'

'Suspicion' hardened to belief when a gas station attendant in Bennet, sixteen miles away, reported Charlie and Caril had stopped for gas and to repair a flat.

Little Red bought a box each of .22 rifle cartridges and .410 shotgun shells.

On January 29 Charlie's car was reported to be parked next to August Meyer's farmhouse. Sheriff Merle Karnopp, with a large body of officers, crept up on the house at dawn.

'Charlie Starkweather!' Karnopp roared through a bullhorn. 'Come out with your hands in the air!'

No response. At Karnopp's signal nine tear gas bombs were shot through the farmhouse windows. The deputies moved in, guns drawn.

An officer kicked open a door and almost vomited. 'Starkweather and the girl are gone,' he told Karnopp. 'They left the farmer with his head nearly torn off by a shotgun.'

A short time later a nearby farmer, Evert Broening, found the bodies of Robert Jensen, 17, and Carol King, 16, shot through their heads in an abandoned storm cellar near the Meyer place.

Police figure that Jensen was killed for his automobile. Carol, the coroner reported, had been stripped naked and viciously raped before being killed.

(From his confession: 'I began to wonder what kind of life I did live in this world, and even to this day, I'm wondering about it, but it don't matter how much I used to think about it. I don't believe I ever would have found a personal world or live in a worth-while world maybe, because I don't know life, or for what it was. They say this is a wonderful world to live in, but I don't believe I ever did really live in a wonderful world.')

Two hundred lawmen combed the plains around Lincoln, but they were too late for wealthy industrialist C. Lauer Ward. A relative got suspicious when the businessman failed to appear at work; he found a 1950 Ford in Ward's garage in place of Ward's '56 Packard.

Officers broke into the Ward home to find Ward sprawled in the foyer with a bullet in his head.

In a bedroom were the mutilated bodies of Clara Ward and her maid, Lillian Fenci. Both women had been tied and gagged, then stabbed repeatedly.

(From his confession: 'Nobody knowed better than to say nothin' to me when I was a-heavin' their goddamn garbage.')

By now 1,200 men, including 200 National Guardsmen were looking for Little Red and his girlfriend. Charlie had made the Big Time.

Luck let Charlie slip through massive dragnets into Wyoming. Outside the small town of Douglas, he came on a car parked along the highway.

Shoe salesman Merle Collison, Starkweather's last victim, had pulled over for a nap. Starkweather sent a bullet through the window.

Collison, frightened, got up.

'Come on outta that car, mister!' Starkweather shouted, gesturing wildly with his rifle.

As Collison stepped out of the car, Starkweather pumped nine bullets into him, killing him instantly and blowing him back into the car.

'We got us another car, honey!' Charlie shouted.

(From his confession: 'People will remember that last shot. I hope they'll read my story. They'll know why then. They'll know that the salesman just happened to be there. I didn't put him there and he didn't know I was coming. I had hated and been hated. I had my little world to keep alive as long as possible, and my gun. That was my answer.')

The killer leaned over Collison's body and tried to release the emergency brake, but it was stuck. Passing oil agent Joseph Sprinkle, pulled over to help what he thought were motorists in trouble. Starkweather brandished his rifle.

'Help me release this brake or I'll kill you!' Starkweather yelled.

Sprinkle spotted Collison's body and knew what he could expect. When Charlie reached forward to help the oil man release the brake, he grabbed the rifle.

'You bastard!' Starkweather screamed. 'Gimme my rifle! Jump him Caril! Get my shotgun!'

The fourteen-year-old girl stared petrified as she saw another car, a police squad car, approaching fast, red warning light spinning. As Deputy Sheriff William Rohmer drove up, Caril Ann ran toward him.

'Help! It's Starkweather!' she yelped. 'He's going to kill me! He's crazy! Arrest him!'

Sprinkle tore the rifle out of Starkweather's hands and the killer darted for his car. Rohmer couldn't fire because Caril Ann was in the way.

The deputy threw the girl into his car and took after Charlie, radioing to police ahead. Another sheriff's car took up the chase at 115 miles an hour. A shot blew out the rear window of Little Red's car.

Outside Douglas, Wyo., Starkweather suddenly braked and staggered out, holding his right ear. 'I'm hit!' he squealed. 'You lousy bastards shot me!'

While Sheriff Earl Heflin held a shotgun on the killer, Police Chief Robert Ainsley looked him over.

'You're a real tough guy, aren't you?' he asked in disgust. Charlie had a superficial cut from flying glass.

At first, Starkweather tried to protect Caril Ann: 'Don't take it out on the girl. She had no part in any of it.' He shouted that Caril had been his hostage.

Later when she cried innocence and branded him a killer in court he turned on her.

'She could have escaped at any time she wanted,' he said. 'I left her alone lots of times. Sometimes when I would go in and get hamburgers, she would be sitting in the car with all the guns. There would have been nothing to stop her from running away.

'One time she said that some hamburgers were lousy and we ought to go back and shoot all the people in the restaurant.

'After I shot her folks and killed her baby sister, Caril sat and watched television while I wrapped the bodies up in rags and newspapers.

'We just cooked up that hostage story between us.'

As Starkweather had no mercy for his playmate in death, the jury ignored her plea of innocence. Caril Ann Fugate was sentenced to life in prison, though she continued to sob her not guilty plea as they led her from the courtroom.

Starkweather went to his death in the Nebraska State Penitentiary only a few miles from the shack he called his home. He entered the death room on June 24, 1959. Only hours before, the Lions Club in Beatrice, Nebraska had asked that he donate his eyes to their eye bank following his death.

'Hell no!' Little Red roared from his cell. 'No one ever did anything for me. Why in the hell should I do anything for anyone else?'

Starkweather sat down in the electric chair at exactly midnight, saying nothing. He wore a badly-fitted death mask that made the ritual all the more grotesque. Five jolts of electricity – 2,200 volts in each charge – were sent into his body and at 12:03 a.m. prison doctor Paul Getscher dramatically announced to witnesses present: 'Charles Starkweather is dead!'

Outside the prison gates, thirty teenagers in blue jeans and bobby socks milled around. A young girl stepped forward and told a reporter: 'Some of us knew him. Some of us wanted to be with him at the end.'

Malcolm Muggeridge

THE TERRIBLE FATE OF MRS STAUNTON

Mrs Harriet Staunton died in a room in Forbes Road, Penge, in the house of a Mrs Chalklin, at 1.30 on Friday, April 13th, 1877. Dr Longrigg, who had been called in the day before to see her, certified that her death was due to apoplexy, and precipitate arrangements were made for her to be buried. A suspicious circumstance was that the four persons who had brought her to Mrs Chalklin's house on April 12th did not remain for the funeral. As Mr Justice Hawkins put it later at the Old Bailey: 'They had appeared at nine on the previous evening; they had brought nothing but the woman herself; they took away nothing; they left only the dead body behind with directions for a funeral to take place in two days.'

These four persons were Lewis Staunton, Harriet's husband, and Patrick Staunton, Lewis's brother; Elizabeth Staunton, Patrick's wife, and Alice Rhodes, Elizabeth's sister. They were arrested and charged with murdering Harriet by starving her, with a strong supposition that they had murdered her child by Lewis Staunton by the same means. All four were found guilty and condemned to death. This sentence was later commuted to penal servitude for life in the case of Lewis and Patrick Staunton and Elizabeth Staunton, while Alice Rhodes was given a free pardon. She was pregnant at the time of the trial, the father of her child being Lewis Staunton.

Lewis and Harriet were married on June 16th, 1875, she being thirty-six and he twenty-four. Harriet was weakminded. The year before her marriage her mother, Mrs Butterfield, took proceedings in lunacy to get her certified as a lunatic. These proceedings failed. The bait, as far as Lewis was concerned, was certainly not Harriet's person; she was large and animal-looking, with black empty eyes and a coarse complexion. What he was after was her money. She had £2,500 in her possession and other reversionary interests. The £2,500 came to him when he married her, and he was able to dispose of the reversionary interests altogether, through his marriage, laying hands on about £4,000. He met her when she was staying with Mrs Hincston, a distant connection of Mrs Butterfield, and formerly Mrs Rhodes, mother of Lewis's sister-in-law, Elizabeth, and Alice Rhodes. Although he had been courting Alice he immediately transferred his attentions to Harriet when he heard how much money she had, and she fell in love with him at once - a little common flamboyant man, a clerk in an auctioneer's office, with restless hopes of getting on in the world. Harriet had always wanted to be married. Mrs Butterfield described how her daughter had often spoken of the husband and children and household she was going to have, and how she had not liked to check her. She married Lewis without her mother's consent.

They set up house in Loughborough Road, Brixton, and some weeks after their marriage Mrs Butterfield called with a view to making peace with her son-in-law. Lewis opened the door when she rang. There was no maid, and a number of rooms were unfurnished. When Mrs Butterfield asked Harriet if she was happy, she said:

'Pretty well, mamma, middling.'

She was not more then ten minutes in the house altogether, and left it full of apprehension. The next day she received a letter from Lewis telling her not to call again, and enclosing a note from Harriet to the same effect. She never saw her daughter alive again.

In March, 1876, Harriet gave birth to a boy. The nurse who attended her during her confinement stated afterwards that her condition suggested neglect. As with most weak-minded persons, Harriet easily neglected her person. She was like a child, requiring to be told to wash and change her clothes. Despondency made her careless and untidy, and without her mother to look after her she became dirty as well. Lewis, inevitably, grew to hate the sight of her. He had married her for a particular purpose, and that purpose was achieved. Her money had enabled him to leave his auctioneer's office and live indolently.

He invested it carefully, always prudent about money, and wondered what to do with himself, appalled when he remembered that his wife was an imbecile whom he daily found more repugnant.

His thoughts turned back to Alice Rhodes. How different she was from Harriet! How gay and vivacious and fresh! He decided to ask Alice to come and keep house for him while Harriet was getting over her confinement, and Alice accepted his proposal. They both insisted at their trial that their relations at this period were innocent. Evidence was produced, however, of Alice's nightdress being found in Lewis's bedroom, and of other suspicious circumstances, and it is probable that Lewis found relief from the horror his wife had come to inspire in him in Alice's arms, even when her heavy stumbling footfall sounded overhead and her meandering voice was likely at any moment to call him to her. There were scenes. Harriet was jealous. At times she showed herself unaccountably sharp. If her mind was undeveloped her instincts were not, and jealousy is a matter of instinct, not mind. It is an animal faculty.

Two months after the child was born the household, still including Alice, moved to Gipsy Hill. Lewis wrote to his brother Patrick – 'My Dear Bay' – about how Harriet was getting on his nerves. 'From the time she gets up in the morning until she goes to bed at night she does nothing but try to aggravate and make me as miserable as she possibly can.' There was no reference in the letter to Harriet having taken to drink, though this was the excuse afterwards put forward by Lewis to justify his treatment of her.

In reply Patrick suggested that it might be a good idea for Harriet to come and spend some weeks at his house in the country. He was living at Cudham in Kent at a house called The Woodlands. It was a lonely spot, some miles from the nearest village. Speculative builders were just beginning to cast an eye towards Bromley, the nearest railway station, and The Woodlands might be regarded as an outpost of Suburbia. Patrick was a painter by profession, and found great difficulty in earning a living. He had two children. By having Harriet as a paying guest, besides doing his brother a kindness, he would be augmenting his meagre income. She came to The Woodlands with her baby, Tommy, in August, and did not leave it again, not even to go for a walk, until she was taken to Penge to die.

The Patrick Stauntons gave Harriet a room upstairs, and at first she came down to meals, except to breakfast, which was taken to her by the maid, a distant relative of the family named Clara Brown. Tradesmen who called at the house did not know of her existence, except one, who saw her once come to the door, and heard Patrick call her back with:

'I've a policeman here, and if you don't go he'll run you in.'

Another remembered hearing someone walking about, and then hearing Clara Brown say:

'Go back, ma'am,' and lock a door.

In October Lewis and Alice came to live at a farm about twenty minutes' walk from The Woodlands. It was called Little Grays Farm, and consisted of some twenty acres of grazing land. Lewis rented it at £70 a year. He used to walk over two or three times a week to see his brother, and then would see Harriet too. She looked forward eagerly to these visits, for she still loved him. After her death this note was found in the sitting-room at Little Grays Farm, where it had slipped, unnoticed, behind a sideboard.

> 'MY OWN DARLING, – I write these few lines hoping this will find you well. Will you be down on Sunday? If not, I shall be disappointed. I hope to see you on Monday. If not, will you let me know when you will be down? Will you bring me a piece of ribbon. I have not had clean flannel for a month. It is time I should be at home. My boots is worn out. – Ever your affectionate wife,
>
> HARRIET.'

Another note, found among Lewis's papers, ended: 'Tommy is quite well, so good-night my dear and God bless you.' Her writing was huge, like a child's, and she could scarcely spell at all. For instance, she spelt 'collar,' 'colour.' Great pains had been taken and a lot of money spent to give her an education, but to no purpose.

It was thought in the neighbourhood that Alice was Lewis's wife. She called herself Mrs Staunton and received letters in that name. Perhaps because of the strange nature of their relationship – living together with Lewis's imbecile wife lodging with his brother a short way away – it continued passionate. When they were separated they corresponded affectionately, Alice in one of her letters quoting:

> 'Though absence parts us for a while
> And distance rolls between,
> Believe, whoever may revile,
> I'm still what I have been.'

and Lewis being indiscreet enough to write in one of his:
'There will be a time when Harriet is out of the way....'
First of all Harriet was treated fairly well at The Woodlands. Lewis paid a pound a week for her board and lodging, and as she was to be 'one of the family.' Gradually, however, she began to be neglected. Her presence at table became irksome, and it was decided to send all her meals up to her. These were sent up after the others had finished, and consisted of their leavings. If there were no leavings, well, it would not hurt her to go without for once. There was not a particular point when it was decided to starve her. It just happened that she often got overlooked, because they all hated the thought of her and wanted to forget that she existed. Then the idea that she might die occurred to them with a pang of hope. Were they to go out of their way to keep such a creature alive? What was her life worth to herself or to any one else? If she didn't eat, if she neglected her person, whose fault was it?

Mrs Butterfield gave them a shock. By chance she met Alice Rhodes, whom she knew through Mrs Hincston, on London Bridge Station, and asked her where Lewis and Harriet were living. Alice said they were living at Brighton. She told this lie, Lewis explained later, to hide the fact that she was living with him as his wife, and not because she was afraid of Mrs Butterfield seeing Harriet. Then Mrs Butterfield noticed a curious thing. She noticed that Alice was wearing a brooch that had belonged to Harriet. It was not a valuable brooch, but happened to be one that Harriet particularly liked. Mrs Butterfield felt certain that Harriet would not have given it to Alice, and determined somehow to see her daughter. She found out that Patrick Staunton was living at Cudham, went there, and was astonished to hear that Lewis Staunton and his wife had moved into Little Grays Farm. She called, but they would not admit her. She pleaded just to be allowed to see her daughter's hand on the bannister, just to see her handwriting, and she would go away and bother them no more. It was of no avail. She went to The Woodlands, but could get no information, and received a letter from Lewis:

> 'I hear from my sister that you called and wished to see your daughter. I only wish I had been there at the time. I will tell you once and for all that for your unnatural conduct she never wishes to see you again, nor will I allow her to do so.'

She approached the police, but they could do nothing for her. The child had been ailing for some time. Harriet was unable to feed him or look after him properly, and one evening Patrick took him to Guy's Hospital, where he died the same night. The cause of his death was starvation and neglect – not uncommon enough among babies brought in at that time to surprise or arouse the suspicions of the hospital authorities. Lewis called the next day and was told of the baby's death. He gave his name as Harris, said that the baby belonged to an employee of the firm to which he belonged, and left twenty-five shillings to pay the funeral expenses.

Harriet's own condition was becoming critical. She scarcely ate anything at all, even when food – often no more than a dry crust – was taken to her. She never washed or had clean clothes. The state of her room was indescribably filthy, its single window boarded up. In this dark room she lived like an animal, no longer able to articulate at all, occasionally making strange noises, scarcely noticing the passage of time, whether it was light or whether it was dark. If she had not had a particularly robust constitution she would have died long before she did. It was noticed, when her dead body was examined, that the soles of her feet were horny, suggesting that she had walked about without shoes or stockings for some considerable time, and that her real and false hair were so matted together that they could not be separated. The false hair was a relic of the time when she had been noticeably vain about her appearance, loving bright-coloured dresses and large flamboyant jewellery – a taste that made it easy for Lewis to find a way to her heart.

What were they to do about her? They did not discuss the question, and decide 'Let her die.' They reached this conclusion each one separately, and spoke it with their looks. Even Clara Brown, the maid, reached the same conclusion. Harriet was friendless. She had none even to pity her occasionally, and to do her an occasional kindness. She was just something horrid that unfortunately existed, and that would soon, to every one's relief, cease to exist. Alice's pregnancy gave Lewis a particular reason for wanting her to die soon.

It would be highly inconvenient if she died in the house. A doctor would have to be called in, and might ask awkward questions. The conditions in which she had lived would become known, and perhaps an inquest be ordered. They decided to take her to Penge to die. Accommodation was arranged in Mrs Chalklin's house, a bedroom and a sitting-room at fifteen shillings a week. They told Mrs Chalklin that the accommodation was for a lady who was quite healthy, but who could not be persuaded to eat. They were bringing her to Penge, they said, so as to be near good medical advice, and asked Mrs Chalklin to recommend a doctor. She recommended Dr Longrigg, whom Lewis saw, telling him that he would be asked to attend a lady who had lost the use of one side, and who was 'thin but hearty.' They then went back to Cudham to fetch Harriet.

She had not left the house since the previous summer when she first arrived there. It was spring now, early April. No attempt was made to tidy her up for the journey, though shoes were found for her. A porter who helped her into the train at Bromley railway station noticed that one of them slipped off. He found the other one on the platform after the train had gone. She had grown unaccustomed to wearing shoes. When they arrived at Penge they took her in a cab to Forbes Road. She was supported on either side by the two men, almost carried by them, and the two women followed along behind. Mrs Chalklin was astonished at her aged appearance, since she had understood that the lady who was to occupy her rooms was Lewis's wife. When she spoke out about this Alice said Harriet was Lewis's mother, not wife.

They had brought a hamper of food with them, but no linen. Mrs Chalklin boiled eggs and made a pot of tea, and Harriet was put to bed. When Mrs Chalklin came in to clear away she saw a half-eaten egg and an empty cup by Harriet, who seemed to be in a stupor. After Harriet's bed had been made up, Lewis went off to see Dr Longrigg, but he was out. Elizabeth and Alice spent the night with Harriet, Elizabeth sharing her bed and Alice sleeping in an arm-chair. Patrick and Lewis stayed in an hotel. Seeing how ill Harriet seemed, Mrs Chalklin suggested that, Dr Longrigg being out, another doctor should be fetched, but Elizabeth said it was not necessary, and Alice agreed.

The next morning (Friday, April 13th), however, they told Mrs Chalklin that Harriet had taken a turn for the worse, and an urgent summons was sent to Dr Longrigg. He sent a nurse and came himself at about ten o'clock. He saw at once that Harriet's condition was critical, and told Lewis and Patrick, when they arrived at noon, that she was unlikely to live another twenty-four hours. The nurse sat with her, noticing how emaciated she was, and her verminous condition; the others sat in the sitting-room, not talking, occasionally one or other of them looking out of the window, waiting. At one o'clock the nurse put her head into the sitting-room to say that Harriet was dying, and that if Lewis wished to be with her when she died he must come without delay. He did not move. At 1.30 Harriet died.

Now the four in the sitting-room got busy. The legal formalities of death were complied with, if not the emotional ones. An undertaker's assistant was in the house half an hour after Harriet had breathed her last; Dr Longrigg signed a death certificate, and the certificate was handed in at the Registrar's office; the nurse was instructed to lay out the body, and was given the key to the room where it lay with instructions to admit no one except the undertaker. The funeral was to be inexpensive but adequate. Its cost was estimated at £9 6s. 0d. If it had been possible Lewis would have had Harriet buried on the Saturday, but the undertaker said that was too short notice, and the funeral was fixed for Monday.

What did they think on their way back to Cudham? Were they exultant? – see her no more, hear no more the strange inarticulate noises she made, no more have a sharp pang of anxiety at the thought of her living, bare-footed and hungry and filthy, in her boarded-up room, whose stench they caught sometimes as they passed by her door. Or were they still uneasy, longing for Monday, when their last doubt would be laid to rest? Did it occur to them now for the first time that they had in effect murdered Harriet? It is doubtful. They so loathed her, had come so little to think of her as a human being like themselves, that murdering her was as inconceivable as murdering a toad. She had been an obstacle to their happiness and contentment. Now she was no longer. She had been an unpleasant appendage to four thousand pounds, and now the appendage was removed and they could enjoy the four thousand pounds to the full. Lewis would be able to marry his Alice, their child be legitimate, and the two households be happy separately and in their relations with one another. They all went to Little Grays Farm, having a distaste for The Woodlands until after Monday. After Monday the little upstairs room could be scrubbed out (it would take some scrubbing), the board knocked away from the window and the spring sunshine let in.

At Penge things were happening. The nurse who had been left to lay out the body and make arrangements for the funeral felt uneasy about the whole affair. There was Harriet's filthy condition (she was more than ever shocked by it when she came to lay her out), and the surprising indifference of her relatives, not even bothering to stay for the funeral; there was the body's terrible emaciation, and the peculiar circumstances of Harriet being brought to Penge, where she knew no one, the day before her death. Lewis had told Dr Longrigg that at Cudham she had been attended by Dr Creasy. The state she was in did not suggest that she had been attended by any one at all for months and months. They had not even brought sheets for her. For the laying out the nurse had borrowed two old ones from Mrs Chalklin.

The nurse talked. She dropped hints that although Dr

Longrigg had given a death certificate things looked very strange. Mrs Chalklin talked, the undertaker talked. This talk got round to someone who knew Mrs Butterfield, and had heard about Harriet's marriage. A wire was sent to Mrs Butterfield. She came to Penge with her son, lodged information with the police, and an order was issued for the funeral to be stopped.

Most murderers – at least most murderers who are caught – make mistakes. They are surprisingly obtuse as well as subtle. The mistake made by Lewis Staunton and his brother and sister-in-law and mistress was in going back to Cudham as soon as Harriet died. If they had remained for the funeral, and made some attempt to play the part of bereaved persons, themselves laying out Harriet's dead body, and watching by it, suspicion would not have been aroused and Dr Longrigg not have withdrawn the death certificate he had signed. Even if they had made some attempt to clean Harriet up before bringing her to Penge their crime might never have been discovered. They were so careless. It was so obvious that they just wanted to see the last of her. Their utter indifference was so apparent. They had grown so used to forgetting about her that it somehow never crossed their minds that in the eyes of the law she might be of some account.

Lewis's greed and social pretentiousness – perhaps more that than greed – had led him to do violence to his nature. He had made love with loathing in his heart, even begotten a child out of loathing. It had been worth it for £4,000, but he could not do more than he had bargained for. He had bargained to pretend to love what was hateful for £4,000; he could not be expected, without further payment, to mourn when he felt no grief, only unutterable relief.

A post-mortem examination was ordered, and it was found that Harriet weighed five stone instead of, as she should have according to her height, between nine and ten stone. There were no signs of poisoning or alcoholism. The state of her organs suggested protracted under-nourishment, and the condition of her body protracted neglect. At the inquest the Coroner sat with a jury, whose verdict led to Lewis and Alice and Patrick and Elizabeth being arrested and charged with Harriet's murder. The Woodlands and Little Grays Farm were searched, and the condition of the room in which Harriet had lived was revealed. It was found that, besides being dark and unventilated and filthy, no fire had been lit there, even in the middle of winter. Public indignation was aroused, especially in Penge; and the newspapers sent special reporters down to Cudham, interviewed whoever was even remotely connected with the prisoners, and tried to piece together the whole story of the crime.

A key witness was Clara Brown, since she was practically the only person, apart from the prisoners, who had seen Harriet after she came to Cudham. The first statement she made agreed roughly with the prisoners' account of what had happened. She said that Harriet had been difficult, and although treated kindly by Patrick and Elizabeth, had refused to eat. She supported them when they said that she had been given to excessive drinking, and that this was the reason Lewis had boarded her out with his brother and sister-in-law. As for food, she insisted that plenty had been provided. On the Tuesday before she was moved to Penge there had been fowl, on Wednesday steak. Then she suddenly collapsed, saying that in her statement to the police she had only said what the prisoners had told her to say, and that now she wished to tell the truth.

It was her evidence which revealed the full horror of what had taken place, and which revolted all who read or heard it. On her own admission she had committed perjury once, and in his summing-up the judge warned the jury against accepting any of her statements unless corroborated. At the same time, her account of Harriet's life at The Woodlands was convincing. It fitted in with what other evidence there was – the tradesman who had seen Harriet come to the door and be pushed back by Patrick with 'I've a policewoman here and if you don't go he will run you in'; the two maids from nearby houses who had once spent an evening with Clara Brown at The Woodlands when Patrick and Elizabeth were away, and who had caught a glimpse of Harriet before Clara drove her back to her room; the porter on Bromley railway station who saw Harriet's shoe fall off and heard Elizabeth whisper to her when she made a strange moan: 'You'll have your supper soon.'

Clara Brown had terrible things to tell. She described outbursts of savagery on Patrick's part, when the wretched creature confided to his care enraged him and he struck her brutally, and the threats they used to prevent her talking to outsiders about Harriet and the way she was treated. She described Lewis's visits, his callousness, and how Alice Rhodes used to wear a wedding ring and call herself Mrs Staunton.

The crime was so horrible that its possibility even had not been envisaged – a human being becoming an animal, padding in bare feet about a dark room, accumulating filth, never washing or changing clothes, forgetting how to speak, just waiting for food and pouncing on it voraciously when it came – and all for £4,000. The four prisoners, people thought, must be monsters, with nothing human in them at all. Even if they'd decided at all costs to get rid of Harriet, they might have poisoned her, or knifed her, or just had her put away in an asylum; but to kill her by inches! 'A crime so black and hideous,' the judge said, 'that I believe in all the records of crime it would be difficult to find its parallel.'

The defence took the line that there had been neglect, certainly; Lewis's guilty relations with Alice gave him a motive for wanting to get rid of his imbecile wife, certainly; but had there been murder? Could it be shown beyond any shadow of doubt that Harriet died of starvation? Might she not have died of, say, tubercular meningitis, encouraged perhaps by underfeeding and harsh treatment, but still the cause of her death.

The trial was postponed once at the request of the defence for the purpose of getting more medical evidence. A second postponement requested on the same ground was refused, and the trial opened on September 19th. The prisoners all pleaded Not Guilty. They hung together. There was no question of one trying to get off by giving away the others. Alice alone broke down and wept bitterly. The others were composed but dejected.

Perhaps the most shocking thing was that it was only as they became aware of the almost universal horror their crime evoked that they themselves realised its horror. If they had not been found out it is doubtful if the crime would have been at all on their consciences. They evinced quite genuine surprise at the public reaction to what they had done, so insensitive were they, so callous had they become in their dealings with Harriet.

The court was packed, and large crowds waited outside. For

several days medical experts were examined and re-examined. Their evidence was conflicting. No one could doubt that the prisoners were morally responsible for Harriet's death, but were they legally responsible? Cases were quoted of imbeciles who, having the best possible attention, died of starvation. The fact that Dr Longrigg had granted a death certificate (though later he had withdrawn it) suggested that Harriet's death might have been primarily due to natural causes. On the other hand, public opinion was solidly against the prisoners, and the judge's summing-up was against them too. The jury took only just over an hour to reach a unanimous conclusion, and the death sentence was pronounced.

Afterwards opinion veered round to a certain extent. A number of eminent doctors wrote to *The Times* supporting the arguments of the defence, and pointing out that sentiment had been allowed to overshadow the discrepancies of expert testimony; a committee was formed and certain points re-investigated, when it was found, for instance, that although, according to Clara Brown, Harriet had been kept locked up, the door of her room had no lock on it. A petition was presented to the Home Secretary, and only three days before the death sentence was due to be carried out, on October 31st, an announcement was made that in the case of Lewis and Patrick and Elizabeth the death sentence was commuted to penal servitude for life, while Alice was given a free pardon. After her short unhappy eminence life swallowed her up and she was heard of no more.

Judge Gerald Sparrow

THE PASSION OF PERVERSION

The trial of Ian Brady and Myra Hindley for murder, arising out of the sadistic torture of children from which they derived their sexual satisfaction, revealed the cruellest and most horrific crime of perverted passion of the twentieth century, even if we include the innumerable Japanese tortures of the Second World War and include the United States which usually has the ultimate in crime as well as in various fields of human progress. No other crime brought to light produced a couple as depraved, as sadistic, and as diabolically lustful as Brady and Hindley. The evidence was made more horrible because these monsters ran short of victims, and when this happened they played back to themselves the recorded tapes which they made of the live torture scene, including the growing terror of the victim, the screams for help, the slow and painful death, and their own sexual consummation. I attended the whole trial at Chester Assizes and when I heard this evidence given, like a number of other lawyers, press men, and authors present, I felt that the vicious young man in the dock and his mistress, who had the pallor of death, were still slaves of a satanism which sane people would never fully understand.

I stayed at Alverston which had formerly belonged to my cousin, and motored each day to the Court to be there in time to take the seat reserved for me before the entrance of the judge.

The figure of the Attorney-General, Sir Elwyn Jones QC, was instantly recognizable, for he gives the impression of being larger than life. This is a senatorial figure with *gravitas*. He has no pomposity, but he was very much the leading actor of this cast. With him prosecuting there were Mr William Mars-Jones and Mr Ronald Waterhouse. Brady was defended by Mr Emlyn Hooson QC, and Mr D. T. Lloyd-Jones, while Mr Godfrey Heilpern QC and Mr Philip Curtis of the Manchester Bar, defended Myra Hindley. Mr Heilpern seemed a taut astringent figure among the host of mellifluous Welshmen.

Then the great moment came. We rose to our feet and the judge entered. The Bar bowed, the judge bowed. He took his seat flanked by the high sheriff and the under-sheriff. He seemed almost incredibly small, but this was misleading. He was neither small nor insignificant. He was spare and neat and commanding, a man of few words, every one of which reached its target. Ian Brady and Myra Hindley were not going to have an indulgent judge in Mr Justice Fenton Atkinson. But they would have a fair one.

The young man described as a stock clerk and the girl with the ash-blonde hair who followed him into the dock were so typical in appearance of two modern young urban workers that the public, expecting perhaps something bizarre, were startled. They were the young couple one might see at the bingo club, the cinema, at the dog track, or shopping at the supermarket on a Saturday morning. But they were not such a young couple, nor anything like it. Their appearance of ultra-normality was misleading to an almost gruesome degree.

As we were sitting immediately behind the prisoners it was impossible to see their expressions and long experience of murderers had taught me that their eyes tell all. Within half an hour I made a move to leave the court as if to telephone. But I stopped under the shadow of a press gallery at the end of the row that contained the Queen's Counsel, the Attorney-General being immediately before me. From here I had a close and perfect view of Brady and Hindley. He was a spare, springy young man with wavy hair. He seemed completely detached, introvert, arrogant. In so far as he showed expression it was one of contempt for the play being acted around him. Myra Hindley's face was a mask. Her eyes showed no flicker of emotion. I had the strongest impression that Brady was still her god, or her devil. She was a shorthand-typist who had been accustomed to taking his dictation, and now she opened and snapped shut her shorthand notebook, taking copious notes of the trial. She was not disinterested. I looked at them harder, certain I had missed something: and I had. It was this. They had a secret alliance one with the other. They were not of our world. They had formed an unholy alliance to pursue a fiendish pleasure and it was we, the morons of the public and the law, who had stopped them. Every gesture they made, every grimace and change of expression showed that they regarded themselves as special people. It was we who did not understand, who clung to all the gibberish about God, and right and wrong, and piety and duty. Their world was different. Their world was one into which one was born briefly and must drink deeply. If this involved murder, what did it matter? We were all going to die anyway.

Thinking I had let my imagination run away with me, I consulted a very experienced reporter and a first-class criminologist at lunch, seeking his impression. To my surprise he said: 'My guess is that they are living in their own world and we don't mean a thing to them. And none of our gods are their gods. They are creatures of a force we do not understand.'

The case for the prosecution concerned three victims, though it was suspected that there were others. Because the case of Lesley Anne Downey was the most devilish, in a short account of this terrible crime of perverted passion I concentrate on this victim.

My note on the opening by the Attorney-General shows him outlining the case for the murder of this child.

> You will hear from the evidence that I will be telling you about, from which I submit the only inference that can be drawn is that before eight o'clock on Boxing Day, she [Hindley] and the accused Brady, in fact, had got that little girl, Lesley Anne Downey, inside the house and were taking photographs of her in the nude in the bedroom of the accused Hindley.
>
> It is just over nine miles to Wardle Brook Avenue from the fairground at Hulme Hall Lane, where Lesley Downey was last seen alive, a journey of about half-an-hour by car. Shortly after the disappearance of Lesley Downey, the ten-year-old girl was in the living room of 16 Wardle Brook Avenue with Brady and Hindley.
>
> Without her knowledge the conversation was being tape-recorded, and the recording will be played to the jury.

I submit it will be admissible evidence, because the voice of Hindley has been identified, and will be heard on the recording. You will hear Hindley inviting the girl to look at the local paper, the *Gorton and Openshaw Reporter* for 1 January 1965.

The headline on the front page was, 'Have you seen ten-year-old Lesley? Big search for lost girl.' On the page was a picture of Lesley and a photograph of police cadets searching the banks of the river.

On 15 October 1965, the police recovered two suitcases belonging to Brady from the left-luggage office at Central Station, Manchester. Among the contents were a number of photographs and negatives, and tape recordings, including one of an extract of a conversation between the dead girl and Hindley. Among the photographs and negatives found there were several of Lesley Anne Downey naked in various pornographic positions.

[Albums of photographs were distributed among the jury.] You will see from the photographs that the child had a scarf tied tightly round her mouth. In the first photographs there is something hanging down below the chin from underneath the scarf which looks like the corner of a handkerchief. She is wearing nothing but shoes and socks.

You will hear evidence from Mr David Noel Jones, Director of North-Western Forensic Science Laboratory at Preston, that from a careful study of an enlargement of the headboard of the bed and an examination of the headboard itself, there was no doubt that the bed and headboard where the child was, were in the bedroom of Hindley.

Mr Noel Jones also tested a camera sold to Hindley on July 1965. He is of the opinion that these photographs, in respect of which no adjective of the English language is appropriate, were taken with that camera.

You will recollect that I told you a little girl was aware that Brady had two tape-recorders. A recorder and a microphone were recovered from 16 Wardle Brook Avenue, and some tape recordings were found in the suitcase. Two of the tapes were recordings of the same sounds.

One of the tapes carried two separate recordings of the same conversation on two separate tracks. In other words, the police discovered one original recording, and two copies of that original made by someone.

Who? Who? Who could it be, you may think, other than Brady or Hindley or both?

You will hear the voices of a man, a woman, and a little girl. The little girl's voice had been identified as that of Lesley Anne Downey. The man's voice is that of Brady. The woman's voice is that of Hindley.

At some stage of this trial you will have to suffer the burden of listening to the tape being played and hearing the little girl's screams and protests.

[The Attorney-General invited the jury to look at a transcript of a tape recording.] When reading that transcript you will have noticed a reference to a man, a woman and a child: in our submission they are Brady, Hindley and the little girl, Downey.

You may think that the transcript shows that it was made on the day this little girl disappeared. She is protesting and saying that her mother expected her home – 'I've got to get home. I'll get killed if I don't. Honest, I will . . .'

That recording was taken before eight o'clock and the recording was also taken before the photographs because you have heard the voice of the man and the girl trying to get the child to put something in her mouth and pack it before she was gagged with a scarf.

If this little girl's mouth was packed in this way and she was then gagged it would, you may think, be a simple matter to smother her.

The scene evoked by the Attorney-General's words and by the transcripts was of such horror that the jury were transfixed. One felt that after this any additional evidence would be quite superfluous that nothing the accused might say would influence the jury one iota.

Apart from the actual playing over of the tape, this was the point in the trial where degradation, cruelty and evil seemed to sweep through the court, gripping us all. Reporters who had been in the business for a lifetime were visibly moved. It was a moment that none of us will lightly forget.

Sir Elwyn continued:

'After reading the transcript and seeing the photographs you may think that if this is what they did to this girl, they dare not let her leave that house alive . . .'

I looked at the jury. They had taken this without any reaction. They accepted this motive. These cold calculating killers had to cover up their awful deed . . . It would indeed have been difficult for the jury, horrified and angry as they must have been, to have seen that this was hardly likely to be the motivation for the crime itself. Though it might well be the motive for burying the body on the moors.

And then the Attorney-General, clinching the matter, said: 'You will in fact hear that the body of this girl was recovered on the moors and when it was recovered it was still naked. The submission of the Crown is that it was naked from the time the photographs were taken and went to its grave in that condition.'

Even when this evidence was being outlined, Brady showed no sign of fear or even of interest. He had heard all this before. Hindley buried her head in her hands and the curious pulsation in a vein in her neck was clearly visible. Apparently this only came in moments of tension. It had a curiously theatrical effect.

From this point the trial had a remorseless quality. One felt that no power on earth could stop it reaching its inevitable conclusion. These two would be convicted of the foulest of crimes but still, with the evidence mounting up ever more damning, the lawyers pursued their objective with undiminished tenacity. Something might go wrong. But nothing went wrong.

The climax of this ghastly trial was the playing back of the tape recording the torture and death of Lesley Anne Downey. She had been told that Brady only wanted to take some photographs of her. 'You are such a beautiful little girl . . .' But it was Myra Hindley who took her into a bedroom to strip her and gag her. Then she was brought down to the room where Ian Brady was waiting with his camera and his tape recorder.

As this particular tape was played back to the jury most of the women in court left. Those of us who stayed, who were concerned to see this horror, listened as Myra Hindley encouraged Brady to add tortures to the child's suffering. At first they played with her and when the child said, 'I have to be back by eight. Honest I do . . .' they laughed at her and said, 'Not yet. Not yet.' And Hindley, apparently revelling in every twist and turn of the obscene torture, said, 'Do you see the terror in her eyes, Ian?'

I think no one in court that day will ever forget the experience. The evidence was equally convincing in the cases of the other victims buried by the accused on nearby Saddleworth Moor. So their conviction and sentence was inevitable. They received it in their usual manner. Brady with arrogant indifference, Hindley with unconcern, her dead face changing not at all, as if she were living in another world. Perhaps she was.

What kind of persons were Ian Brady and Myra Hindley? Horrible, obviously, but how did they come to be what they were?

Although the psychiatrists are not agreed as to the real nature of obsessional-compulsive neurosis, they are agreed that most young men and women who fall victim to this terrible state have developed over the years a grudge against society. A great deal of research has been done in kleptomania and pyromania, but the old conception of mental illness affecting only one section of the mind, leaving the personality as a whole totally unaffected, has been abandoned. Modern psychiatry realizes that a person who develops an overriding compulsive urge directed against others cannot be regarded as otherwise normal.

Remarkably little research, considering the importance of the subject, has been done in the field of compulsive sexual perversion, but we know that like the victims of kleptomania and pyromania, the compulsive sadist achieves sexual excitement and perhaps satisfaction from his acts. Thus the act of touching and handling the forbidden goods in a store gives the kleptomaniac sexual excitement, and the sight of fires raging is the stimulant to the compulsive maker of arson. In the case of the compulsive sadist the results may be more hideous. Almost certainly the normal development of the man or the girl has been arrested, and cannot flow on in the normal course; it had been diverted into cruelty. The sexual act itself is usually an act of aggression, and the trade-mark of the perverted and compulsive sexual act shows this aggression greatly inflamed. Thus it is possible that two young people who find themselves diverted towards perversion may build up a whole secret life which is their reality, the object of which is from time to time to satisfy their craving which, of course, tends to increase rather than to abate. If we attempt to distill the consensus of psychiatric opinion, it seems fairly clear that the compulsive sadists will usually be or rather appear to be 'perfectly normal' when engaged in their day-to-day business. They will be extremely introvert, regarding themselves and their secret life as supremely important, and consequently other people as essentially unimportant. They will have no feeling whatever for their victims who have suffered pain or have been sacrificed to satisfy their perversion, and usually their background will be of the kind that one would expect to give rise to a certain amount of resentment and anger.

If these theories are valid, and they would seem to be, it is extraordinary how exactly Ian Brady and Myra Hindley fit into them. For instance, they never personalized their victims. The victim was always 'it'. Even the murders were 'it'. When 'it' was all over they would say, we did this and that. And their complete calm after the consummation of their compulsion is what one would expect from people suffering from this kind of coercive compulsion.

It does seem as if it is time that the law took a big step forward and attempted in conjunction with the psychiatrists and alienists to review the whole field of mental aberration in relation to crime. At present outright insanity is only admitted in law when the criminal has completely lost control, at all times, of this volition, that is he does not know what he is doing or, if he does, he does not know that what he is doing is wrong. He has failed to distinguish between right and wrong, being incapable of making this distinction. It is true that to this has been added the fairly modern doctrine of diminished responsibility, but by and large the medical realities that cover people like Ian Brady and Myra Hindley are not recognized by the law. This is a serious and important defect. It is no good saying that English law evolves gradually as public opinion demands. As we know more and more about the science of psychiatry, the law becomes more and more out-of-date. It is no good leaving the matter to the specialized committees who study legal reform under either the Bar Council or the Law Society, because we know from long experience that these committees are dominated by the intense conservatism of the legal profession. In the Postscript on page 262 this matter is explored more fully, but at least we have now indicated the answer to those who say: 'They must have been insane otherwise they would never have done these dreadful deeds,' and likewise the answer to those who say: 'Ian Brady and Myra Hindley were not insane. They were calculating and cunning murderers who plotted and planned their crimes with great care and who took great pains to cover their tracks after each murder.'

In fact, of course, the premeditation of the subsequent concealment of their crime is typical of the category of criminal we are discussing. They procured the body they needed. They used it for the purposes of their compulsion. Immediately 'it' was all over they calmly set about washing-up and tying up the body in such a way that 'it' looked like an innocent bundle of clothes. But during the hour or two or even longer that the compulsion was raging, they had lost their volition. They were the creatures of an irresistible power so that we get here the classic difference of view between the lawyers who see in Brady and Hindley calculated and cunning murderers, and the psychiatrists who at least understand something of the compulsive terror of the world Brady and Hindley lived in, and moreover believe that psychiatric therapy might be able to cure them. For cure surely is necessary. They have been sentenced to life imprisonment. If they are released after, say, fifteen years and have had no effective treatment will they not be perhaps as potentially dangerous as they are now? Is prison likely to make them less or more resentful towards the society to which they may one day return?

Turning over these approaches and speculations in an attempt to arrive at the truth, we now pass to the kind of people Ian Brady and Myra Hindley were.

Ian Brady was illegitimate, and started life in the Gorbals slums of Glasgow. His mother was a waitress. It was necessary for her to keep on working, so she handed her baby to a Mrs

Sloan who lived in Camden Street in the Gorbals. Mrs Sloan brought up Ian Brady with her own four children with great kindness. But the child seemed to resent from the beginning his fate, and he had an extraordinary record of cruelty from his earliest days. If he saw an animal, such as a dog or a cat, his first instinct was to stone it. If a playmate was weaker than he was, it was not very long before he or she was being either bruised or cut or burnt by Ian Brady. He went to Camden Street Primary School, and there is a story that he cut the heads off four white rabbits. This was not proved, but certainly he did bury a number of cats alive. So that the picture at this stage is of a most abnormal boy. He was quite intelligent, he could charm if he wanted to, but usually he did not want to. He did not mix well with other children, appearing to regard himself as a special person who knew things the others would not dream of. Perhaps he did. In 1949 he was entered at Shawlands Academy, Glasgow, and he had not been there long before he became obsessed with Nazism. He read all the usual Nazi literature and would give the Nazi salute. What appeared to appeal to him in the Hitler regime was the cruelty of the racial philosophy directed against races other than the purely Aryan. The beating-up of those who opposed Hitler gave him immense pleasure and, as a logical sequence of this kind of thinking, the comparatively compassionate welfare-state philosophy that prevailed in England moved him to contempt.

He began his criminal career at thirteen, and was placed on probation for two years for theft and attempted housebreaking. He was before the courts again the following year, again for housebreaking; and in the year after that, when he was fifteen, he was again charged with housebreaking and theft. But on all these occasions, presumably because of his extreme youth, he was bound over. In fact, he had become an expert thief and had acquired the skill in forcing doors, locks and windows which is the basic asset of the petty housebreaker. On the last occasion on which he was bound over, the court made it a condition that he should return to his mother, now married, because they felt that Mrs Sloan had too difficult a task in attempting to control him. Needless to say, Brady resented this intensely, but he had no alternative and took the train to Manchester where eventually he got a job as a stock-clerk in a reputable firm. There, Myra Hindley, a shorthand typist, helped him in his work, which was to complete the records each day, so that they would give an accurate summary of the stock remaining in the warehouse.

Myra Hindley was born in Gorton, Manchester, an industrial district which includes the Peacock Motor Works. She was born on 23 July 1942. Her father, serving in the army, was a Catholic, her mother a Protestant. After the birth of her sister Maureen, she was sent to live with her grandmother, Mrs Ellen Maybury, who resided in Bannock Street, Gorton. It is probable that living with an elderly person whom she could easily hoodwink was extremely bad for her. The death of a school friend in 1957 turned her towards religion, and she became a Roman Catholic and fairly devout. She seems to have had some small literary talent and her headmaster, a Mr Lloyd Jones, commented on this. But she spent her evenings either at the cinema or the bingo hall, occasionally, dancing. She became engaged to be married, but it came to nothing, Myra complaining that the young man was 'immature'. Probably she was very dissatisfied with life when she met Ian Brady and ready to discard the satisfaction she derived from her religion. At twenty-one she was probably subconsciously hoping to meet a man with a strong character, and Brady was such a character. There were no half-measures about Brady. The political aspect of his development was very much overlooked and underplayed at the trial. But the more we look into this, the more certain we are that this Nazi philosophy meant a great deal to him, and fitted in admirably with his sadistic sexual compulsion. He began drinking when he was about twenty, and was twice convicted of being drunk and disorderly. He does not seem at any time to have become an alcoholic, but he used alcohol for his own purposes. The only work that he could get at first was casual work in Manchester market. It was heavy and dirty and he loathed it. In 1959 he answered an advertisement for a job as an invoice clerk at Millwards Merchandise Ltd, a firm of chemical suppliers in Gorton. They offered £12 a week. Brady applied for the job and got it. He worked in a dark, somewhat smelly office overlooking a back yard which was crammed with chemical drums. Myra Hindley worked in a small typists' pool, the other side of the passage. Myra Hindley became attracted to the lank, laconic, six-foot-tall young man who daily dictated to her the details of the firm's stock. They started having lunch together. Brady introduced Myra to the books which fascinated him, political books on the Nazi regime, an apologia for Eichmann, a number of books on Hitler, including of course *Mein Kampf*. Myra read them all. Then Brady gave her books from his small library of erotica including *Justine* by de Sade and two excrutiatingly badly written books entitled *The Kiss of the Whip* and the *Pleasures of the Torture Chamber*. She also read at his command several rather better books on the history of torture and the cult of satanism.

Apparently this diet of sadism was exactly what Myra Hindley was seeking. With her square jaw and prominent forehead she had an almost masculine aspect, and during the time she was being corrupted by Brady, she acquired the language of the lorry drivers and porters who used to come to the firm carting chemicals.

Brady carried his fanatical Nazi theories into practice. He ordered a very large number of records of Hitler's marching songs, as well as records of the Nuremberg trial. But he remained intensely lonely, apart from his friendship with Myra Hindley. He did not seem to be able to get on with people, partly because he despised them. If Brady corrupted Myra, it appears to have been a reciprocal affair. She considered herself in love with him. The entries in her diary at this time contain such phrases as 'Ian smiled today.' 'Today he would not speak to me at all,' 'I wonder if he will ever take me out.' 'He is cruel and selfish, and I love him.' Her reaction to Brady's sadistic talk was to cap it whenever she could, playing that part of provocation which came naturally to her.

A Mr Clitheroe introduced Myra to the Cheadle Rifle Club of which he was captain. He arranged for her to buy a .22 rifle from some gunsmiths in Withy Grove. After this she bought two pistols, a .38 and a .45, probably at Ian Brady's request. In a period of less than two years she had forsaken her religion, taken to drinking with Brady, experimented with him in taking the more easily obtainable drugs, and completely changed her personality. Like Brady, she became completely indifferent to the feelings of other people, especially regarding any misfortune or pain that might come their way. Both of them developed the raucous 'anti-nigger' attitudes that arose out of Brady's political leanings.

In the autumn of 1964 Myra moved with her grandmother to Wardle Brook Avenue, and six months later Brady joined them. Grandmother lived upstairs and knew remarkably little of what was going on in other parts of the house. Myra had one weak spot, her dog called 'Puppet'. She was devoted to 'Puppet'. Her attitude in this manner was the only relic of her former self that seemed to remain with her. She bought a van and later a blue Mini shooting brake, and it is remarkable that the guns and car which Brady considered very necessary acquisitions were both procured by Myra. Nor was Myra without character. She had become a very heavy smoker, but she was able to break this habit by a sudden decision.

This was the background of Ian Brady and Myra Hindley. Undoubtedly it did nothing to discourage their anti-social behaviour but, in my opinion, it cannot be said to account for it. Ian Brady was bound over three times before he was sent to Borstal. He had an uninteresting but secure job which gave him the leisure he required, and Myra Hindley had never been really ill-treated by her family or by her friends. True, in both cases, the early fluctuating family background could have unsettled them, but it seems much more likely that sadistic perversions were deeply part of Ian Brady's nature, and that he met Myra Hindley at just that point in her life when she was prepared to throw aside the rules which had guided her, and plunge into the kind of pleasures that Brady offered.

Probably the fact that Brady does not seem to have had a normally happy friendship with any girl, and that Myra Hindley was unsuccessful in her only attempt to get married, accounts for a great deal. It is easy to read too much into the influence of environment; conditions far worse than Ian Brady or Myra Hindley had to endure, could have been cheerfully overcome by a normal young man or girl. Neither of them was normal and the growth of their perversion was accelerated by their meeting and later by their living together. We do not know if in fact they had sexual intercourse together. It is quite conceivable that they did not, for their lives began to centre around Brady's plans for acting out his own philosophy. As soon as he had conceived the idea that the infliction of pain brought the greatest pleasure, lovemaking in the normal sense seemed to him inadequate or unnecessary. It seems quite clear that Myra Hindley was able to follow the evil convolutions of his mind, and that she was an eager and only too willing tool in planning the murder of Edward Evans. Her remark, 'Did you see it? The terror registered in his eyes,' shows that she, as well as Brady, was achieving her sexual satisfaction from the horrible infliction of pain on the young man.

The rate at which their compulsive perversion grew might have alarmed them because, having found that what they wanted to do would lead to killing, they must have known that the dreadful game was dangerous to a degree. But, far from stopping they egged each other on.

The case of Regina versus Brady and Hindley will never be forgotten, but out of its ultimate evil some good may arise if both the public and the professions involved realize that it is a challenge to all of us. We cannot just sit back and regard it as an interesting and gruesome case. There was something basically wrong here. In murder at any rate, truth must come out. In the case of Brady and Hindley it had no opportunity to do so. This is the verdict on the Moors Murders. We must hope that before this crime or something like it is repeated, a full realization of the scope and horror of compulsive perversion will be achieved and effective reform will not only be debated, but will reach the Statute Book.

I travelled back to London with a friend who had covered the trial as a journalist. We compared notes and both of us felt that for fourteen days we had been in the presence of overwhelming evil. As the train sped southwards, the clouds lifted and the sun came out. It was a relief to rejoin the society of harrassed, preoccupied, cheerful, normal human beings again.

EDITOR'S POSTSCRIPT

Ian Brady was found guilty of the murders of John Kilbride, 12, Lesley Ann Downey, 10, and Edward Evans, 17, and received three life sentences which were to run concurrently. Myra Hindley was found guilty of the murders of Downey and Evans, and of being accessory in the murder of Kilbride. She received two concurrent life sentences and, on the accessory charge, a further concurrent sentence of seven years. Hanging had been abolished in Britain just one month before they were arrested.

The story did not end there, however, for as Judge Sparrow points out in his account above, 'truth must come out', and in this case a whole series of questions remained unanswered; questions which have nagged away at the nation's sense of justice ever since. There were more children who had disappeared during the period that Brady and Hindley were active, but despite large-scale searches on the moors and prolonged questioning no more bodies were found and no more charges could be brought at the time. But truth does eventually come out, and more has emerged, slowly and tantalisingly, during the years since Brady and Hindley were jailed.

To begin with, they were solidly together, Brady taking most of the blame at the trial and pleased that he had enabled Hindley to get off at least one of the murder charges, and Hindley stating from the dock 'I loved him. I still . . . love him'. During the committal proceedings they had tried to get married, and when they were at last separated in their respective jails they wrote to each other and petitioned to be allowed to meet again on the grounds that in common law they were man and wife. This was not permitted, and eventually the spell began to break. While Brady seemed to accept his sentence and suffer it fairly stoically (electing solitary confinement rather than suffer the hostile attentions of fellow-prisoners, who detest child-molesters and killers, and frequently attack them), Myra Hindley began to change.

Brady, isolated in Durham jail, went on hunger strike in protest at the authorities' refusal to let him see Hindley, but she had been visited in Holloway by Lord Longford and was writing to him:

> I wish I could put complete trust in God, but I'm frightened to do so for my faith is full of doubt and despair that I'll never be good enough to merit complete forgive-

ness. I don't think I could adequately express just how much it means to me to have been to confession and to have received holy communion. It is a terrifyingly beautiful thing – terrifying because I have taken a step which has taken me on to the threshold of a completely new way of life which demands much more from me than my previous one, and beautiful because I feel spiritually reborn. I made such a mess of my old life and I thank God for this second chance.

More hunger strikes from Brady produced no response, but he still wrote to Myra every week. In December, 1970 she wrote:

I feel so mashed up mentally that it is taking all my energy just maintaining my equilibrium and keeping my head above the waterline. The truth of the matter is that after only five years of a life sentence I am obsessed with an inordinate desire to be free. In other words I have rampant 'gate fever'. I've always lived with both feet well and truly inside the prison gates which is, I think, the sensible thing to do with a long and indeterminate sentence. But now, not only have I got one foot outside but, which is much worse, my spirit has left me and is hovering restlessly on the other side of the wall.

And in 1972 Lord Longford caused a national furore by suggesting that she was a reformed character and should be considered for parole. The British press made a meal of it, quoting the outraged comments of the murdered children's parents and relatives and carrying out unofficial opinion polls which found – predictably enough – that more than 90 per cent of the population felt that neither Brady nor Hindley should ever be released. A fair proportion also voted to 'bring back hanging.' All this abruptly scotched any idea of parole, and Myra reportedly hatched an escape attempt with a fellow-prisoner, which set her hopes back even further. In 1974, she wrote:

Something is slowly dying inside me, and it's the will to live . . . I don't know whether it's because of the acute depression which makes me feel, deep in my heart, that I'll never be released, or if so, not until I'm quite old. I feel tortured with grief and remorse about the disaster I have caused others and I can hardly live with myself. I feel I just want to drag myself into a corner in the dark, as does an animal when it knows it is dying, and if I had no moral responsibilities and didn't owe so much to so many people I think I could quite easily do so now.

Brady took a dim view of all this. He was deeply cynical about Myra's reported return to the church and scathingly sarcastic about it in his letters to her, and gradually the rift between them grew. It was not until 1978 that he made any public pronouncement about it, but when he did it was damning. Lord Longford had found Myra depressed, and told *The Times* that 'No-one who knows her seriously supposes that she would be a serious public menace if she was released.' Brady wrote:

Noting the alacrity with which the quality and popular press publish L.L.'s lamentably frequent utterances re the question of parole for Myra Hindley and myself, it is not widely known that he does not and never has represented my opinion on this subject.

Over the years I have repeatedly made strong requests, verbal and written, that he desists from publicly using my name in connection with parole. He has ignored all such requests . . . Lord Longford is well aware, as is the Home Office, that I have never applied for parole and have no intention of applying, and that I have always accepted that the weight of the crimes both Myra and I were convicted of justifies permanent imprisonment, regardless of expressed personal remorse and verifiable change.

From here on the two of them were adversaries, not allies. There were reported suicide threats from both of them, but as they grew into middle age they both changed. Myra's hair reverted from the bleached blonde to its natural auburn, she grew plumper, and she started regretting that she could never herself have a child. Ian Brady, the reports said, was deteriorating both mentally and physically. He had been a healthy eater but now (perhaps because of poison threats, real or imagined) he lost weight alarmingly and became increasingly remote, although he occupied some of his time in transcribing books into braille for the blind. Myra studied through the Open University and took a degree in sociology. Both were moved from one prison to another, Myra eventually being settled in Cookham Wood – an open prison – and Brady at Gartree in Leicestershire.

She was still trying periodically for parole, and was now condemning Brady outright:

> Curse all goddamned *bad* men . . . and curse the bad luck we women have – and the bad judgement – when we meet them and fall for them and lose our sense of perspective and just about everything else we have to lose.

Brady still refused to apply for parole, but he now had his sights set on being transferred to a mental hospital. *Sham remorse!* shrieked the newspapers whenever Myra made a move. *Feigned madness!* some of them now screamed about Ian Brady – although others took the line that only a monster could have done the things he did, and took a certain delight in portraying him as a 'gibbering husk'.

By the mid-eighties public interest in the case had, if anything, grown and matters reached a head when Myra began to show signs of responding to the pleas from the mothers of the missing children. Most commentators had always assumed that two children who vanished in 1963 and 1964, Pauline Reade and Keith Bennett, were victims of Brady and Hindley and that their bodies were also buried on the moors; tormented by uncertainty and – if the suspicions could be confirmed – wishing to give these children a proper burial, they pressed harder for an answer. Myra did help, and after twenty years the grim search on the moors began again. In a widely publicised exercise, Myra Hindley was taken by police back to Saddleworth Moor in an effort to pinpoint the site of the graves, and another body was found which was identified as that of Pauline Reade, who had vanished in July 1963, shortly after Brady had moved in to live with Hindley at her grandmother's house. Brady too was taken to the moors from the mental wing to which he had succeeded in being transferred, and he also tried to help, but memory had faded:

> It was weird seeing the place again, all that space and vastness. And when we reached the slope where Keith Bennett was I couldn't find the ravine.
>
> We searched from early morning till late afternoon, and I wanted to continue, but a police convoy picked us up and I kept repeating to Mr Topping [the officer in charge of the search] that I needed a second chance at it, but without any success.

Keith Bennett's body has not so far been found, but Brady's statement after the visit to the moors continued to devastating effect:

> I've also given Mr Topping details of 'happenings' [Brady's term for murders] but he doesn't seem interested in them . . . i.e. a man on a piece of wasteland near Piccadilly [in Manchester], a woman in a canal, a man in Glasgow, and another on the slopes of Loch Long etc. . . . There's another on the opposite side of the moor road.

At least five more victims. Myra Hindley's solicitor was quick to issue a statement that she was shocked by Brady's claim and that 'she has no knowledge of any other killings.' It is possible that she does not, for Brady has hinted that he committed murders before he met Myra, and he may even have continued with occasional solo efforts after they joined forces – just possibly without her knowledge, though this is hard to believe.

If Myra had hoped that her new helpful attitude would bring sympathy and help her fight for parole she was again disappointed, for the media used the occasion to go over the horrors of the crimes all over again and public revulsion has never been higher, with a new generation now all too familiar with the Moors Murders. As the first edition of this book went to press, a front-page headline proclaimed HINDLEY WILL NEVER GO FREE. There may be two new murder charges to be faced, and Brady's recent statement would seem to dash any hopes that the case will soon be closed.

So Judge Sparrow's remarks about this case have been justified by subsequent events, and now we do know the answers to at least some of the questions it raised. There are conflicting reports about Brady; according to some he is now approaching total madness, while others suggest that he has responded to treatment, gained weight, and is benefiting from contact with other patients after all those years of virtual isolation. His chief complaint over the years has been that his imprisonment was useless. If it was meant to be a punishment it was half-hearted and it would have been better to have hanged him; if it was aimed at rehabilitation it was an utter failure; and if it was meant to help society by learning from him, the attempt has scarcely been made. Brady's willingness to accept his fate has even earned him a certain amount of respect, and his treatment does indeed seem pointless, satisfying no-one and helping no-one.

Only a handful of the killers discussed in this book are still alive. Percy Stoner, now an old man, is reportedly free and living quietly under another name, and it would be wrong to bother him now. Pauline Parker and Juliet Hume were released from prison some years ago and have now disappeared from view. The murders of Brady and Hindley, so symptomatic of the times we live in, present problems beyond those of the murders themselves, of which the main one is, as Colin Wilson has written,

> the relationship between Brady and Hindley. Was this another 'master and slave' relationship, like Leopold and Loeb? Was Brady also a homosexual? Were the murders genuinely sadistic or were they a sort of anarchic gesture, like Ravachol's? The only thing that can be said is that there is no precedent for this type of murder – that is, for an intellectually unbalanced male to persuade a perfectly normal and affectionate girl to take part in child murder ... The couple will probably spend the remainder of their

lives in prison, but it would be more to the point if a psychologist could get them to explain exactly why they committed the murders.

Brady and Hindley are, more than any other killers, available for study, and it is a tragedy that as far as understanding them is concerned we have in more than twenty years learned virtually nothing more about them.

SOURCES AND ACKNOWLEDGEMENTS

'The Incredible Lovers' by Bruce Sanders from *Murder Behind the Bright Lights* (London: Barrie & Jenkins, 1958). Reproduced by permission of Random House UK Ltd.

'The Double Life of Edith Thompson' by Max Pemberton from *Stranger Than Fiction* (New York: Howell, Soskin Publishers, 1947).

'Superman's Crime' by Miriam Allen de Ford from *Murderers, Sane & Mad* (New York: Abelard-Schuman, 1965).

'The Amateur Gangsters' by Rupert Furneaux from *They Died by a Gun* (London: Herbert Jenkins, 1962). Reprinted by kind permission of Random House UK Ltd.

'Clyde, Bonnie, Buck and the Boys' by Lew Louderback from *Pretty Boy, Baby Face – I Love You* (Fawcett Publications Inc., 1968).

'In the Interests of Science' by George A. Birmingham from *Murder Most Foul!* (London: Chatto & Windus, 1929). Reprinted by kind permission of A. P. Watt Ltd on behalf of Susan Harper and Althea C. Hannay.

'The Murder in Le Mans' by Janet Flanner: this article was originally published in *Vanity Fair*. Copyright © 1934 (renewed 1962) by The Condé Nast Publications Inc.

'Alma Rattenbury' by Charles Franklin from *World-Famous Acquittals* (London: Odhams, 1970). Reprinted by kind permission of Reed International Books.

'The Widow Gras' by H. B. Irving from *A Book of Remarkable Criminals* (New York: George H. Doran Company, 1918).

'The Kray Twins' by Edgar Lustgarten from *The Illustrated Story of Crime*. Reproduced by permission of George Weidenfeld & Nicolson Limited.

'Corsets and Chloroform' by Leonard Gribble from *Adventures in Murder* (London: John Long Ltd, 1954). Reproduced by kind permission of Lois Gribble.

'Death in a Cathedral City' from *Famous Australian Crimes* (London: Muller, 1957).

'A Little World All Our Own': from *Bloodletters and Badmen*, copyright © 1973 by Jay Robert Nash, revised 1983, 1991. Reprinted by permission of the publishers, M. Evans & Company, Inc., New York, NY 10017.

'The Terrible Fate of Mrs Staunton' by Malcolm Muggeridge from *The 50 Most Amazing Crimes of the Last 100 Years* (London: Odhams, 1936). Reprinted by kind permission of Reed International Books.

'The Passion of Perversion' by Judge Gerald Sparrow from *Crimes of Passion* (Arthur Barker, 1973). Reproduced by kind permission of George Weidenfeld & Nicolson Limited.

While every effort has been made to trace authors and copyright holders, in some cases this has proved impossible. The publishers would be glad to hear from any such parties so that omissions can be rectified in future editions of the book.

LADYKILLER

by Christopher Berry-Dee and Robin Odell

In July 1986, three days after John Guise Cannan was released following an eight-year sentence for rape, estate agent Suzy Lamplugh went alone to meet a prospective client. She was never seen again. In April 1989, after Cannan's conviction for the murder and rape of newlywed Shirley Banks, the judge recommended that he 'never again be at liberty outside of prison walls' and the Lamplugh file was finally closed...

Handsome and charming, John Cannan wooed women with flowers, champagne and flattery, and boasted of over a hundred one-night stands in three years. But how did such a violent man win his way into so many women's hearts? And what turned him into a vicious rapist who killed at least once?

Drawing on the latest psychological profiling knowledge developed in America by the FBI, and on an intense three-year correspondence between Cannan and the authors, *Ladykiller* provides a chillingly personal and comprehensive portrait of a complex and intelligent man. Rarely has a book delved so deeply into the mind of a convicted murderer.

'A balanced, sensitive psychological portrait'
Diana Lamplugh, *Mail on Sunday*

ISBN 0 86369 690 2

MASSACRE AT WACO
The Shocking True Story of
Cult Leader David Koresh and
the Branch Davidians

by Clifford L. Linedecker

With his rock-star good looks and dark sexual charisma David Koresh wooed hundreds of followers from Britain, America and all over the world to a desolate spot in Texas, where he preached Armageddon and lived like a king, with a harem of nineteen 'wives' and girls as young as twelve to share his bed.

When Federal agents stormed Koresh's compound on 28 February 1993, his Promised Land exploded in a bloodbath, and fifty-one days later the world watched in horror as scores of men, women and children were lost in the flames.

Massacre at Waco gives a startling insight into how a guitar-playing Seventh Day Adventist called Vernon Howell transformed himself into David Koresh, Messiah, convincing his followers to join him in the coming Apocalypse. But were the 87 horrifying deaths at Waco the result of a mass suicide by God's chosen people, or the avoidable outcome of a siege bungled by government agents too eager for fast results?

ISBN 0 86369 713 5

THE ENCYCLOPEDIA OF CRUEL AND UNUSUAL PUNISHMENT

by Brian Lane

As old as mankind, the use of institutionalised punishment and execution has been known in virtually every culture; time and again man has shown appalling ingenuity in devising ever crueller and more effective ways of inflicting pain and death on his fellow human beings, however serious or trivial their offence. This shameful but seemingly universal trait has eaten away at mankind's claim to civilisation.

The Encyclopedia of Cruel and Unusual Punishment is an A–Z history of the systematic use throughout the ages of various means of punishment and coercion, up to and including the death penalty. From the iniquities of the Emperor Nero, through the atrocities of the Inquisition and the purge of the Knights Templar; from cutting up alive in China to the horrors of the Spanish *auto da fé* – this is a shocking and compulsive study of the shameful methods and motives of the torturer and executioner, and of the hideous duty they have performed throughout the centuries.

ISBN 0 86369 670 8

THE SERIAL KILLERS

by Colin Wilson and Donald Seaman

White. Twenty-eight years old. High IQ. And a law student. Yuppie success story?

No, portrait of a serial killer. Ted Bundy, one of the most notorious serial killers of recent years, confessed to killing 23 women. But he was no aberration. Statistics show that most serial killers are young, white, intelligent males. Triggered by either sexual fantasies or a need to inflict pain and fear, their sadistic addiction to frenzied killing is the most horrifying of all crimes. And serial killers are increasing at an alarming rate.

But with the formation of the world's first National Centre for the Analysis of Violent Crime in Virginia, made famous in the hugely popular *The Silence of the Lambs*, the methods of tracking down these killers have been revolutionised.

Using their privileged access to the centre's sophisticated techniques of pyschological profiling, Colin Wilson and Donald Seaman have produced the most comprehensive study to date of this terrifying modern phenomenon. *The Serial Killers* is the definitive study of the psychology of the criminal mind.

ISBN 0 86369 615 5

THE RED RIPPER

by Peter Conradi

He was a soft-spoken grandfather. The 'perfect' family man. A former Russian literature teacher. And a serial killer.

Beneath Andrei Chikatilo's model-citizen exterior lurked the warped mind of one of the most prolific killers of all time. At his 1992 trial, watched in his cage by the world's media, Chikatilo was convicted of murdering a horrifying total of 52 women and children over twelve years.

Peter Conradi, an English journalist based in Moscow, has interviewed key figures – from the police who finally caught Chikatilo (six years after an initial arrest in 1984) to the psychiatrist who helped track him down – to lay bare a damaged mind in a damaged society.

ISBN 0 86369 618 X

PRECIOUS VICTIMS

by Don W. Weber and Charles Bosworth Jr

Who would believe a mother could murder her own baby? It seemed the least likely explanation to the Jersey County police when they heard Paula Sims' story of a masked kidnapper in June 1986. But then, in April 1989, her second newborn daughter suffered an identical fate. This time the police would not stop searching until they had discovered the whole, horrifying truth.

Written by the lawyer who won the case, and the reporter who covered it from beginning to end, *Precious Victims* is a riveting journey into the twisted heart of a family with a dark and murderous secret.

ISBN 0 86369 598 1

DYING TO GET MARRIED
The Courtship and Murder of Julie Miller Bulloch

by Ellen Harris

At 30, Julie Miller was a successful executive who dreamed of a white knight who would come and bring romance to her well-ordered life. Then, after placing an ad in a St Louis personal column, Julie met Dennis Bulloch. Movie-star handsome, an MBA, a member of the young Republicans, he seemed to be the perfect husband.

But underneath the perfect façade was a violent, disturbed man. A compulsive womaniser and social climber, Bulloch married Julie for her money and connections. Just ten weeks after their wedding, Julie's burnt body was discovered after a fire in the garage. Naked, she had been bound to a rocking chair with more than 76 feet of tape.

The shocking true story of Julie Miller Bulloch's desperate search for love and her tragic death is the story of an American dream that turned into a brutal nightmare.

ISBN 0 86369 638 4